Classic
BROOKE BOND
PICTURE CARD
COLLECTIONS

Classic
BROOKE BOND
PICTURE CARD
COLLECTIONS

12 COMPLETE BROOKE BOND ALBUMS
WITH EVERY CARD IN PLACE

Mark Knowler

PRION

Published in 2009 by Prion
an imprint of the Carlton Publishing Group
20 Mortimer Street
London W1T 3JW

1 3 5 7 9 10 8 6 4 2

Introduction and Chapter Opener text © Carlton Books Limited 2009
Cover design © Carlton Books Limited 2009

A CIP catalogue record for this book is available from the British Library.

ISBN 978 1 85375 720 4

Printed in China

Contents

Tea-picking in Assam, India

At first, packing beautifully illustrated picture cards along with the nation's favourite drink might not seem like an obvious idea but for Brooke Bond in the early 1950s it was a masterstroke. Giving away picture cards was a tried and tested marketing device (principally with cigarette manufacturers) to encourage brand loyalty amongst customers. The lure of the 'free' gift and the fact that the gift formed part of a collectable series helped to keep tea drinkers buying Brooke Bond. Promoting the brand in this way was essential as tea rationing, a throwback to the austere days of the Second World War, ended in 1952 and the market was becoming ever more competitive.

For Brooke Bond, the smell of fresh tea and the sight of great picture cards was the recipe for success. It seems appropriate, then, to look back over the history of Brooke Bond's tea card collections. Brooke Bond tea cards were issued for 45 years from 1954 to 1999 and in that time millions of cards were printed. Cards were given away free not only with tea but also with coffee and appealed to a huge number of people.

The cards were a convenient size to collect and followed the example set by the old cigarette cards, each set coming with its own display album. They were interesting to study, generally educational and the early sets have easily stood the test of time to become even more collectable nowadays. The fine illustrations have influenced a generation of collectors and over the years a whole plethora of collectables have grown up around Brooke Bond cards.

Right from the outset Brooke Bond enlisted the foremost artists and writers of the time to contribute to each set. The attention to details and colour, and the printing technique made these cards stand out. They were hugely desirable items for collectors young and old. When a new box of tea was ready to be opened the whole family would gather round in great anticipation, waiting to see if the cards inside would be an exciting new set, or cards missing from the current set. Tea packets had an added challenge in trying to remove the cards without damaging them and coffee had the cards in cellophane packets. No doubt more tea was drunk than might otherwise have been in order to finish off the tea and get down to the shops to buy a fresh supply!

Visits to previously boring aunts and uncles were suddenly exciting. Family friends would always keep the cards in a drawer or cupboard and on those occasional visits the kids' reward might be a large handful of cards. In the school playground, the traditional forum for swapping or trading collectables, tea cards faced stiff competition from football cards, with bubble gum cards following later.

Brooke Bond produced their first set of cards in August 1954, a series of 20 **British Birds**. These photographic studies were prepared by Francis Pitt a well-known naturalist, photographer and writer of the time, who also wrote the supporting descriptive text. Right from the start they were designed to appeal to a wide market, and children in particular were readily drawn to them. Such was the demand for this set that when the cards were withdrawn Brooke Bond were inundated with requests for odd cards and albums.

THE

Frances Pitt

SERIES OF
BRITISH BIRDS

PICTURE CARD ALBUM
Price 3d.

At the same size as cigarette cards, the sets appealed to older collectors as well as children, making them an instant success. From the outset each set was issued with its own display album and for **British Birds** an album priced 3d (threepence) was available. These delightful booklets contained further information of interest to the collector and could initially be purchased from greengrocers, although later you had to send for them from Brooke Bond direct. They were subsequently available free for the cost of postage and packaging.

The second set produced was of 50 **Wild Flowers** (commonly known as **Wild Flowers** series 1) about seven months after **British Birds**. This fine photographic set was so popular that both cards and album had to be reprinted. A large base of keen collectors had clearly been quickly established.

The third set is probably the most iconic set produced. Still highly collectable over fifty years since it first appeared, **Out Into Space** is a wonderful set of 50 cards, which for the first time were illustrated with paintings rather than photographs. Both cards and album were again reprinted, something that was to become an ongoing trend over the years.

WILD FLOWERS

A Series of 50 Picture Cards
from originals by
John Markham, F.R.P.S.

PICTURE CARD ALBUM
PRICE 3ᴰ

Bird Portraits (1957) is another fine set, illustrated by the renowned artist C.F. Tunnicliffe OBE, RA, who was to be involved in several subsequent sets. No doubt these cards were the inspiration for many a young bird watcher.

Francis Pitt and Charles Tunnicliffe collaborated on the fifth set, *British Wild Life*, and Brooke Bond also produced a wall chart to accompany the cards and album. Available only to schools as a classroom teaching aid, these were to become another popular collectable item in years to follow.

A second series of flowers came out in 1959 and this time the flowers were illustrated, again by C. F. Tunnicliffe. The frequency of issues was reduced slightly now with a new set being produced approximately every eight months, so collectors did not have to wait too long for new sets. Brooke Bond had also set up a picture card department so that odd cards for sets could easily be obtained.

BIRD PORTRAITS

A series of
BRITISH BIRDS
Illustrated and described by
C.F. TUNNICLIFFE R.A

PRICE 6D

Another very popular subject was featured on the seventh set of cards; *Freshwater Fish* released in February 1960. Even today the fine illustrations by E.V. Petts are sharp, clean and detailed.

African Wild Life followed with both cards and album illustrated and described by the prolific Charles Tunnicliffe. He followed this up with *Tropical Birds* in November 1961, the vivid colours and exotic locations adding to the appeal for collectors. *Asian Wildlife* complimented the earlier *African Wildlife* to give children and collectors a wealth of information. *British Butterflies* continued the theme of cards based around nature.

Another landmark set came out in 1963, *Wildlife in Danger*. For the first time the cards highlighted the plight of a number of animals at risk of extinction. Written and illustrated by Peter Scott, the son of Antarctic explorer Robert Falcon Scott and a famous naturalist and artist of

the time, the album cover really fired the imagination and still catches the eye today.

A third series of **Wild Flowers** followed, giving the collector a great reference of 150 different species. 1964 also saw a second series of **Butterflie**s, this time from around the world. Illustrated and described by Richard Ward, who had also prepared the earlier **British Butterflies** set. **Wild Birds in Britain** saw Tunnicliffe again illustrating and writing the series.

The type of card used for printing was changed around this time. A thinner, glossier card replaced the more traditional thick card and led to subsequent sets having many more printing colour variations.

BROOKE BOND PICTURE CARDS

The saga of
SHiPS

6D

BROOKE BOND PICTURE CARDS

British Costume

Illustrated by Michael Youens. Described by Madeleine Ginsburg, B.A., A.M.A.

PRICE SIXPENCE

January 1966 brought a change in theme with the release of **Transport Through the Ages**. This set had some great illustrations that again captured the interest of young collectors. The wallchart for this set was also the first created for the mass market, not just schools, another trend that continued for years to come with almost fifty different wallcharts ultimately being printed for collectors. These were obtained by sending off to Brooke Bond directly using forms provided within the albums.

Trees in Britain was a study of 25 trees and their flowers, also published in 1966, while in 1967 the magnificent **Flags and Emblems of the World** first appeared.

The wonderful **British Costume**, illustrated by Michael Youens, the same artist for **Trees in Britain** was published in 1968 as was **History of the Motor Car**, establishing a run of collections that were not linked to the world of nature. The **Motor Car** series proved to be a hugely popular set of cards, superbly rendered by Kenneth Rush. Angus McBride illustrated **Famous People**, the last set of the 1960s.

Next came **The Saga of Ships**. The subtle illustrations by David Cobb cannot really be appreciated on cards of this size but the album cover shows how good they would have appeared at larger size.

Brooke Bond Picture Cards **THE RACE INTO SPACE**
Man's first 50 steps into the universe

5p (1/4)

As **Out Into Space** was such a huge success in the 1950s so was the **Race Into Space** in the early 1970s. Man had only recently walked on the moon when this set was released. Previous sets had largely been attributed to one or two writers or artists but this set credited no less than six scientists and illustrators and included a foreword by the eminent astronomer Patrick Moore.

Brooke Bond picture cards were now in their heyday, with the next new set offering yet another favourite subject for children and collectors. **Prehistoric Animals** (1972) formed a delightful set of 50 cards. The 1970s continued with the highly colourful **History of Aviation**, **Adventures and Explorers**, **The Sea – Our Other World**, **Inventors and Inventions**, and **Wonders of Wildlife**.

Moving away from the subjects of science and nature, **Play Better Soccer** (1976) saw a radical change when for the first time the set count was reduced to 40 cards. At the same time, albums no longer showed a price on the front cover. The reduction in numbers was a bit of a shock to collectors at the time but did make it easier to complete sets without having to send off for missing cards. **Police File** (1977) was a fact packed set about the workings of the police force. Very much a snapshot of the time, this would have made an interesting second series today.

The distinctive art of Graeme Sims shone on the artwork of **Vanishing Wildlife**, a set which updated the much earlier **Wildlife in Danger**.

Olympic Greats was a photographic study produced using both black & white and colour photographs in 1980, the year that Moscow hosted the summer games.

The 1980s witnessed the first set to run for a full year, **Woodland Wildlife** creating a trend that continued with **Small Wonders**. **Queen Elizabeth I to Queen Elizabeth II**, a historical set regularly referred to for school projects, was a return to the 50-card set as was **Features of the World** (1984) illustrated with a fine selection of photographs. Brooke Bond allowed both sets to run for over a year.

The card count dropped to 40 again for **Incredible Creatures** which broke new ground as far as collectors were concerned. The set ran for a whopping 18 months and it seemed at the time as if it would never end. A transition period at Brooke Bond meant that these cards can be found with three different addresses on the text sides and collectors can obtain seven different versions of this one set (eight including the set issued in Ireland). This was also the first time a traditional display album was not produced for the cards. Instead, a set of four wall charts with spaces for the cards were printed.

To celebrate 30 years of chimps a set of 12 stickers were released in 1986. Only three months later came **Unexplained Mysteries of the World**, another great production stimulating the minds of young and old alike with its amazing variety and well-written texts. Another set of 12 stickers followed with **The Language of Tea**, the second and last time that no display album was printed, although a wall chart was available. Collectors were delighted when a new 50-card set, **Discovering our Coast**, featuring some

beautiful photographs from around Britain, became the next Brooke Bond offering.

A cartoon set of 25 cards celebrating the **Magical World of Disney** was very popular with younger collectors but possibly detracted from the educational theme of previous releases. Brooke Bond had clearly decided to focus on the younger age group when **A Journey Downstream** (25 cards) was then followed by **Teenage Mutant Hero Turtles** (12 cards). This latter

set was around for a whole year and for such a small collection it was very easy to make up many duplicate sets. **Olympic Challenge** and **Natural Neighbours** (both 40 cards) preceded another fine dinosaur issue. **The Dinosaur Trail** (20 cards) was beautifully illustrated but was the last set of cards released at the standard size that had been used for almost 40 years. It was the end of era.

Creatures of Legend (April 1994) was a set of 24 cards which were about 1cm larger in both dimensions than the traditional cards and the quality of board they were printed on was entirely different. They had a rougher texture and often the card edges had a slightly ragged feel to them. They appeared to be thicker but were easier to crease. **Going Wild** (40 cards) was produced on the same size card. It led to many long term collectors voicing their disappointment at the quality of the cards.

The Secret Diary of Kevin Tipps was the last set of fifty cards to be released. At an even larger size (approx 90mm x 64mm) these were unusual in that they were not numbered but are sequenced in date order. This photographic set showed Kevin the chimp and his friends throughout the year and were aimed once more at younger collectors. With cards this size it was even more difficult for serious collectors to keep loose cards crease free. The size was more in keeping with commercially produced trading cards but they were not printed to their same high quality. This is entirely understandable as they were being given away free, but for lifelong collectors it added to discontent regarding size, set themes and overall quality.

40 years of the Chimps Television Advertising (1995), another photographic set, was also at this new large size as were all subsequent issues.

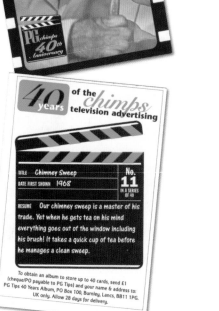

Pyramid Power was released as part of Brooke Bond marketing strategy for their new revolutionary pyramid (in fact tetrahedron) tea bags. Beautifully illustrated, unusual and very desirable, these showed Brooke Bond could still create great collectable cards.

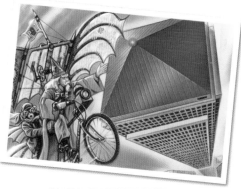

Demand for these led to an official reprint, the last set to enjoy this level of success. Slightly more basic in appearance *The Wonderful World of Kevin Tipps* was a series of 30 cards, showing both natural and man made wonders.

1998 saw the release of the last official set: *International Soccer Stars*. This set of 20 cards showed photographs of football stars of the time in action and was a nicely produced finale. One further unnumbered series appeared in 1999 called *Tea Leaf Oracle* comprising 19 cards all with similar fronts of a dark brown circle in the middle of a tea cup. When heated, three symbols are revealed which are matched to a legend on the reverse of the cards. No supporting album or wallchart came with these cards and they were deemed to be 'just for fun' rather than collectable items.

That, of course, made them very collectable and they are still much sought after today! Tantalisingly they also stated 'New card series starts soon' on the reverse side.

Also in 1999, Brooke Bond issued a Survey Card asking Brooke Bond customers for their opinions of the cards.

Disillusioned collectors had been voicing disappointment for some period of time as Brooke Bond seemed to have lost their enthusiasm for tea cards. The traditional look and feel, plus the original intention to produce educational material seemed to have gone. A "Thank You" for taking part in the survey card followed.

THANK YOU!

PG Tips would like to thank everyone who replied to our recent questionnaire about our PG Tips picture cards.

We are now busy looking at the responses and will let you know the results soon.

THANK YOU!

In September 1999 Brooke Bond sent an open letter to the Brooke Bond collectors club (TEAMS) informing them of their decision to discontinue producing any

further series of cards. Finally, a group of three cards were released all with the title "Farewell to Picture Cards". On the backs of the cards was a message which read "Our many thanks to everyone who filled in our questionnaire. Your feedback was invaluable and although some of you felt a fondness for the cards, the majority of you indicated to us that there are other things you would prefer us to be doing to continue to bring you the best quality and value tea possible. So we say farewell to our long tradition of picture cards and instead look forward to some exciting new ideas. So watch this space!"

Our many thanks to everyone who filled in our questionnaire. Your feedback was invaluable and although some of you felt a fondness for the cards, the majority of you indicated to us that there are other things you would prefer us to be doing to continue to bring you the best quality and value tea possible. So we say farewell to our long tradition of picture cards and instead look forward to some exciting new ideas. So watch this space!

PG

So ended a great tradition, despite many letters and calls for them to reverse their decision it wasn't to be. Ten years later many collectors still buy Brooke Bond PG Tips tea, some still collect any related ephemera and all yearn for the cards.

These days it is actually easier than ever before to buy cards on the internet using web sites such as ebay where many thousands of cards are listed every day. Even the scarcest can be found and where once it might have taken years to finish a set now it can be a matter of hours. Car boot sales are another place to find cards and albums in large numbers.

Over the years Brooke Bond issued cards in Ireland, Canada, USA, Southern Rhodesia & Eastern Africa and South Africa. The cards issued in Canada and the USA were produced in an entirely different way with each set having 48 cards and the cards themselves having rounded corners. The cards were also printed on a bright white stiff card and were beautifully illustrated by such great artists as Charles Lewis "Chuck" Ripper.

In Great Britain Brooke Bond released 56 sets and officially reprinted 22 sets in addition to those that were reprinted whilst in production. The official reprints can be distinguished by different colour backs to the originals. Double cards

CREA

- Ghosts a
who return
- They are
died a viol
the person w ... m harm.
- Some people claim to have seen Ghosts but there are never any good photos of them!
- Many old houses and inns are said to be haunted, usually by someone who lived or died there.
- Near Edinburgh, a ghostly hound can be heard baying at night for its master who did not return from the Crusades hundreds of years ago!
- Ghosts of people who were beheaded usually carry their head under their arm.

I could tell mum a ghost keeps messing up my room.

Illustration: Mark Longworth

... t for all the mishaps that befell RAF pilots.
- The name first appeared in print in 1929, in The Aeroplane, and was probably invented at the end of World War I.
- It may have started as a jokey reference to a goblin that came out of a bottle of beer. (Fremlin are well-known brewers.) G-oblin + F-remlin = Gremlin.
- Gremlins that get tangled up in propellers are called Spandules.
- In the film Gremlins, unsuspecting families adopted cuddly baby gremlins as pets, only to discover that they grew into hideous monsters who wrecked homes.

I'm certain my skateboard has Gremlins.

Illustration: Mark Longworth

Special album or wallchart for 24 picture cards. Just send 50p (p&p) & name and address to: Picture Card Dept (B49), PO Box 100, Burnley. Lancs BB11 1PG. UK residents only.

were found in packets of loose tea and were pairs of cards that had not been trimmed in two. The earliest type of these cards were in **Queen Elizabeth I to Queen Elizabeth II** and in total thirteen sets can be found in this format, including the larger size **Creatures of Legend** and **Going Wild**.

Of course, the collectors' sets don't get time to gather dust, many still being used as a great source of reference for school projects. Web sites and newsletters have continued sharing information and enabling collectors to finish those difficult sets they were unable to complete at the time of release.

Collectors continue to find various anomalies within the sets and variations in the cards. Scarce sets that do not come up very often at auction or on ebay can be sold for many hundreds of pounds. On the other hand, anyone wishing to start a collection of Brooke Bond cards can purchase many of the cards, albums and wallcharts with ease and, with gentle encouragement, the tradition of collecting Brook Bond cards will hopefully continue for years to come.

This book is a review of 12 of the finest albums from the early years of Brooke Bond tea cards, each album shown slightly larger than they were originally produced to make the most of the fabulous illustrations. The albums are also displayed in a way that many collectors will never have seen them before – with every card in its correct place. That was a mouthwatering prospect for anyone building up a tea card collection in the 50s and 60s, so for those who never quite attained the entire collections, here's what your albums would have looked like!

Out Into Space was the third set issued by Brooke bond and was first issued in tea in 1956. This iconic set is wonderfully illustrated and the backs of the cards were packed with information not only about the planets and the stars, but also about the signs of the Zodiac and how they relate to the constellations in the night sky.

The eye-catching illustrations of the heavens captivated collectors young and old and became the inspiration for many to take up stargazing. Subjects included the Sun, Moon, Planets in the Solar System, and the Zodiac amongst others. The earth-based pictures are particularly vivid, especially those showing the 'Astrolabe', 'Composition of a Star', or the 'Radio Telescope'. No artist is credited to this set but it is described as being approved by the Secretary of the Royal Astronomical Society.

While explaining something of the relationship between astrology and astronomy, the texts on the backs of the cards concentrated on historical and scientific fact rather than straying into the mystical realm of astrology. The texts were not lost, of course, when the cards were pasted into the album because, as was usual with Brooke Bond albums, the captions on the pages repeated the text from the back of the cards.

The album was printed with a dark and light blue cover and gave a great impression of the earth in the heavens, and was priced at 6d – twice the price of the previous two albums.

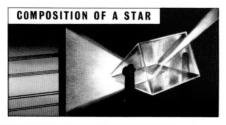

Of further interest to collectors this set was the first set where the *reprinted* cards could clearly be identified by the text on the back. One version contains wording at the bottom of the text side (within the thick blue band) "ISSUED WITH BROOKE BOND 'CHOICEST & EDGLETS' TEAS", whilst the other reads "ISSUED IN PACKETS OF BROOKE BOND 'CHOICEST', 'P.G. TIPS' & 'EDGLETS' TEAS".

The album was also reprinted, with wording on the back reflecting the different wording on the card backs.

The first well known Brooke Bond error card is also to be found in this set which is of great interest to collectors. Card number 11 can be found with and without the wording "INNER PLANETS" and "OUTER PLANETS" printed on the front of the cards.

It is also interesting in that the next time Brooke Bond issued a set not related to nature was the 16th set, *Transport Through the Ages*, issued some ten years later.

OUT INTO SPACE

A series of 50 picture cards
on Astronomy approved by
A. Hunter, Ph.D. Secretary of
the Royal Astronomical Society.

PRICE 6d.

27

HERCULES
No. 43

CYGNUS
No. 40

PEGASUS
No. 42

VIRGO
No. 29

URSA MINOR
No. 38

POLE STAR
No. 36

CASSIOPEIA
No. 44

URSA MAJOR
No. 37

PISCES
No. 35

LEO
No. 28

PERSEUS
No. 45

ARIES
No. 24

CANCER
No. 27

GEMINI
No. 26

TAURUS
No. 25

CANIS MINOR

GUIDE TO THE NIGHT SKY

All you need is clear weather, a warm overcoat, and these cards. Only half the sky is above the horizon at any one time, so you cannot see everything at once. Your chief guide is the Plough (main part of Ursa Major No. 37). It may be upright close to the northern horizon, or upside down overhead, but it is always above the horizon in Great Britain. The Pointers will give you the Pole Star (No. 36), due north. From the adjoining map of the northern hemisphere you can then find, card by card, many of the other constellations, for they never change position relative to one another.

As the Earth rotates, the whole sky, carrying all the stars, swings overhead from east to west, once round in 23 hr. 56 min. You will therefore lose some constellations as they set but gain others rising. Furthermore, the stars gain on the clock by four minutes each night, so if you keep watch at a fixed time every evening, they appear to creep forward, once round the sky in a year.

Watch out for the Moon (No. 2), changing phase every week; and follow the planets (No. 8) as they wander through the Zodiac (No. 21). There is always something happening in the sky.

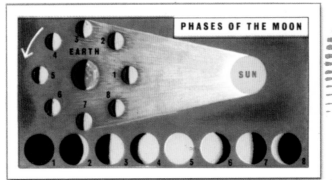

PHASES OF THE MOON

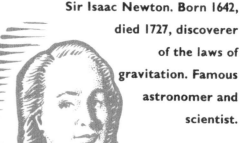

MOON AND ITS PHASES The Moon does not emit light, but only reflects light emitted by the Sun. It travels around the Earth in 27 days 7 hours and rotates on its axis in the same time; consequently, the same face of the Moon is always turned towards us. During its journey we see first a narrow crescent (new moon) which gradually widens until the whole surface is visible (full moon), then it gradually diminishes until nothing at all is seen. Period from New Moon to New Moon averages $29\frac{1}{2}$ days: 1st Quarter $7\frac{1}{2}$ days; Full $14\frac{3}{4}$ days.

THE SUN is the centre of our life and the main body of the solar system. It is only one of millions of stars, some larger and others smaller. The nearest star is 25 million million miles away from the Earth whereas the Sun is only just under 93 million miles away—hence its apparent size, brilliance and power. The Sun's temperature is calculated to be 6,000° Centigrade. The diameter of the Sun is over 100 times greater than the Earth's.

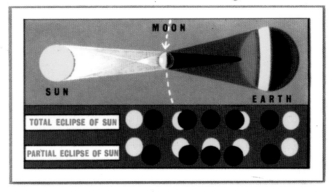

ECLIPSE OF THE SUN When, as shown, the Moon comes in a direct line between the Sun and Earth it hides the Sun from view for a few minutes causing a "Total" eclipse in that part of the Earth touched on the diagram by the black pointer, but only a "Partial" eclipse in the shaded part surrounding that point. It may happen occasionally that although the Moon is central over the Sun a thin rim of sunlight can be seen round Moon's edge. This is called an "Annular" eclipse, and happens if the Moon is farther than usual from the Earth, and so looks smaller.

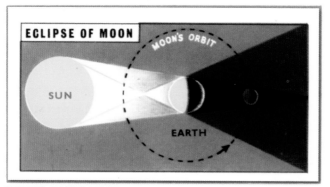

ECLIPSE OF THE MOON The Moon is eclipsed when the Earth is in a direct line between the Sun and Moon, and the Earth's shadow covers it. This can only occur at Full Moon. Even when the Moon is totally shadowed it may still be observed because sunbeams which have touched the edge of the Earth have been refracted by the Earth's atmosphere and turned *inwards* into the shadow, illuminating the Moon with a coppery colour. This is due to the great thickness of atmosphere through which sunbeams pass. Colour effects at sunset are from the same cause.

GALILEO. Born 1564, died 1642. The famous Italian astronomer, the first to use a telescope to examine the stars.

SEASONS These are the four quarters of the solar year, namely: Spring, beginning when the Sun enters the constellation of Aries, the Ram, at the time of the Vernal Equinox, March 21st; Summer (the Summer Solstice, June 21st) starting when it enters Cancer, the Crab; Autumn, when it enters Libra, the Balance, at the Autumnal Equinox, September 23rd; Winter (Winter Solstice, December 21st) when it enters Capricornus, the Goat. The difference between these seasons is caused by the varied angles the Earth's surface presents towards the Sun at different times of the year.

MOON—EFFECT ON TIDES The rise and fall of the sea is produced by the attraction of the Sun and Moon. The Moon is the principal factor. High water to high water is about 12 hours 25 minutes. The greatest or 'Spring' tides occur when Sun and Moon act together at New Moon or when the Earth is immediately between them at Full Moon. The smallest or 'Neap' tides occur when the Sun, Moon and Earth form a right angle. This is at Half Moon, when the Moon's pull acts against the Sun's, and causes tides then to be at minimum.

ROTATING EARTH

ROTATING EARTH The Terrestrial Equator is an imaginary circle around the Earth equidistant from the Poles, separating Northern from Southern hemisphere. The Celestial Equator is an extension of the Terrestrial Equator and is equidistant from the Poles of the heavens. The Ecliptic is the path of the Earth's revolution around the Sun, and is inclined to the Celestial Equator at an angle of $23°\ 27'$, called "Obliquity of Ecliptic". Direction of the Earth's axis never varies. Tropics are circles on celestial sphere $23°\ 27'$ on each side of Equator.

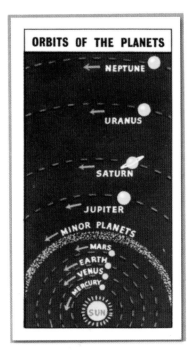

ORBITS OF THE PLANETS

PLANETS—ORBITS All Planets revolve around the Sun anti-clockwise as seen from the north, and differ in size, speed, velocity of axial rotation, etc. Their paths or orbits are not circular but elliptic. The Sun is their focus. Every orbit lies within $7°$ of the plane of the Earth's orbit except Pluto's (too distant to include in picture), which is inclined at $17°$. Mercury takes 88, Venus 224, Earth 365 and Mars 687 days to complete their orbits. Jupiter takes approx. 12 years, Saturn 29, Uranus 84 and Neptune 165 years. Pluto takes 248 years.

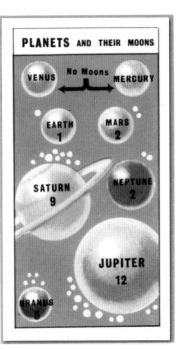

PLANETS AND THEIR MOONS

PLANETS AND THEIR MOONS All planets with the exception of Mercury, Venus and Pluto have their moons (or "satellites") which revolve around them. Each takes a definite time to complete its orbit. The period of the four largest Jupiter satellites is 2, 4, 7 and 17 days. Mars has two tiny moons, both approximately only 10 miles in diameter. One is approximately 6,000 miles from the planet and the other 15,000 miles. Although as telescopes have become more powerful, more satellites have been discovered attached to other planets, our Moon is the Earth's only satellite.

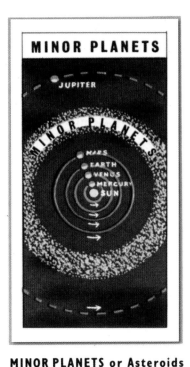

MINOR PLANETS

MINOR PLANETS or Asteroids Thousands of very small bodies form a ring between Mars and Jupiter, the largest being only 480 miles in diameter. The smallest known are considered to be only a few miles across. They are mostly invisible to the naked eye and are called Minor Planets. The first minor planet to be discovered was Ceres, by Piazzi, on 1st January, 1801, and so named after the Goddess of Corn and Harvest. Vesta, the brightest, was discovered in 1807. Those now discovered number nearly 2,000. They may be parts of a larger planet, broken up or not yet formed.

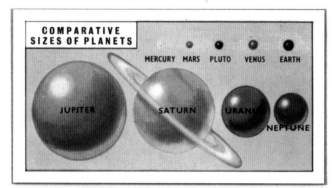

PLANETS—SIZES Of the nine Major Planets, Mercury, Venus, the Earth and Mars are known as Inner Planets; Jupiter, Saturn, Uranus, Neptune and Pluto as Outer Planets. The diameters of the planets in thousands of miles are approximately Mercury 3, Mars 4, Pluto 4, Venus 7½, the Earth 8, Neptune 28, Uranus 31, Saturn 75, Jupiter 88. Owing to their greater distance from the Earth, the big Outer Planets appear to be about the same size as the others. Mercury and Venus are also known as Inferior Planets. Others whose orbits are outside the Earth's are called Superior Planets.

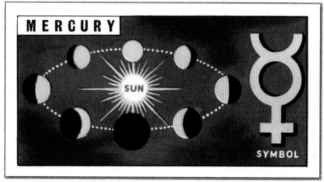

MERCURY is 3,000 miles in diameter, a much larger globe than the Moon. First record of its observation was in 265 B.C. Owing to its proximity to the Sun, it is difficult to see, never appearing in a dark sky; but every few years it may be found near the horizon, an hour after sunset, in April-May. Often it is crescent-shaped like the Moon. Mercury takes about 88 days to revolve around the Sun at a mean distance of 35,750,000 miles. Its velocity varies between 23 and 35 miles a second, being quicker when nearer the Sun.

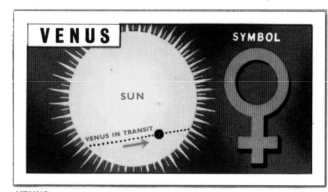

VENUS Named Lucifer (Morning Star) and Hesperus (Evening Star) by the Ancients, Venus comes nearest to the Earth and is the brightest planet. At its greatest brilliance it can be seen by the naked eye in full sunlight within an hour of noon. Venus is nearly the same size as the Earth, diameter 7,600 miles. Mean distance 67,000,000 miles from the Sun, around which it revolves in approximately 225 days. At rare intervals it can be seen in transit across the Sun and observations of its transit in 1769 resulted in the first accurate knowledge of the Sun's distance.

MARS Fourth Planet from the Sun. Distinguished from others by its reddish light. Mean distance from the Sun is approximately 141,500,000 miles. Nearest distance from the Earth is 34,500,000 miles. Diameter 4,200 miles. Revolves around the Sun in 687 days. Rotates on axis in 24 hrs. 37 mins. Possibility of life on Mars has always intrigued observers. Markings once thought to be continents and seas can be seen; some observers have seen long straight "canals". White patches near the poles are probably hoar-frost.

JUPITER An aeroplane travelling at 500 m.p.h. would take 90 years to reach Jupiter, the largest of planets. Its diameter is 88,000 miles and its bulk 1,250 times that of the Earth. It is 300 times heavier than the Earth. Jupiter takes nearly 12 years to complete its elliptic orbit around the Sun at a mean distance of 483,000,000 miles. Its surface is cloud-covered so cannot be seen, and it rotates on its axis in 9 hrs. 50 mins. Two of Jupiter's moons exceed Mercury in size and were first thought to be fixed stars not connected with the planet.

SATURN is a huge globe surrounded by three rings and has nine satellites or moons. The rings are composed of myriads of very small moonlets, the middle ring being the most brilliant. They form a circular band 40,000 miles wide with a thickness of 100 miles. Saturn is 887,100,000 miles from the Sun and takes 29 years to complete its orbit. During its course the rings are observed at various angles, being nearly invisible when the plane passes through the Earth and Sun. They are not visible to the naked eye, and were not known until the telescope was invented.

URANUS is rarely visible to the naked eye. Its diameter is four times greater than that of the Earth, and its volume about 64 times greater; but it is only 15 times as heavy because it is composed of lighter materials. Period of rotation is 10 hrs. 45 mins. and it takes 84 years to complete its orbit, the diameter of which is 3,600,000,000 miles. Its orbital speed is 15,110 m.p.h. approximately. The orbits of its satellites are unique in that they all lie in the same plane, nearly at right angles to the plane of the orbit of Uranus round the Sun.

NEPTUNE has a pale bluish hue. Its mean distance from the Sun is 2,793,000,000 miles. Seen from Neptune, the Sun would appear as large as Venus does when viewed from the Earth, but intensity of the Sun's light would be about a million times greater. Diameter of Neptune is 27,800 miles. Rotation time 15 hrs. 40 mins. Takes 164 years and 7 months to complete its orbit around the Sun travelling at about 12,080 m.p.h. Its orbit is more nearly circular than that of any planet except Venus. Neptune weighs about one 19,314th part of the Sun. Its density is less than half that of the Earth.

COMETS are common, curious and impressive visitors. They move amongst the stars like planets. Most are small and can be seen only with a telescope. Their orbits vary: some are parabolic, but most are elliptic. Sometimes they increase enormously in size and likewise diminish. Coming from afar they go round the Sun and then disappear from whence they came. Majority have no 'tail', but some have a large 'tail' which always points away from the Sun; these 'tails' caused the Greeks to call them "the long-haired ones", hence name Comets . . . Komëtës (Gr.) 'long-haired'.

BAILY'S BEADS. The bead effect round the rim of the sun during a total eclipse, was first discovered by Francis Baily (1774 — 1844).

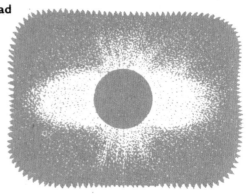

METEORS (Meteorites) (sometimes called Shooting Stars, Aerolites or Bolides) are very common. Millions enter the Earth's atmosphere daily. Friction, resulting from terrific speed at which they travel, makes them ignite and vaporize. Although most are completely burnt out, some ultimately explode, scattering debris far and wide. Some Meteors are of stone, others are metal—usually an alloy of iron and nickel with traces of other metals. Largest Meteorite ever found fell at Groetfontein in South West Africa; it weighs about fifty tons and consists of iron and nickel.

The surface of the moon, showing the craters, probably caused through meteors.

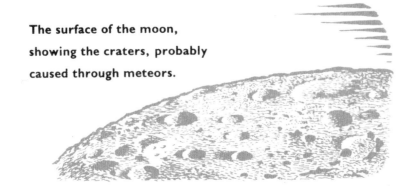

ZODIAC (Path of Creatures) is a zone or girdle extending round the heavens, including all the heavenly bodies within eight degrees on each side of the Sun's path. It contains twelve constellations called the Signs of the Zodiac. The Northern Signs are: (1) Aries, the Ram; (2) Taurus, the Bull; (3) Gemini, the Twins; (4) Cancer, the Crab; (5) Leo, the Lion; (6) Virgo, the Virgin. The Southern Signs are: (7) Libra, the Balance; (8) Scorpio, the Scorpion; (9) Sagittarius, the Archer; (10) Capricornus, the Goat; (11) Aquarius, the Water-carrier; (12) Pisces, the Fishes.

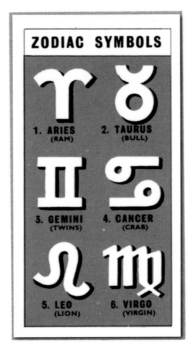

ZODIAC SYMBOLS (Northern) It is considered that the science of Astronomy was born of Astrology. For carrying out their 'trade', soothsayers and magicians had gained knowledge of the Signs of the Zodiac. On this knowledge, mathematicians and other scientifically-minded men laid the foundation of Astronomy. The soothsayers had invented symbols as a sort of shorthand for the twelve Zodiac signs. These are still used, immediately recognised and accepted by astronomers. This card shows the symbols of Aries, Taurus and Gemini (Spring signs) and Cancer, Leo and Virgo (Summer signs).

ZODIAC SYMBOLS (Southern) The six Southern Zodiac signs, like the Northern ones, are divided into two groups of three. Each has its symbol originating in astrology. Libra, Scorpio and Sagittarius are Autumn signs, Capricornus, Aquarius and Pisces Winter signs. Capricornus is also known as a Tropical and Libra as an Equinoctial sign. Astrology was practised in Babylonia as far back as 3000 B.C. and in Greece in the 4th Century B.C. and, although we may not now take it seriously, let us remember that to its scientific offspring, Astronomy, we owe our present wide and useful knowledge of the heavens.

ARIES "The Ram" is mentioned by Eudoxus (4th Century B.C.); in Mythology it is said to be the Ram with Golden Fleece sacrificed to Zeus who placed it in the Heavens as a constellation. It is the first sign in the Zodiac. Only main stars, easy to identify, are illustrated, but over 50 can be seen unaided and even thousands by using a powerful telescope. North of Aries is Triangulum, Cetus is South, Pisces is on the West and Taurus East. The bright star Hamal is used for navigation.

GREENWICH OBSERVATORY. The famous English astronomical observatory, now moved to Herstmonceux, Sussex.

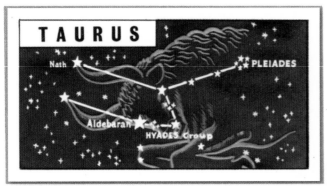

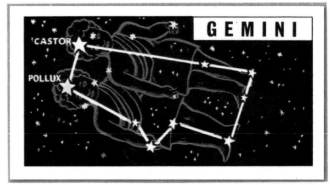

TAURUS (Bull), second of the Zodiacal Signs, has two main groups of stars in the constellation. One is Hyades, a V-shaped group; the other is the Pleiades cluster. According to fable, the Pleiades are the seven daughters of Atlas turned to stars with their sisters, the Hyades, on account of their virtues and mutual affection. The red star Aldebaran (Follower) so named for following the Pleiades, is principal star in Hyades group, and a navigation star. Mythology says that the god Jupiter took the shape of a bull when he abducted Europa and carried her to Crete.

GEMINI (Twins), third Zodiacal sign, is between Taurus and Cancer. It contains several double stars, and is represented on most Celestial maps by male twins of mythology . . . Castor and Pollux. Castor is a binary or 'double star' consisting of two white stars of approximately same magnitude, but appears as one very bright star, except when seen through a telescope. Pollux is a navigational star. Castor, Pollux and other principal Gemini stars are very noticeable, because the adjoining areas of Cancer and Lynx constellations have few stars of great magnitude.

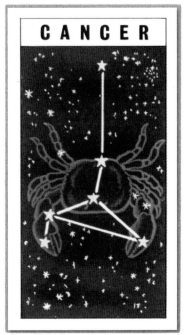

LEO (Lion), fifth sign of the Zodiac, is bounded on the West by Cancer, on the East by Virgo. It is easy to locate . . . a straight line from the Pole Star to Plough Pointers leads to Leo. February to end of June is good time for viewing, but evenings in March and April are best. Principal and very prominent star is Regulus . . . also known as Cor Leonis (Lion's Heart) or Royal Star. Regulus, Gamma Leonis and several smaller stars form a group shaped like a sickle. From near these stars most of November meteor showers known as Leonids radiate.

CANCER (Crab) is fourth sign, and first of Summer Signs, of Zodiac. The sun enters Cancer on 21st June, giving the Northern Hemisphere their longest day and the Southern their shortest. The Sun, reaching its greatest height in the North, moves backward along ecliptic, which accounts for the Crab being used as symbol for this sign. Cancer contains several 'double' stars and a 'triple' star. Over 90 stars can be seen with the naked eye. One cluster of over 150 stars of sixth and lower magnitudes was known to ancients as Praesepe or Beehive.

VIRGO (Virgin) sixth Sign of the Zodiac, is bounded on East by Libra, West by Leo, North by Bootes, and on South by Corvus and Hydra. Best seen from April to July. Virgo was sometimes represented as Ceres (Goddess of Corn and Harvest) or as an angel holding ears of corn in her hand, because the Sun enters this sign when cereal crops are ready for harvesting. Over 180 stars are visible to naked eye. Most brilliant is Spica (Ear of Corn), a navigational star of first magnitude, easy to locate because of its isolated appearance.

Sir Isaac Newton's original Reflecting Telescope, the first of its kind, made in 1668.

LIBRA (Balance), seventh Sign of the Zodiac, and first Autumnal Sign. The Sun enters this part of Ecliptic at Autumnal Equinox when days and nights are equal in length—hence its name. Libra is bounded by Virgo on the West, Scorpio on the East, Serpens on the North and Centaurus on the South. It is an inconspicuous constellation, having no stars of great magnitude, although there are several double and triple stars; also two clusters in one of which Herschel observed 200 different stars of eleventh and less magnitude.

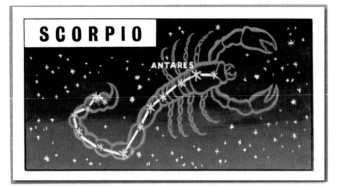

SCORPIO (Scorpion) is the eighth Sign of the Zodiac. Not large but a brilliant constellation. Can be seen in Europe only in June and July owing to its low altitude. Bounded on the West by Libra, on the East by Sagittarius, on the North by Serpens, and on the South by Lupus and Ara. Most prominent star is Antares, known also as Cor Scorpii (Heart of Scorpion), its diameter being over 400 times as large as that of our Sun, but its density very small. Ancient astrologers deemed Scorpio accursed—a source of war, discord and universal evil.

SAGITTARIUS (The Archer) The ninth Sign in the Zodiac and third of the Southern Signs, symbolized by the Centaur, part man and part beast, shooting an arrow. The main part of the group lies in the Milky Way. Old astrologers considered it a lucky sign. Nunki, the uppermost and brightest star, and Kaus Australis, are navigational stars. Can be seen in July and August and in early evening in September, but not well as it is low on the horizon.

GALILEO'S TOWER, near Florence in Italy, from which Galileo made his astronomical discoveries.

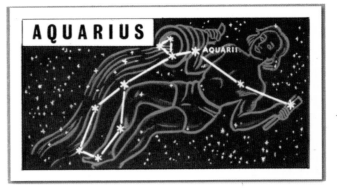

AQUARIUS (Water-carrier), 11th Sign of the Zodiac, is seen from August to October. Bounded on the East by Pisces and Cetus, on the West by Aquila, on the North by Pegasus and Equuleus, on the South by Piscis Austrinus. About 150 stars are visible to the naked eye. When the Venerable Bede changed the names of the Zodiac signs to those of Saints, he called Aquarius 'John the Baptist', probably because it marked the rainiest of months. Principal star Alpha Aquarii, a pale yellow double star of 3rd magnitude, is known as King's Lucky Star.

CAPRICORNUS (Sea Goat), tenth sign of the Zodiac and fourth Southern Sign, is bounded on the West by Sagittarius, on the East and North-East by Aquarius, on the North by Aquila, and on the South by Piscis Austrinus. It was mentioned by Eudoxus in 4th Century B.C. The two main stars are Alpha and Beta Capricorni. Ancients represented it sometimes as a goat but mainly as a creature having forepart of a goat and hind-part of a fish, probably because of amount of rain at this season. Capricornus is seen from August to October.

PISCES (Fishes) is the twelfth Sign of the Zodiac. Greek legend states Aphrodite and Eros jumped into the Euphrates when surprised by Typhon and were changed into two fishes. Bounded on North by Andromeda, on South by Cetus, on West by Pegasus and Aquarius, and on East by Aries and Triangulum. Pisces was mentioned by Eudoxus (famous Greek astronomer and mathematician 4th Century B.C.). Alpha Piscium, a close double star of 3 and 4 magnitude—pale green and blue in colour—is its largest star.

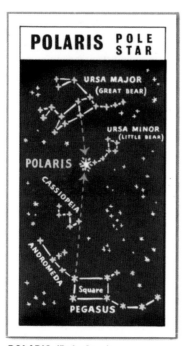

POLARIS (Pole Star) though not the most brilliant, is the most important star in the heavens owing to its situation close to the Celestial North Pole, and it has become known as the Pole Star. In the Northern Hemisphere it is always visible and is used by astronomers and navigators. Stars near the Pole seem to move slowly around it and those far away quickly; this is because they have to cover much larger circles in the same time. At the North Pole, the Pole Star is exactly overhead, but as one travels south it sinks downwards towards the horizon.

URSA MAJOR (The Great Bear) main part of which is also known as The Dipper, Plough, David's Car, Bier of Lazarus and Charles' Wain, is always visible in Great Britain. It is a guide to other constellations. It seemingly makes a complete circuit of the sky around Polaris (the Pole Star) in 23 hours 56 minutes; this is actually due to the Earth's rotation. The Plough consists of seven white stars. Dubhe and Merak are pointers to Polaris.

URSA MINOR (The Little Bear) Like Ursa Major, though smaller, it is easily distinguished by seven main stars. It contains Polaris (North Pole Star), a yellow star of second magnitude of utmost use to mariners and astronomers. To ordinary observers, Polaris appears to be the only star which never changes position; actually it does so very slightly, describing a circle of 2° 25′ daily about the true Pole. Illustration shows position of Little Bear at 11.30 p.m. on first day of the month indicated. Thales, Greek astronomer in 7th Century B.C., recommended its use for navigation.

CANIS MAJOR

CANIS MAJOR (The Great Dog) Old legends say Canis Major was 'the hound of Orion when hunting'. It is visible from December to March, below Orion on the horizon. Its main star is Sirius (Dog Star), brightest of all stars, and one of the nearest to the Earth, being only about nine light years distant. Sirius means 'sparkling' and appears to change colour quickly as it sparkles . . . mainly a blue-white. Eastern nations looked to its rising as the precursor of great heat, hence 'the dog days', Sirius being overhead in our dog-days, though invisible.

CYGNUS (SWAN)

CYGNUS (The Swan) A Northern Hemisphere constellation (known also as the Northern Cross) in the Milky Way, directly east of the Lyre, and nearly on the same meridian as the Dolphin. Seen from May to December. Its brightest star, Deneb, is in the tail of the Swan, and always above the horizon in England. One named 61 Cygni (a small variable star in this constellation and almost invisible to the naked eye), was the first to have its distance from the Earth determined—50 billion miles.

CRUX SOUTHERN CROSS

CRUX (Southern Cross) One of the smallest constellations consisting of few stars visible to naked eye; yet it is most attractive, so varied are the coloured stars contained therein. Situated in the Southern Hemisphere, it is always visible at Cape Town and in Australia. It stands out from the Milky Way, and is near a hollow region, destitute of stars, known as 'Coalsack' because of its seeming blackness. Upper and lower stars in centre of the cross point downwards to position of the South Pole, which is approximately 27° 38′ from lowest star.

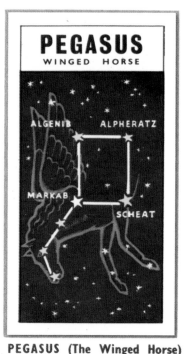

PEGASUS
WINGED HORSE

PEGASUS (The Winged Horse) is seen upside down in our latitudes. Only half of Pegasus is illustrated in celestial maps—one star, Alpheratz, forming part of the adjoining constellation of Andromeda. It is prominent on the meridian at midnight in September. There are many small stars within and in clear atmosphere over 100 may be observed. Markab, a white star of second magnitude, is a navigational star. Scheat is a deep yellow star also of second magnitude. According to mythology Bellerophon tried to ride to heaven on Pegasus' back and was thrown off.

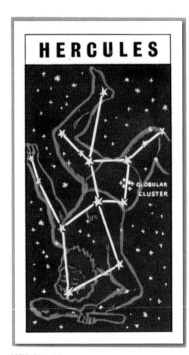

HERCULES

CASSIOPEIA

PERSEUS

MILKY WAY

HERCULES This is a summer constellation and is best seen May to October. It is large and very interesting although containing no star of greater than 3rd magnitude; within it there are numerous double stars, clusters and nebulae. One great cluster is estimated to contain over 1,500 stars concentrated into a very small space in a roughly globular form, and has always been of intense interest to astronomers. Kneeling figure of Hercules, son of Jupiter, is seen upside down. This constellation was mentioned by Eudoxus (4th Century B.C.).

CASSIOPEIA is on the opposite side of the Pole Star from The Plough. It consists notably of a group of five very bright stars forming a W. Two of these, Ruchbah and Caph, are navigation stars. This constellation contains about 60 stars visible without the aid of a telescope. It is named after Cassiopeia, wife of Cepheus, King of Ethiopia, and mother of Andromeda who was saved from a sea monster by Perseus (Greek Mythology).

PERSEUS This Northern Hemisphere constellation is called after the Greek legendary hero, Perseus, son of Jupiter, who rescued Andromeda, daughter of Cassiopeia, from the sea monster. Heis records 136 stars visible therein without telescopic aid. Its main stars are Mirfak, a navigational star, and Algol—a star which varies from second to fourth magnitude, then back to second in about seven hours, and remaining at its greatest lustre for nearly 3 days. Perseus is in the Milky Way, north of Taurus, south of Cassiopeia, east of Triangulum and west of Auriga.

THE MILKY WAY called by the Greeks 'Galaxy' and by the Latins 'Via Lactea' on account of its colour and appearance, is a soft zone of luminous misty light forming a broad but very irregular girdle around the heavens. It covers about one tenth of whole sky. This light is formed by myriads of tiny faint stars, mostly too small to be observed independently (even with powerful telescopes), with a scattering of larger, brighter stars shining here and there. Dark spaces in it are not due to absence of stars, but to dark nebulous matter veiling the stars beyond.

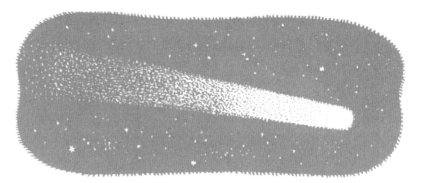

Halley's Comet, which has appeared every 76 years since the third century B.C.

AURORA BOREALIS The Aurora Borealis is a phenomenon of the night sky. In the atmosphere are seen long quivering streamers of light, usually seeming to radiate from an arc. These bands of light are often white, but sometimes red, green, or yellowish. It is most frequently seen between 65 degrees and 80 degrees northern latitude and is believed to be caused by discharges of electricity in the rare upper atmosphere, travelling along the lines of magnetic force which point towards the magnetic North Pole. A similar phenomenon in the Southern hemisphere is known as the Aurora Australis.

Edmund Halley. Born 1656, died 1742. Famous English Astronomer who predicted the return of Halley's Comet.

RADIO TELESCOPES for study of the heavenly bodies have been in use for some time, and a giant one is being erected in Cheshire to transmit and receive ultra-short-waves. These waves are picked up by a large curved wire mesh in a framework, shaped like a bowl fire, which can be pointed anywhere; they are then focused on to an aerial. Disturbances on the sun (sun-spots etc.) emit short radio waves. These affect ordinary radio transmissions by disturbing the upper atmosphere but such interferences may be obviated through discoveries made by Radio Telescopes.

A spiral nebula,
a vast cloud
of stars like
our Milky Way.

ASTROLABE

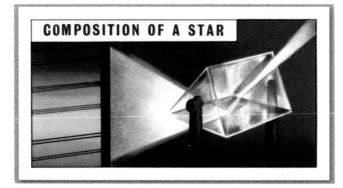

COMPOSITION OF A STAR

COMPOSITION OF A STAR To find out what the stars are made of, we study their light. Starlight is studied by using a spectroscope, in which it is passed through a glass prism and broken up into a coloured band like a rainbow. Dark lines across this 'spectrum' are due to substances in the star's outer layers which have absorbed certain colours. By comparing the colours with those produced by known chemical substances in the laboratory, it has been found that stars consist almost entirely of hydrogen, with small amounts of gaseous iron, chromium, nickel, and other metals.

ASTROLABE One of the earliest instruments used by astronomers. Originally they were spherical in shape and consisted of divided metal circles corresponding to ecliptic, meridian, etc., with which the position of the Sun, Moon and Stars could be measured with fair accuracy. Hipparchus, Greek Astronomer, used one before 100 B.C. Tycho Brahe, Danish astronomer who died in 1601, had one similar to that illustrated. Portable astrolabes varying in size from two inches to a foot were first made in the East in 15th Century and later were used in India, Persia and Arabia.

GLOSSARY OF TERMS

Constellation:
Collection of stars in the same region of the sky which the eye groups naturally together.

Double (triple) stars:
Stars which seem single to the naked eye but appear in the telescope as two (three) close together.

Ecliptic:
Apparent path of the Sun amongst the fixed stars. Centre line of the Zodiac.

Ellipse:
Oval curve resembling a circle compressed along one diameter.

Equinox:
Point where the Sun crosses the equator, northwards at the spring equinox (March 21), southwards at the autumn equinox (Sept. 23).

Magnitude:
Number expressing the brightness of a star. The brightest stars are magnitude 1, those just visible to the naked eye are 6.

Meridian:
Line going from the north point of the horizon overhead to the south point.

Nebula:
Hazy patch of light in the sky which may mark a cloud of gas and dust, or a more distant cloud of stars.

Period:
Time taken by a planet or comet to complete its path once round the Sun.

Revolution:
Motion of an object around a centre of attraction outside itself.

Rotation:
Spinning of an object around an axis inside itself.

Solstice:
Point on the ecliptic midway between the equinoxes. The Sun is farthest north at the summer solstice (June 21) and farthest south at the winter solstice (Dec. 21).

DIAGRAM SHOWING POSITIONS OF THE CONSTELLATIONS
SOUTHERN HEMISPHERE

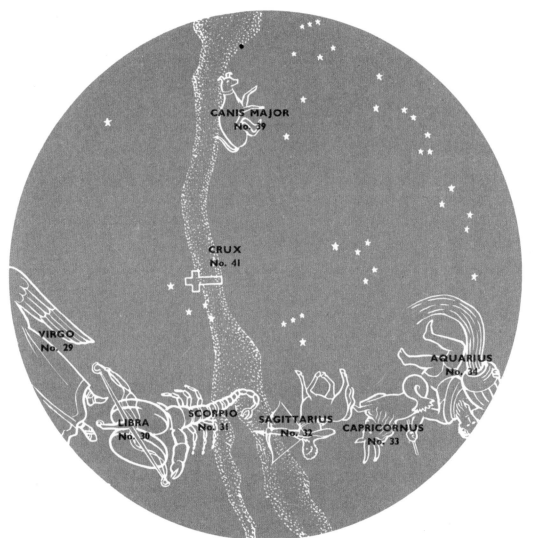

This series of picture cards is offered
in the interests of education by

Brooke Bond & Co. Ltd.

A card is given free in every packet of

Choicest, Edglets and P.G. Tips Tea

The symbol of Brooke Bond service
throughout the world.

THE BERKSHIRE PRINTING CO. LTD.
READING, BERKS

The third of the 'animals' natural history sets following **British Birds** and **Bird Portraits, British Wild Life** was the fifth set from Brooke Bond, first issued in tea in 1958. The set combined the talents of Frances Pitt, who had previously produced **British Birds**, as the writer and the great C. F. Tunnicliffe, the artist whose illustrations had been seen in **Bird Portraits**.

The 50 creatures featured in the wonderful illustrations range from ponies and deer to bats, voles and newts with detailed descriptions of their habits and habitat on the reverse of the cards. This fascinating collaboration between Pitt and Tunnicliffe provided a reference work that is still of value today. How else could you tell the difference between a stoat and a weasel? The fact that most of us are unlikely ever to see either in the wild is beside the point. Knowing that the weasel has a shorter tail without the stoat's dark hairs at the tip was the important thing when it came to settling playground disputes.

BRITISH WILD LIFE

Described by Frances Pitt
illustrated by C. F. Tunnicliffe, R.A.

THE WELSH MOUNTAIN PONY

The Welsh mountain pony is a delightful little animal and makes a very good child's mount. It was formerly much used in the pits, but mechanisation has largely done away with the need for ponies in the mines. Welsh ponies vary in colour—bays, greys, chestnuts and blacks are all to be met with, and a pretty sight they are when seen on a green hillside or wandering over a gorsy common, the little mares followed by their foals, with a proud stallion leading the party.

GET A PICTURE CARD ALBUM FROM YOUR GROCER—Price 6d.

ISSUED IN PACKETS OF BROOKE BOND 'CHOICEST' 'P.G.TIPS' & 'EDGLETS' TEAS

Brooke Bond Tea Ltd.
35 Cannon Street, E.C.4

A SERIES OF 50. No. 6

BRITISH WILD LIFE

Described by Frances Pitt
illustrated by C. F. Tunnicliffe, R.A.

THE ROE DEER
(Capreolus capreolus)

The roe is the smallest of the three well known species of deer found in Britain, it being only about twenty-four inches in height at the shoulder. It is a shy, retiring animal sheltering in woods and thickets in many parts of the country, where it may be found in family parties consisting of a buck, doe and their offspring. The male has small, sharp pointed antlers. The female often has two young at a time.

GET A PICTURE CARD ALBUM FROM YOUR GROCER—Price 6d.

ISSUED IN PACKETS OF BROOKE BOND 'CHOICEST' 'P.G.TIPS' & 'EDGLETS' TEAS

Brooke Bond Tea Ltd.
35 Cannon Street, E.C.4

A SERIES OF 50. No. 29

BRITISH WILD LIFE

Described by Frances Pitt
illustrated by C. F. Tunnicliffe, R.A.

THE WATER VOLE
(Arvicola amphibius)

The water vole must not be confused with the rat, for it is a very different animal, yet it is often called a "water rat", a sad misnomer seeing what a charming inoffensive creature it is. The water vole resembles in many particulars the little meadow vole of the fields. It too is a strict vegetarian and loves to nibble the succulent grasses, but its home is a burrow at the water side and it is semi-aquatic in its habits. It swims well and dives like an expert, and loves to nibble the reeds and rushes. We find it on rivers, canals, lakes and in damp places.

GET A PICTURE CARD ALBUM FROM YOUR GROCER—Price 6d.

ISSUED IN PACKETS OF BROOKE BOND 'CHOICEST' 'P.G.TIPS' & 'EDGLETS' TEAS

Brooke Bond Tea Ltd.
35 Cannon Street, E.C.4

A SERIES OF 50. No. 36

BRITISH WILD LIFE

Described by Frances Pitt
illustrated by C. F. Tunnicliffe, R.A.

THE NOCTULE OR GREAT BAT
(Nyctalus noctula)

The noctule is one of the largest of our more common British bats, to be compared with the greater horseshoe in point of size. We may see it flying strongly, high against the sunset, or we may find it at rest in the church tower, an old barn, or a hole in a tree, of course hitched up by its heels as is customary with bats, which prefer to hang head downwards. Its chief times of activity are at dusk and dawn for, like so many bats, it is largely vespertine in its habits.

GET A PICTURE CARD ALBUM FROM YOUR GROCER—Price 6d.

ISSUED IN PACKETS OF BROOKE BOND 'CHOICEST' 'P.G.TIPS' & 'EDGLETS' TEAS

Brooke Bond Tea Ltd.
35 Cannon Street, E.C.4

Alongside the animal tracks on the inside back cover, there was information about how to obtain cards and albums from the previously issued sets. Of further interest to collectors, this set has no less than three distinct printings with the difference being on the text sides, at the very bottom of the cards just above the address line. The different versions are a) Brooke Bond & Co Ltd, b) Brooke Bond (Great Britain) Ltd, and c) Brooke Bond Tea Ltd.

The display album included an introduction by Frances Pitt, who seemed confident that our moors, woodlands, hedgerows, mountains, waterways and coastline were so teeming with wildlife that we would inevitably come across most of the creatures described in the album at some point. If he encouraged youngsters to become serious naturalists, then he was undoubtedly right. As well as the illustrations on the cards, the album included sketches of "Footprints in the snow" to help identify creatures that may have passed across your path in deepest winter. The quality of this album has certainly stood the test of time and it has lost none of its relevance, with the latest crop of domestic television nature shows concentrating on exactly the same creatures that Pitt and Tunnicliffe presented to us over half a century ago!

The artwork for this set can also be found in books and other cards of the time.

British Wild Life

Described by
Frances Pitt

Illustrated by
C.F. Tunnicliffe R.A.

PRICE SIXPENCE

THE animal life of Britain is very interesting, including as it does creatures so diverse as the red deer, the pigmy shrew and the grey seal, and mammals so beautiful as the red squirrel and the hare, also beasts so highly specialised as our various bats and the subterranean mole.

Our fields, our hedges, our coppices, hills and valleys provide a variety of animals. There is the brown hare on the windswept arable ground, the fox slipping home at dawn to his lair in the wood, and the mouse in the cupboard raiding our stores.

All these are on the list of British mammals and if we give them our attention we shall meet with them and many others, such as the dormouse, the bank vole, perhaps the shy and secret badger, or even that elusive fisherman, the otter.

On the cards of this series you will find pictures of these animals and many more, and you will find much information about them and about their ways.

Frances Pitt

THE SHETLAND PONY   Here we have a picture of a Shetland pony mare and her foal. In days gone by these tiny horses did nearly all the agricultural work of the crofts, but today they are largely replaced by tractors, and the Shetland pony is quite scarce on its native islands. However, there are many to be found in the south, where it is highly esteemed as a children's riding pony. Lucky indeed is the small child who has one of these delightful and docile ponies as his first mount.

THE WELSH MOUNTAIN PONY   The Welsh mountain pony is a delightful little animal and makes a very good child's mount. It was formerly much used in the pits, but mechanisation has largely done away with the need for ponies in the mines. Welsh ponies vary in colour —bays, greys, chestnuts and blacks are all to be met with, and a pretty sight they are when seen on a green hillside or wandering over a gorsy common, the little mares followed by their foals, with a proud stallion leading the party.

WILD WHITE OR PARK CATTLE
Wild white or park cattle are kept in several places in Great Britain. They are fine white cattle with black or red points and date back to the Middle Ages, when the great noblemen enclosed areas of land for sporting purposes. In these parks were deer, wild boars and wild bulls. Whether the cattle were really wild or gone wild is not certain. They may have been the latter. Anyhow the breed still survives, for example the Chillingham herd in the great park at Chillingham in Northumberland, and the Chartley Cattle at Woburn Abbey in Bedfordshire.

FEMALE RED DEER,
OR HIND

THE RED DEER (*Cervus elaphus*) The red deer is the largest and finest of the land mammals that live wild in Britain. Formerly widespread, wild herds today are limited to Devon and Somerset, the Lake District and the Highlands of Scotland. They are mostly found in the Highland deer forests. A deer forest is a treeless area of country where deer are allowed to go their own way. The male red deer has antlers and is called a stag. The female is called a hind. The calves are usually born in June, and are at first prettily spotted. Normally a hind has only one calf at a time.

THE ROE DEER (*Capreolus capreolus*) The roe is the smallest of the three well known species of deer found in Britain, it being only about twenty-four inches in height at the shoulder. It is a shy, retiring animal sheltering in woods and thickets in many parts of the country, where it may be found in family parties consisting of a buck, doe and their offspring. The male has small, sharp pointed antlers. The female often has two young at a time.

THE FALLOW DEER (*Dama dama*) The fallow deer, the beautiful animal with palmate antlers so often kept as an ornamental park species, but also known as a wild beast in the New Forest and many other districts, may or may not be truly indigenous. Opinions differ on this point. Some people believe it was brought here in historic times, but others maintain that it is a true native.

RED DEER CALF

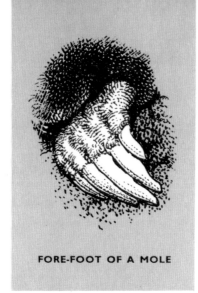

FORE-FOOT OF A MOLE

THE FOX (*Vulpes vulpes*) The red fox is widely distributed throughout Europe and nowhere does it flourish more than in the British Isles, being common from the fringe of London to the outer wilds. It lives on mice and frogs, rabbits and hares, it takes ground-nesting birds and raids fowl pens, and has many foes, from huntsman and hounds to the irate poultry keeper, but it is a cunning creature. In nursery rhyme, in poetry and story it is a popular hero, depicted as the personification of guile, usually winning in a war of wits—it is indeed the cunning fox.

THE MOLE (*Talpa europaea*)
The mole is a marvellous example of adaptation to an underground existence. Its dark velvet-like fur does not easily get dirty, its forepaws are wonderfully strong digging implements, and its nose is remarkably keen so that it can easily detect the earthworms on which it lives. In 24 hours it eats its own weight of worms. Its eyes are so reduced that it is questionable if they can do more than distinguish light from darkness. It works and sleeps in short alternate spells resting in a nest under an extra large hillock known as the mole palace or castle.

THE HEDGEHOG (*Erinaceus europaeus*) We usually know the hedgehog as an inanimate prickly ball, but when unalarmed and unafraid the hedgehog, or urchin, is a sleek, eager active animal as will be seen in the picture. Hedgehogs are fond of worms and grubs in general. They also eat carrion. There is nothing a garden urchin appreciates more than a saucer of bread and milk. Hedgehogs are creatures of the night and most of their activities are undertaken under cover of darkness.

FOX CUBS

53

THE BADGER OR BROCK (*Meles meles*)   The badger or brock is an animal that has survived in some numbers despite much persecution. It has never received any protection for sporting purposes—it is a truly wild beast. It lives in a large burrow known as a "sett" and is strictly nocturnal in its habits, hence its presence in a neighbourhood often goes unsuspected. Sometimes, particularly in the autumn, it may make itself known by long, loud yells, which are probably a love song. The cubs, generally two or three in number, are born in February or March.

THE OTTER (*Lutra lutra*)   The otter has webbed feet, a waterproof coat and is an expert fisherman, yet it is not entirely wedded to an aquatic life. It hunts rabbits and even birds with gusto and is not averse to a cross country excursion, especially in winter when snow lies around. Few animals are more playful than the otter and it loves to romp in the snow, when it often toboggans head first down the banks. Otters are vagrant in their habits, fishing part of a river, then moving on several miles, next exploring a stream, but eventually working back to their original headquarters.

THE POLECAT (*Putorius putorius*)   Here we have a picture of a Welsh polecat, an animal that closely resembles a big, dark, ferret; indeed some people think that the ferret, whether dark or white, is a domestic form of the polecat. Polecats used to be common throughout Great Britain, living on rabbits, frogs, field voles and maybe a hen or two, but persecution reduced them until today we must go to the valleys and bogs of central Wales, before we can have much hope of meeting with this handsome outlaw. Usually it is dark brown-black in colour, but occasionally a sandy-red variety occurs.

THE PINE MARTEN (*Martes martes*)   The pine marten looks like a cross between a fox, a squirrel and a little cat, but it belongs to the stoat tribe. It was formerly common in the woods of the British Isles, but it is now a rarity of the wilds. A few survive in the west of Ireland, one or two in North Wales and the Lake District, and a few in the Highlands of Scotland. Very active and a great climber, it used to chase squirrels and birds through the tree-tops. The picture shows a marten aloft on a branch. The winter fur of the marten is as lovely as that of the sable.

THE STOAT (*Mustela erminea*)   The stoat or ermine is a native of Great Britain and Ireland. It is also widespread on the Continent of Europe, in the north of which it regularly adopts a winter coat of white, though it always retains the dark pencil of hairs at the end of its tail. It is then known as the ermine and is the origin of the lovely white fur used to trim State robes and so on. The dark spots on the white fur are tails. The stoat is a great hunter of rabbits but when rabbits are few it turns its attention to mice, voles, rats, frogs, birds, etc. The picture shows the stoat in its summer coat.

THE WEASEL (*Mustela nivalis*)   Hardly more than a finger-thickness of life and devilment, the weasel is a great hunter of small game particularly mice and voles and is a valuable factor in keeping these prolific rodents within bounds. Its world is the jungle of grass, weeds, ferns and other vegetation. Here we find small tunnels, along which passes the weasel, more like a snake than a fur-clad animal, hunting the little rodents with ruthless efficiency. The weasel may be distinguished from the stoat by its lesser size, sandy hue and its short tail without any terminal tuft of dark hairs.

THE COMMON SEAL (*Phoca vitulina*)   The common seal is the smaller of the two species of seal that breed on our shores. It prefers quiet coasts, with sand banks, to the rocky haunts so loved by the grey or Atlantic seal and is plentiful on the East coast of England where it may be seen in large herds. This seal has a spotted coat but may be distinguished from the grey seal by its much rounder head. It has its single young one in summer.

THE GREY SEAL (*Halichoerus grypus*) The grey or Atlantic seal is the bigger of the two species of seal that breed in British waters, and is essentially an animal of our rocky shores, whereas the smaller common seal loves sand banks. Its single young one is born in the autumn, in caves, in sheltered coves and on islands along the Welsh coast, the Scottish shore, on the Orkneys and Shetlands and on the Farne Islands off the coast of Northumberland. The last named colony is a strong one, and here the calves do not appear until November.

SCOTTISH WILD CAT (*Felis silvestris*)   There are gone-wild cats and truly wild cats and they are very different animals. The real wild cat, *Felis silvestris*, is one of the most untamable of savages. In the British Isles it is now found only in the Highlands of Scotland, where it roams the hills and glens, living on grouse, ptarmigan and mountain hares, plus voles and mice. The old male is a fine fellow and most devoted mate. The wild cat is a striped rusty-coloured tabby, with a handsome black tip to its tail and black soles to its feet, and does not vary in colour.

THE GREY SQUIRREL (*Sciurus carolinensis*) The grey squirrel was brought from North America to England in the middle of the nineteenth century. Today it is widespread and numerous and is spreading into Wales and the Lowlands of Scotland. It was at first regarded as a delightful addition to our fauna, but soon this opinion was reversed. Where it appeared our native red squirrel disappeared and, as it grew more numerous, it began to do damage, particularly in orchards and young plantations. Today it is regarded as a pest.

THE RED SQUIRREL (*Sciurus vulgaris*)
Formerly a common inhabitant of the woods of Britain, the red squirrel has lately been displaced in wide areas by the grey squirrel. However, it is still found in many woods and is widespread in Continental forests. The British red squirrel differs slightly from that across the Channel, for example its fur is more liable to fade and its tail becomes very bleached in summer, so it has been given subspecific rank and the lengthy name of *S. vulgaris leucourus*. But by whatever title it may be known, a red squirrel is one of the most graceful and beautiful of animals.

THE MOUNTAIN OR BLUE HARE (*Lepus timidus*)   Whereas the brown hare is a lowland species that likes cultivated land, the smaller, greyer mountain hare is an animal of the wilder, northern, more mountainous regions. The mountain, blue or variable hare owes its last name to the fact that it changes colour in winter, when it grows a white coat, which is excellent camouflage among snowy surroundings. The hare shown here is in full winter coat, completely white save for the black tips of its ears. The Irish hare is a subspecies of *Lepus timidus* that does not turn white in winter.

THE BROWN HARE (*Lepus europaeus*)   The brown hare is the common hare of the lowlands and loves well-cultivated fields. It usually rests in a "form" by day and explores the countryside by night. The young ones, called leverets, are born in one of its "forms". They have furry coats and large bright eyes. The mother does not worry much about them and soon they are nibbling grass and going their own way. The female hare is known as a "doe" and the male is called the "jack". When two jack hares meet they may rear on their hind legs and beat each other with their fore paws, but such combats are seldom serious.

THE RABBIT (*Oryctolagus cuniculus*)
The rabbit is one of the best known mammals met with in the British Isles. It came to Northern Europe from the Iberian Peninsula, and was probably brought across the English Channel by some of the sporting Norman barons. Anyhow the rabbit soon made itself at home and spread to most parts of the land. Efforts to keep it within bounds met with small success, until the disease called myxomatosis broke out when rabbits vanished from wide areas. They have, however, reappeared in many places.

THE BLACK OR OLD ENGLISH RAT (*Rattus rattus*) Rats are of Asiatic origin and came to Western Europe comparatively recently. The black rat, which may be grey or fawn as well as black, arrived about the time of the Crusades. It is a mouse-like animal of lighter build than the brown rat. It is very active and easily invaded the old wooden houses, where being susceptible to the dreaded bubonic plague, it was, by means of its fleas, an agent in the spread of the disease. In early Georgian days the brown rat came and ousted the black, but the latter is still to be found in many ports and frequently on ships.

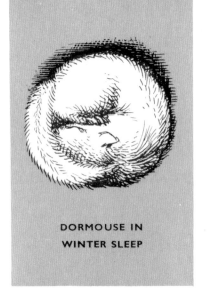

DORMOUSE IN WINTER SLEEP

TEETH OF A RODENT—BROWN RAT

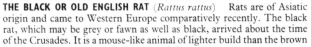

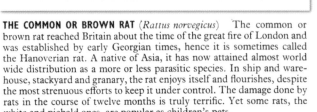

THE COMMON OR BROWN RAT (*Rattus norvegicus*) The common or brown rat reached Britain about the time of the great fire of London and was established by early Georgian times, hence it is sometimes called the Hanoverian rat. A native of Asia, it has now attained almost world wide distribution as a more or less parasitic species. In ship and warehouse, stackyard and granary, the rat enjoys itself and flourishes, despite the most strenuous efforts to keep it under control. The damage done by rats in the course of twelve months is truly terrific. Yet some rats, the white and piebald ones, are popular as children's pets.

THE DORMOUSE
(*Muscardinus avellanarius*) The dormouse with yellow-buff fur, large dark eyes and a long rather fluffy tail, is a beautiful little animal. It haunts thickets, dingles and hazel coppices, where it climbs aloft to feed on nuts and insects. It builds a breeding nest in the bushes but when autumn comes it seeks a safe refuge down a hole or under a tree stump. Here it falls asleep, only waking from hibernation when the temperature rises. Formerly common and well-known as a child's pet, the dormouse has recently become much scarcer. Today it is most numerous in the south west counties of England.

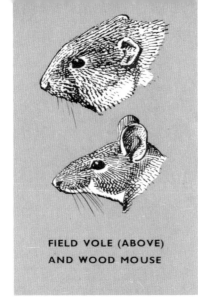

**FIELD VOLE (ABOVE)
AND WOOD MOUSE**

THE WATER VOLE (*Arvicola amphibius*) The water vole must not be confused with the rat, for it is a very different animal, yet it is often called a "water rat", a sad misnomer seeing what a charming inoffensive creature it is. The water vole resembles in many particulars the little meadow vole of the fields. It too is a strict vegetarian and loves to nibble the succulent grasses, but its home is a burrow at the water side and it is semi-aquatic in its habits. It swims well and dives like an expert, and loves to nibble the reeds and rushes. We find it on rivers, canals, lakes and in damp places.

THE BANK VOLE

(*Clethrionomys glareolus*) The bank vole or red mouse is a dapper little animal. It is clad in red-brown above and white beneath. It is a common inhabitant of hedge-bank and thicket in most parts of the British Isles. Allied but slightly different forms occur on certain Hebridean islands and on Skomer Island off the Welsh Coast. The Skomer vole is somewhat bigger and a brighter brown in colour than the common bank vole, however all the bank voles are very smart, indeed they are most attractive wee beasts.

THE FIELD VOLE OR GRASS MOUSE (*Microtus agrestis*) A small, brown, furry, short-eared, short-tailed mouse, the meadow vole depends on grass for both food and shelter. It is widespread in Europe and varies a good deal but, whatever the subspecies, it is ever the same inoffensive beast watched over by owl and kestrel, buzzard and fox, weasel and stoat. Yet, despite the efforts of these predators, it is subject to periodic fluctuations when it may become excessively numerous. A vole plague is a serious thing, the swarming voles eating all greenery, but disease breaks out and they vanish for the time being.

WATER VOLE SWIMMING

59

THE WATER SHREW (*Neomys fodiens*) The water shrew is a beautiful little animal, clad in black velvet with a white underneath, that lives at the waterside and feeds on grubs, aquatic insects and the small things of damp places. The water shrew is an expert swimmer and dives with ease, when bubbles of air caught in its fur make it look like a pencil of quicksilver. Like all the shrews this species is very keen and active, racing and chasing around with great energy. If strangers meet they may go for one another and fight desperately, indeed they will probably battle to death.

THE LESSER OR PIGMY SHREW (*Sorex minutus*) A pencil-thickness of life, fur and hectic energy, the lesser or pigmy shrew is a widespread yet little known animal. Shrews are highly specialised hunters, living on insects, grubs and so on, and have no kinship with the rodents, yet they are sometimes spoken of as "Shrew mice". There are three species on the mainland of Britain, the black and white water shrew, the grey-brown common shrew and the pigmy shrew, which is the smallest of living mammals. But it has spirit out of all proportion to its size, racing and chasing its tiny quarry with amazing ferocity.

THE HOUSE MOUSE (*Mus musculus*)
The house mouse is indeed well-known to us all. Of Asiatic origin it early linked its fortunes with those of mankind and journeyed along the trade routes, to attain practically world wide distribution. The pretty white and fancy mice often kept as pets are of this species, but normally the house mouse is of plain grey hue. Its musty smell is an unpleasant characteristic, yet however we wage war against it, aided by the cat, it continues to flourish and there are few houses without a mouse or two, raiding the store cupboards and making themselves at home.

THE LONG-TAILED FIELD MOUSE OR WOOD MOUSE (*Apodemus sylvaticus*)
This pretty, long-tailed, sleek-coated mouse, is an inhabitant of field, hedge bank, thicket and wood, nor is it averse to the garden where it often raids our seeds. A dainty wee creature it runs here and there under cover of night, for it is strictly nocturnal in its habits. However the owls keep watch on its doings and help to limit its numbers. Even so it is not only widespread, but probably the most numerous of our smaller mammals, particularly in those seasons when the mouse population rises to a peak.

THE YELLOW-NECKED MOUSE
(*Apodemus flavicollis wintoni*) In many parts of the west of England, in the midland and southern counties, we meet with a large and very beautiful long-tailed or wood mouse. To country folk it is known as the greyhound mouse and to scientists as *Apodemus flavicollis wintoni*, the yellow-necked mouse of de Winton. It owes its name to a fawn band across its chest. It was first recognised as a British species in Herefordshire, our form being slightly different from the yellow-necked mouse found on the Continent.

THE HARVEST MOUSE
(*Micromys minutus*) One of the most delightful of the smaller mammals found in Europe is the sandy-hued harvest mouse. So small and light that a corn stem does not bend beneath it, it is a wonderful acrobat, its climbing ability being enhanced by its prehensile tail. In Britain today it is chiefly found in south-eastern England, where in summer it frequents the cornfields, building a neat nest slung between the stems of the grain. In winter it seeks refuge in hedges, ditches, and even the stacks, though the latter retreat is only a temporary one, as it is driven out at threshing time.

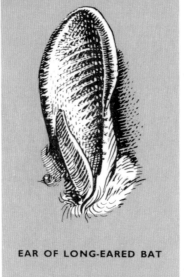

EAR OF LONG-EARED BAT

THE NOCTULE OR GREAT BAT (*Nyctalus noctula*) The noctule is one of the largest of our more common British bats, to be compared with the greater horseshoe in point of size. We may see it flying strongly, high against the sunset, or we may find it at rest in the church tower, an old barn, or a hole in a tree, of course hitched up by its heels as is customary with bats, which prefer to hang head downwards. Its chief times of activity are at dusk and dawn for, like so many bats, it is largely vespertine in its habits.

THE GREATER HORSESHOE BAT (*Rhinolophus ferrum-equinum*) This strange-looking, most remarkable bat, with its horse-shoe-like appendage on its nose, shares with the Noctule the distinction of being one of our bigger members of the order *Chiroptera*, it having a wing-span of thirteen to fourteen inches. It loves rocky recesses and may be found quite numerously in many of the caverns of south-west England, where it seems to enjoy the damp atmosphere and the equable temperature.

THE LONG-EARED BAT (*Plecotus auritus*) The long-eared bat is a remarkable little animal. Its immense ears are nearly as long as its head and body, and it waves them around like great antennae. It is fond of moth hunting and pursues its quarry around bushes and in and out of branches. Its eyes though bright are not large and it is believed that it hears rather than sees its way. In flight, it utters shrill supersonic squeaks inaudible to even the keenest of human ears. These sounds are reflected from its surroundings and picked up by its 'radar' outfit, of which the extraordinary ears are part.

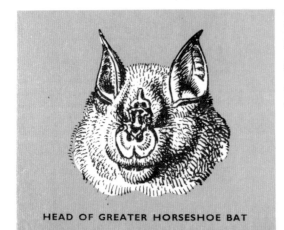

HEAD OF GREATER HORSESHOE BAT

WING AND LEG OF A BAT

THE PIPISTRELLE

(*Pipistrellus pipistrellus*) The pipistrelle or flittermouse is one of the most numerous of that remarkable clan, the bats, which chase insects through the summer twilight. The country name of "flittermouse" recalls the old belief that the bat is half mouse and half bird. In fact it is a member of an extraordinarily specialised order of mammals, the *Chiroptera*, far removed from the rodents and having nothing whatever to do with birds. The pipistrelle is one of our smallest bats. The little bats that flutter about the house and up and down the garden path are usually of this species.

THE SAND LIZARD (*Lacerta agilis*) This lizard is a southern species so far as the British Isles are concerned, being as its name suggests a creature of sandy situations. It varies much in colour and markings, being sometimes of brown hue and sometimes quite green. Its usual colour is brownish-green. It lays eggs, a dozen or more in the sand, carefully covering them up and leaving the sun to hatch them. In the case of the common lizard the young hatch before birth and come into the world as perfect little lizards.

THE COMMON LIZARD

(*Lacerta vivipara*) The common lizard loves the heath lands, sun-warmed rocks and places where it can sit and bask, but it is a quick nimble little thing, and is not easy to surprise. Make a movement towards it and it vanishes as if by magic. It lives on flies and other small things, and its young, which are miniature editions of the parent, need similar fare but of even smaller size. The lizard has its foes. The watchful kestrel hovering on high may see it, drop swiftly groundwards and pick it up before it is aware of the danger. A fox may also snap it up and even the cat may spring on it.

THE GRASS SNAKE (*Natrix natrix*) The grass snake, the largest reptile found in Great Britain, which may attain as much as 30 ins. or more in length, may be distinguished from the adder by the absence of pattern on the back and the presence of dark marks on the flanks. Its ground colour is olive-buff. It is quite harmless to all things bigger than frogs, newts and similar creatures on which it feeds. It lays eggs under piles of decaying vegetation, in manure heaps and such situations, the small snakes that emerge being miniature editions of their parents.

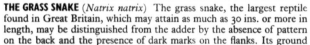

HEAD OF GRASS SNAKE

BLINDWORM OR SLOW-WORM (*Anguis fragilis*) The blindworm or slow-worm is not blind and it is not slow, moreover it is not a snake despite the fact that it looks like one. Without mark or pattern, olive-buff in colour, this legless lizard is quite common. It is generally about 18 ins. in length and is often thought to be a "poisonous snake", a belief enhanced by its "sting". The so-called "sting" is nothing but the black forked tongue which the blindworm flicks in and out of its mouth and uses as a feeler. In truth the blindworm is perfectly harmless and quite safe to handle.

THE ADDER (*Vipera berus*) The adder or viper is the only poisonous snake found in Great Britain. It does not occur in Ireland, although it is widespread on the Continent. It varies a good deal in colour, but the typical specimen is grey-buff with a dark diamond pattern down the spine. It is an inoffensive creature and does not attack if left alone. Its bite is not dangerous to a healthy person, though by no means a thing to trifle with. It can be fatal to dogs and sheep. An average adder is 20 ins. or a little more in length. Its favourite haunts are moors and heaths.

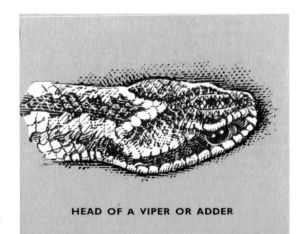

HEAD OF A VIPER OR ADDER

THE SMOOTH SNAKE (*Coronella austriaca*)   This is a small snake, seldom more than twenty-four inches in length. It varies a good deal in colour but is usually prettily spotted on a greyish-brown ground and has a narrow head. It owes its name to its smooth feel. Its scales lack the ridges that give a grass snake a rough feel. It is a local species haunting dry stony places in the south of England, places that appeal to the sand lizard upon which it preys. Its food consists of lizards, blindworms and such things.

THE COMMON FROG (*Rana temporaria*) The frog is a well-known inhabitant of the British countryside, haunting damp meadows and marshy ground. It hibernates in winter but emerges at the first hint of spring, when it seeks water, chooses a mate and lays quantities of jelly-like spawn. From this mass of eggs there emerge numbers of small dark tadpoles. These swim about in the pond and grow rapidly. As they grow they undergo a transformation. Legs appear, the tail is absorbed and gills give place to lungs. The juvenile frog leaves the water for the waterside vegetation where it hunts insects and grubs.

THE EDIBLE FROG (*Rana esculenta*) This is the frog well known on the Continent for its edible qualities. Whether it is a native of Britain is doubtful though it occurs in various places in south eastern England, where it has probably been introduced. The male has a very loud strong voice. The globular sacs one on each side of the head are noticeable. The common frog does not possess such sacs. The edible frog is a much more aquatic species than the common frog and does not wander far from the water in which it dives and swims with such skill.

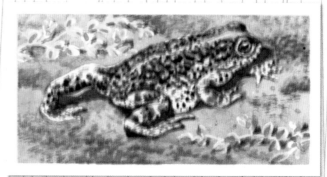

THE COMMON TOAD (*Bufo bufo*) The common toad is a familiar inhabitant of garden and field. It leaves its hiding-place in the evening to search for insects and grubs. It may be known from a frog by its rough warty skin; from these warty glands it can, when annoyed, emit an acid secretion that makes it distasteful to dogs, cats, foxes, owls, etc. The toad breeds in the spring in some favoured pond. Its spawn is in long strings of jelly-like eggs, from which little black tadpoles emerge. These are eventually transformed into tiny toads which leave the pool for the land.

THE NATTERJACK TOAD (*Bufo calamita*) The natterjack is a small greyish toad, of very local distribution in Great Britain, though occurring in widespread places from Scotland to the south of England. It also occurs in Ireland. Where it is found it may be quite numerous. It has a creamy line down its spine which is a useful means of identification, and it is not so warty in appearance as the common toad, moreover it is more brisk in its movements and gives the impression of being longer in its limbs.

THE PALMATED NEWT (*Triturus helveticus*) We have three newts in the British Isles, the great crested newt, the common newt and the palmated newt which owes its name to the webbing between the toes of its hind feet, a characteristic that distinguishes it from the two first-mentioned species. This webbing is shown in our picture. All three species breed in water and their young begin life as tadpoles similar to those of the frog. After breeding in the spring the newts come ashore and in winter hide in some convenient nook to hibernate until spring returns.

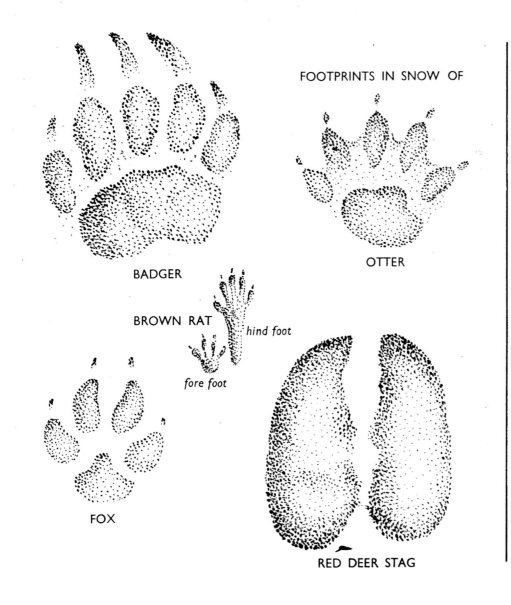

FOOTPRINTS IN SNOW OF

BADGER

OTTER

BROWN RAT

hind foot

fore foot

FOX

RED DEER STAG

Previous Picture Card Series obtainable as long as stocks last:

WILD FLOWERS

50 cards with album....2'6d

OUT INTO SPACE

50 cards with album....2'6d

BIRD PORTRAITS

50 cards with album....2'6d

From :

Brooke Bond (Great Britain) Ltd., 35 Cannon Street, London E.C.4. Write your name and address in BLOCK letters and mark envelope 'Picture Cards'.

This series of picture cards is offered
in the interests of education by

Brooke Bond

A card is given free in every packet of
Choicest, Edglets and P. G. Tips Tea

The prolific C. F. Tunnicliffe provided a breathtaking series of illustrations for **Wild Flowers Series 2**, the sixth set from Brooke Bond. Issued in 1959, this set followed up the earlier **Wild Flowers** to give collectors a wealth of information on 100 different species. To emphasise that this album portrayed an entirely new collection of plants, a note below the contents listing on the inside front cover read "None of the above flowers appear in the first WILD FLOWERS series."

While the previous book had been photographic, produced by the celebrated nature photographer John Markham, this time both illustrations and descriptions were prepared by Tunnicliffe. The cards displayed an incredible level of detail and variety of shape and colour, yet Tunnicliffe himself pointed out in his introduction to the album that "The living flowers, especially when examined through a good magnifying lens, would reveal even more variety".

Clearly with the idea in mind to show as much detail as possible, Tunnicliffe provided additional line illustration inside the album that showed some of the flowers in a different way, concentrating on the roots, seed pods or other aspects of the plants' life cycle.

There were also supplementary illustrations on the inside back cover to explain how insects helped to pollinate flowers. As with British Wildlife, these extra illustrations sat alongside details of how to obtain cards and albums from the previously issued sets.

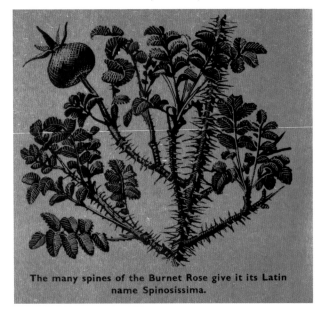

The many spines of the Burnet Rose give it its Latin name Spinosissima.

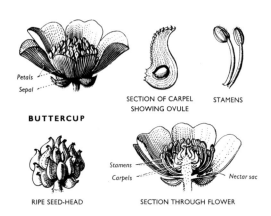

Petals
Sepal

BUTTERCUP

SECTION OF CARPEL
SHOWING OVULE

STAMENS

RIPE SEED-HEAD

Stamens
Carpels

Nectar sac

SECTION THROUGH FLOWER

Collectors will be interested to know that this set has two different original printings with the difference being on the text sides, at the very bottom of the cards. The first version states "Brooke Bond Tea Ltd. , 35 Cannon Street, E.C.4" (on two lines) while the second version has "ISSUED BY BROOKE BOND TEA LTD. 35 CANNON STREET, E.C.4" (on three lines).

The set was also officially reprinted in 1973, along with a number of other sets, and is the earliest to enjoy this status. The cards can easily be identified from the originals as the card texts are printed in black instead of blue. At the same time the album was also reprinted, this time without the price on the cover.

ALBUM FOR

Wild
Flowers

(SERIES 2)

BROOKE BOND PICTURE CARDS

ILLUSTRATED AND DESCRIBED BY
C. F. TUNNICLIFFE R.A.

PRICE SIXPENCE

*I*F you compare the following fifty flower portraits you will note the great variety in their shapes and colours. The living flowers, especially when examined through a good magnifying lens, would reveal even more variety, and yet all these flowers exist for the one purpose—to produce fertile seeds so that the species may continue. We are fortunate that they do this in so many different ways, for as you study them you will be entranced by their intricate beauty, a beauty which is common to them all, from the lowliest buttercup to the rarest orchid. These cards are arranged approximately in the order of flowering.

Beautiful flowers sometimes have poisonous properties, and it is most unwise to eat the berries or seeds of wild plants in case they are harmful.

CARD NUMBERS OF FLOWERS IN THIS ALBUM

1	LESSER CELANDINE	26	AMPHIBIOUS PERSICARIA
2	WOOD ANEMONE	27	WHITE WATER-LILY
3	BUTTERBUR	28	YELLOW WATER-LILY
4	DAFFODIL	29	CENTAURY
5	PERIWINKLE	30	ROCK SAMPHIRE
6	WILD GARLIC	31	SEA-PINK
7	VERNAL SQUILL	32	SEA LAVENDER
8	PURPLE SAXIFRAGE	33	HORNED POPPY
9	EARLY PURPLE ORCHIS	34	SEA HOLLY
10	YELLOW FLAG	35	FOXGLOVE
11	WATER CROWFOOT	36	GREATER BINDWEED
12	COWSLIP	37	SOAPWORT
13	GLOBE FLOWER	38	COLUMBINE
14	PASQUE FLOWER	39	HERB ROBERT
15	MARSH HELLEBORINE	40	CHICORY
16	WILD ARUM	41	RAGGED ROBIN
17	GRASS OF PARNASSUS	42	HENBANE
18	BEE ORCHID	43	TUFTED VETCH
19	MARSH GENTIAN	44	HOUSE LEEK
20	ARROW-HEAD	45	WALL PENNYWORT
21	SUNDEW	46	TANSY
22	BUTTERWORT	47	ROSE-BAY WILLOW-HERB
23	SWEET VIOLET	48	CARLINE THISTLE
24	YELLOW or BITING STONECROP	49	PURPLE LOOSESTRIFE
25	BURNET ROSE	50	MEADOW SAFFRON

None of the above flowers appear in the first WILD FLOWERS series.

LESSER CELANDINE (*Ranunculus ficaria L.*) Weeks before Spring really arrives the yellow stars of the Celandine flowers grace the hedge-banks and the waste ground, braving the snows of February, and the bitter winds of March, to open at the first touch of sunlight. The first flowers usually appear about mid-February, and the blooming continues into May. In spite of its rather fragile appearance it is a virile plant, storing food in its swollen and tuberous roots in readiness for its next flowering.

WOOD ANEMONE (*Anemone nemorosa L.*) This exquisite fragile plant often carpets the ground of deciduous woodlands. It blooms early in the year. The flowers grow on slender stems which look as though the slightest breeze would break them, but they survive the roaring winds of late March and, turning their faces away from the blast, are none the worse; indeed the plant's other name is Wind-flower. It is at its best in late April—early May, but will continue to bloom until early June.

BUTTERBUR (*Petasites hybridus L.*) A plant of the damp places and river banks. The flowers appear early and before the leaves, and the club-shaped flower heads are either male or female. They are rich in honey, and the bees love to visit them. The leaves, when they are fully grown, are huge and resemble giant rhubarb leaves. They can attain a diameter of three feet and are borne on strong hollow stalks. Its flowering period is March to May.

DAFFODIL (*Narcissus pseudo-narcissus L.*) The wild Daffodil is very local in its distribution. It favours damp woods and pastures in England and Wales and is a true native. In its chosen place it grows in great profusion, and seen thus it is a beautiful and gladsome sight, for at that time—in mid-March—there are few other flowers in bloom. The true wild form has a perianth of pale yellow and a crown of deeper yellow.

PERIWINKLE (*Vinca major L.*) A plant of the milder parts of Britain, growing in hedgerows and rough copses. It has long trailing stems, from which grow the erect flower stalks, and from which it puts down roots at every node. Its flowers may be seen in greatest numbers in April and May, but blooms appear throughout the year. This painting was made from a flower in early February. It retains its leaves all through the Winter. Not a native although it has grown in Britain at least since Chaucer's time.

A COMPLETE PLANT OF VERNAL SQUILL

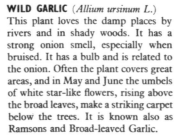

Note the unusual 'lop-sided' shape of each lobe of the Periwinkle flower.

WILD GARLIC (*Allium ursinum L.*) This plant loves the damp places by rivers and in shady woods. It has a strong onion smell, especially when bruised. It has a bulb and is related to the onion. Often the plant covers great areas, and in May and June the umbels of white star-like flowers, rising above the broad leaves, make a striking carpet below the trees. It is known also as Ramsons and Broad-leaved Garlic.

VERNAL SQUILL (*Scilla verna Huds.*) On dry grassy slopes and headlands by the sea, especially on the western coasts of Britain, this beautiful little plant may be found though it is not common. On favourable sites it will grow in great profusion, and in Spring the blue of its flowers appears, from a distance, as a mist over the ground. The flower stems are rarely more than five inches high, and in the more exposed situations are usually three to four inches.

PURPLE SAXIFRAGE (*Saxifraga oppositifolia L.*) This exquisite alpine plant grows on mountains in north Britain. Its pink-purple flowers, each growing singly at the tip of an inch-long stem, are often so thickly packed that they form a cushion of colour which almost conceals the tiny leaves. It blooms in Spring and early Summer, and is usually found growing on damp rocks, high on the mountains, and often in the most inhospitable situations, in patches which may reach twelve inches in diameter.

EARLY PURPLE ORCHIS (*Orchis mascula L.*) This is the commonest and one of the earliest of the many species of British Orchids. It blooms from April to June and may be found in pastures and meadows, downland and sand dunes, and in woods which are not too dark. In colour and size it is very variable, and can range from deep purple-red to almost white, and from six inches to eighteen in height. Usually its leaves are spotted, but not invariably so.

FLOWER AND ROOT OF EARLY PURPLE ORCHIS

YELLOW FLAG (*Iris pseudacorus L.*) From May to July the conspicuous yellow flowers of this Iris, guarded by their long, blade-like leaves, adorn the margins of rivers, ponds, lakes and lowly ditches. The flowers are of more than usual interest as all their parts are arranged in threes, and the larger petal-like forms are really sepals, the true petals being quite narrow and in the centre of the flower. The arched and re-curved form on the sepal is the style.

COWSLIP (*Primula veris L.*) The Cowslip grows in open fields and downland, and favours a clayey soil. Often it may be found in large colonies. It blooms in April and May. Like its relative the Primrose its flowers are of two kinds, one having a long style and the other a short one. The two forms are not found in the same flower-head but are borne on separate plants. A well-grown plant is about six to seven inches high.

GLOBE FLOWER (*Trollius europaeus L.*) A plant very beautiful in both leaves and flowers, growing in damp places in mountainous districts. Its ball-like flower is composed chiefly of large petal-like sepals which overlap and do not open. The real petals are enclosed in these and are quite small. It grows to a height of about two feet and blooms from May to July. It is a true native wild flower but is not common.

WATER CROWFOOT (*Ranunculus aquatilis L.*) A plant of the still waters, sometimes covering large areas, its floating leaves often completely hiding the water surface. The leaves below the surface are quite different in form from the floating leaves, being little more than thin, branched filaments. The flowers are white tinged with yellow at the base of the petals, and are carried singly on erect stems two to two and a half inches long. There are several very similar related species, the differences being concerned with the shapes of the leaves.

WATER CROWFOOT
Note the two kinds of leaves—the lobed surface leaves and the linear submerged leaves.

PASQUE FLOWER (*Anemone pulsatilla L.*) A rare and beautiful flower found wild only on chalky pastures and downs in England, though it is grown in many gardens. Its stalks and leaves are covered with silver hairs and even the flowers are hairy on their outer sides. It flowers in May, and at first the flowers are erect but later they droop. The bright flowers attract many insects, particularly bees, which help to pollinate them.

MARSH HELLEBORINE (*Epipactis palustris L.*) As its name implies this Helleborine grows in damp places particularly where the soil contains lime. It likes the damp hollows in sand dunes and the specimen depicted grew in such a place. It was fifteen inches high, but taller plants are often found. It blooms in July. It is an Orchid, and the flower stalk springs from a long-creeping root stock or rhizome. Though nowhere common it is widely distributed throughout Britain.

WILD ARUM (*Arum maculatum L.*) Sometimes called Lords and Ladies, and Cuckoo Pint. The glossy green leaves appear early in the Spring under trees and shady hedges; later, in April, the flower stalk appears bearing a large rolled up bract which subsequently uncurls to disclose a purple column. This uncurled bract is not the flower, several of which are enclosed in the throat of the bract and cannot be seen. Pollination is effected by flies, which become imprisoned in the throat until fertilisation is completed.

GRASS OF PARNASSUS (*Parnassia palustris L.*) This flower is very localised in its distribution and requires bogs and swampy ground for a habitat. Where conditions are suitable it often flowers in profusion, but it cannot be considered common. The blooms appear in August and are of an exquisite wax-like quality which contrast strongly with their sometimes forbidding surroundings. It has a peculiar arrangement of stamens which ensures cross pollination between flowers. The only British species, its nearest relatives being the Saxifrages.

BEE ORCHID (*Ophrys apifera Huds.*) On dry limestone or chalk soil you may find the Bee Orchid, but there is nothing certain about its appearance. One year it will grow in great numbers, and on the same site in the following year only one or two plants may appear. The flower does indeed resemble a bumble bee with its head in a pale flower, but as a rule is self-pollinated by means of a very ingenious mechanism. It blooms in June and July.

MARSH GENTIAN (*Gentiana pneumonanthe L.*) A rare and beautiful plant which is decreasing. It grows on boggy heathlands usually in hilly mountainous districts, and is in bloom in August and September. The average height of the plant is about seven inches though it can attain twelve inches. In England and Wales it is a true wild native, and no doubt one of the causes of its decrease is the reclamation of land, on which the plant grows, for grazing and ploughing.

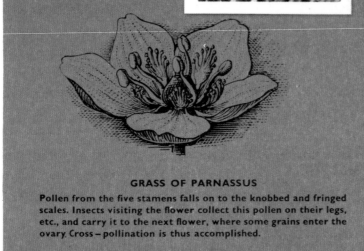

GRASS OF PARNASSUS

Pollen from the five stamens falls on to the knobbed and fringed scales. Insects visiting the flower collect this pollen on their legs, etc., and carry it to the next flower, where some grains enter the ovary. Cross – pollination is thus accomplished.

ARROW-HEAD (*Sagittaria sagittifolia L.*) Arrow-head likes to have its feet in water, and may be found by the edges of canals and ponds. The shape of the leaves gives it its name. Leaf and flower stem are three-sided; the flowers have three sepals and three petals and they are arranged in groups of three up the stem. The upper flowers are usually male, the lower ones female. It flowers from July to September.

SUNDEW (*Drosera rotundfolia L.*) This interesting plant grows in bogs and damp hollows. It is insectivorous, its round leaves having a ring of red filaments which exude a sticky substance. Flies touching this are held. Their struggles cause the leaf-margins to curl up and the flies are imprisoned, and then absorbed by the leaf juices. The tiny white flowers on their slender stem appear in July and August. Sometimes the flower-stem divides into two sprays of flowers.

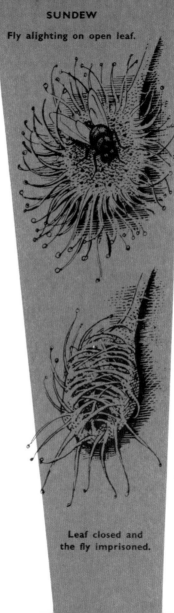

SUNDEW

Fly alighting on open leaf.

Leaf closed and the fly imprisoned.

BUTTERWORT (*Pinguicula vulgaris L.*) Like the Sundew the Butterwort grows in boggy and damp places and it too is insectivorous. The fleshy leaves are sticky and, when small insects adhere to them, the edges of the leaves curl inwards and the leaf-juice eventually absorbs the insects. The bluish-purple flowers are borne singly on slender stems, three to six inches high, which spring from the centre of the rosette of leaves. It flowers from May to July.

79

SWEET VIOLET (*Viola odorata L.*) The painting was made from a plant in bloom in mid-February. It was growing on a sheltered bank-side below a limestone wall in Anglesey. Its usual flowering period is March to May. After the flowering has finished the heart-shaped leaves increase in size and, with them, the plant produces flower-buds which never open but which provide seeds. The sweet perfume is peculiar only to this member of the order Viola.

YELLOW, OR BITING STONECROP (*Sedum acre L.*) Sometimes called Wall-pepper this plant seems to require the minimum of soil to sustain it, for it may be found on old stone roofs, stone walls, rocks, sand dunes and chalk downs. In June the patches of small fleshy-leaved stems gradually become yellow when the flowers at their tips open. In full bloom the plant makes fine solid patches of colour. The names "Biting" and "Pepper" refer to the bitter flavour of its leaves.

The many spines of the Burnet Rose give it its Latin name Spinosissima.

BURNET ROSE (*Rosa spinosissima L.*) A dwarf of the Rose family for it rarely attains a height of more than nine inches. It prefers to grow laterally, spreading by suckers, and often covering large areas. It is fond of sand dunes and rough turf near the sea, but is also found on dry hills and heaths. It begins to bloom in May and will continue through the Summer. The stems are armed with numerous prickles and hairs.

The shape of its fruit gives the Yellow Water-lily one of its names—"Brandy-bottle".

AMPHIBIOUS PERSICARIA (*Polygonum amphibium L.*) The painting depicts the aquatic form of this plant with its floating leaves and stems. It requires the still waters of ditches, ponds and lakes in which to grow. The terrestrial form grows in the mud by the water-side and has ascending or erect stems. It flowers in July and August. Whether growing in water or on land it is capable of covering large areas.

WHITE WATER-LILY (*Nymphaea alba L.*) This fine and decorative plant likes the still water of ponds and lakes. It is widespread throughout Britain, and I have seen it blooming on a lochan in the high hills of Sutherland. When young the leaves are folded and are red, but they soon uncurl and flatten on to the water-surface. The wax-like flowers are very exquisite. They first appear, enclosed in their four sepals, in June, and the flowering continues until August.

YELLOW WATER-LILY (*Nuphar lutea L.*) Sometimes called "Brandy-bottle" because of the flagon-shaped fruit. This Water-lily bears its flowers above the water surface. The conspicuous outer cup is made up of five sepals. The true petals are almost concealed between the numerous stamens and the sepals. The leaves differ from those of the White Water-lily for whereas the veins in this form radiate from the centre, those of the Yellow Water-lily are parallel and spring from a mid-rib. It flowers from June to August.

**PART OF A WOODLAND
SPECIMEN OF CENTAURY**

Compare this with the
duneland type.

CENTAURY (*Centaurium umbellatum Gilib*) This is a plant which varies much in size according to its situation. On sand dunes and open sites it remains small—two to four inches, but by the edges of woods and other sheltered positions up to ten inches. It has a long flowering period—June to September, and on the sand dunes it is one of the most beautiful flowers. The painting depicts a dune specimen.

ROCK SAMPHIRE (*Crithmum maritimum L.*) On the west and south coasts of Britain this plant may be found growing from crevices in the rocks and cliffs, sometimes in great masses. It flowers in mid-Summer and, in spite of the peculiar fleshy appearance of its leaves and stems, it belongs to that large family the Umbelliferae. In the old days housewives used Samphire for pickling, and it was regularly harvested.

SEA-PINK (*Armeria maritima Willd.*) On cliffs and rocks, on saltings and salt marshes around Britain the Sea-pink enlivens the scene with its patches and drifts of pink flowers. The grass-like leaves pack close and form cushions from which the flower stalks spring. The Sea-pink has a long flowering period—April to September, and even when the blooms have lost their colour they still retain their form, often into late Autumn and the beginning of Winter.

A
**FLOWER-HEAD OF
SEA LAVENDER**

SEA HOLLY (*Eryngium maritimum L.*)
Like many other plants which grow
near the sea this plant has blue or
glaucous foliage. It is called Holly and
looks like a Thistle but actually it is a
member of the Umbelliferae. The
plant, from one to two feet high,
flowers in July and August. It grows on
sandy shores and shingle around the
coasts of Britain, and as far north as the
Shetlands.

SEA LAVENDER (*Limonium binervosum
G.E. Sm.*) As its name indicates this
plant may be found on rocks by the sea.
Essentially the rocks must be above the
high-tide mark. It grows also on cliffs
and pebble banks not affected by the
tides. It is an elegant plant with flowering stems six to ten inches high which
are in bloom from July to September.
The leaves are very variable in
shape.

HORNED POPPY (*Glaucium flavum
Crantz.*) This striking plant with its
large yellow flowers, three to four
inches across, and its bold bluish
leaves, grows on the sandy shores and
shingle banks of our coasts. Its name
"Horned" refers to the seed pods
which, after the plant has flowered,
may reach a length of from six to
twelve inches. The plant may attain a
height of two feet. It has a long flowering period—from June to October.

One of the small flowers, greatly
enlarged, which make up the umbel, or
flower-head, of the Sea Holly.
Two of the five stamens have uncurled.

83

FOXGLOVE (*Digitalis purpurea L.*)
On banks and by hedges, in rough heath, and in woods and copses, the Foxglove grows and thrives. Its tall spike of rosy-purple flowers springs from a rosette of large downy leaves. The flower sprays may reach a height of from two to four feet. It often grows in large colonies which, when in full bloom, can provide a wonderful mass of colour. It flowers from July to September.

FOXGLOVE

GREATER BINDWEED (*Calystegia sepium L.*) A common plant of the southern part of Britain, found in hedges, woods, and gardens. It is a climbing plant, the stems extending many feet, and gardeners abhor it. However, it bears a fine flower, pure waxy white and bell-shaped, and where it does no harm is very beautiful. The flowers open in the daytime and close at night. It blooms from June to August.

SOAPWORT (*Saponaria officinalis L.*)
There seems to be some doubt as to whether this plant is a true native or an introduced species. Certain it is that it is often found near villages on waste ground, and by the roadside. It often grows in colonies, when the large heads of pink flowers make a pleasing patch of colour. The flower-stems are from one to two feet high. It is beloved by hawk-moths, the flower being visited both by day and night.

HERB ROBERT (*Geranium robertianum L.*) Herb Robert is a cheerful little plant, its fern-like leaves, red stems and pink flowers gracing many an old dry-stone wall and dry bank. In Autumn when the plant may still be in flower it becomes increasingly attractive for some of the leaves turn bright red, especially in those which grow on stone walls. It blooms from May to September. It is a Cranesbill and has the beaked seed heads characteristic of the family.

CHICORY (*Cichorium intybus L.*) This plant, sometimes called Succory, grows on the dry roadsides, in waste ground and by the edges of fields, particularly in chalky soil. Its stiffly upright flowering stems are from one to three feet high, these growing from a rosette of leaves upon the ground. It flowers from July to October. On the Continent the roots of this flower are roasted and ground, this serving as a substitute for coffee.

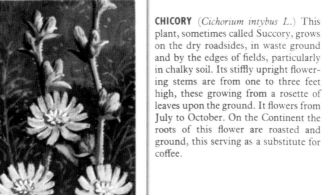

COLUMBINE (*Aquilegia vulgaris L.*) Only one Columbine found in Britain is truly wild. Others have been introduced or are garden escapees. The typical wild plant grows in copses and open woods. It is a tall plant two feet or more high, and elegant in all its parts. The curved hollow tubes which terminate the five petals give the flower a unique shape. The leaves too are beautiful for they are divided and sub-divided in forms of three.

SEED-HEADS OF HERB ROBERT

FLOWER OF RAGGED ROBIN

TUFTED VETCH (*Vicia cracca L.*)
From June to August the long bright flower sprays of the Tufted Vetch create gay spots of colour on many a bank and in thickets. It is a rambling, scrambling Vetch, with stems often four feet long, and with tendrils at the ends of the leaves which enable it to cling to branches and twigs for support. It is a native, and common throughout the British Isles.

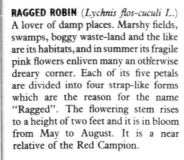

RAGGED ROBIN (*Lychnis flos-cuculi L.*)
A lover of damp places. Marshy fields, swamps, boggy waste-land and the like are its habitats, and in summer its fragile pink flowers enliven many an otherwise dreary corner. Each of its five petals are divided into four strap-like forms which are the reason for the name "Ragged". The flowering stem rises to a height of two feet and it is in bloom from May to August. It is a near relative of the Red Campion.

HENBANE (*Hyoscyamus niger L.*)
This is a strange, sinister plant. It is poisonous, and has an evil smell. Its flowers with their dark purple centres and veinings are distinctive, and quite beautiful. They appear from June to August. The plant may grow to a height of two feet. Stems and leaves are covered with glandular hairs, and the plant is sticky. It grows in sandy places near the sea, on waste ground and chalky soils.

TANSY   A flower-head.

A single flower.

Section of half
a flower-head.

TANSY (*Tanacetum vulgare L.*) A common plant of the roadsides, waste places and hedge-banks throughout Britain, growing to a height of two feet or more. It flowers from July to September. Each flower-head, cupped in green, leathery bracts, is a close-packed mass of florets, so close that they appear like felt. The plant has a strongly aromatic smell, and in olden days it was used as an ingredient of certain dishes, as well as a medicine.

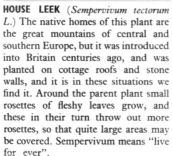

HOUSE LEEK (*Sempervivum tectorum L.*) The native homes of this plant are the great mountains of central and southern Europe, but it was introduced into Britain centuries ago, and was planted on cottage roofs and stone walls, and it is in these situations we find it. Around the parent plant small rosettes of fleshy leaves grow, and these in their turn throw out more rosettes, so that quite large areas may be covered. Sempervivum means "live for ever".

WALL PENNYWORT (*Umbilicus rupestris Dandy*) The name Pennywort refers to the circular leaves which resemble coins with a depression in the centre. On rocks and old stone walls, and on stony banks, it may be found, the new leaves appearing in the early Spring. The flowers appear from May to August, and the flowering spike varies from six to eighteen inches in height. Its distribution is mainly along the western side of Britain.

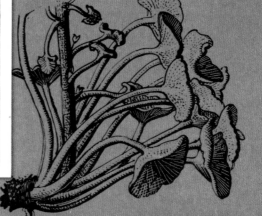

Leaves and base of flower stem of Wall Pennywort.

CARLINE THISTLE (*Carlina vulgaris L.*) A Thistle of the chalk and limestone country, and of sand dunes. Its single flower-stem armed with prickly leaves, rises from a rosette of dead leaves—those of the previous year, for this plant is a biennial and flowers in the second year from July to October. Even after the flowering season the flower retains its form, in a dry state, through the Winter. The name is supposed to commemorate Charlemagne who used the plant to cure his army of plague.

MEADOW SAFFRON (*Colchicum autumnale L.*) In the Autumn months the delicate blooms of the Meadow Saffron may be found growing in damp pastures and meadows, and in woods; its flowers quite unprotected by leaves of any kind. Its broad leaves and fruits appear in Spring, and by the time the flowers appear are no longer to be seen. Though it may be found in England and Wales it is very local in its distribution, and cannot be considered common.

ROSE-BAY WILLOW-HERB (*Chamaenerion augustifolium Scop.*) This fine plant often grows in large colonies. Waste ground, woodlands—particularly in the areas where timber has been felled, embankments and bombed sites are its favourite situations, and when a large colony is in flower it is a brilliant sea of colour. The shape of the four-petalled flower is interesting for the petals are arranged in the upper part of the disc. Its seeds are borne by the wind by means of a tuft of long slender white hairs at one end, and the plant rapidly spreads if not interfered with.

PURPLE LOOSESTRIFE (*Lythrum salicaria L.*) This fine plant is found near water, and often in great quantities. By river banks, and pond margins its tall spires of flowers make vivid patches of colour in late Summer. The plant may be from three to five feet in height. It has three forms of flowers on different plants—long, medium, and short styled, and with each, six differing lengths of stamens. Three different sizes of pollen grains are found in the three types.

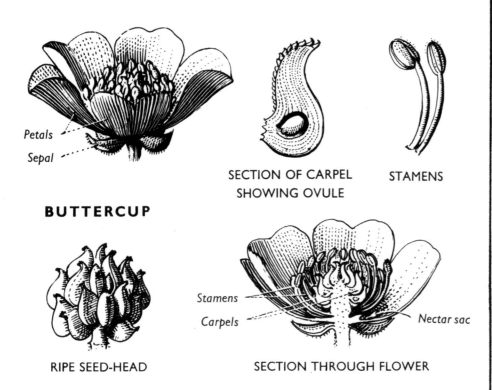

Petals

Sepal

SECTION OF CARPEL SHOWING OVULE

STAMENS

BUTTERCUP

Stamens

Carpels

Nectar sac

RIPE SEED-HEAD

SECTION THROUGH FLOWER

POLLINATION Insects visiting the flower for the nectar in the sacs at the bases of the petals touch the stamens and become dusted with pollen. This is carried to the next flower, and some grains fall on the tips of the carpels. These pollen grains then pass down tubes to the ovules and fertilise them. The ovules ripen, sepals, petals and stamens fall away, and eventually the ripe seeds fall to the ground.

Previous Picture Card Series
(50 cards with album)
obtainable as long as stocks last:

2/6d. per set
and four price—end labels from
any Brooke Bond tea packets

WILD FLOWERS (Series 1)

OUT INTO SPACE

BIRD PORTRAITS

WILD LIFE

Postal Order should be crossed '& Co'
and made payable to

Brooke Bond Tea Ltd., (Dept. P.C.), 35 Cannon Street, London, E.C.4.

Write your name and address in **BLOCK** letters.

THE BERKSHIRE PRINTING CO. LTD., READING, BERKS.

This series of picture cards
is offered in the interests of education by

Brooke Bond

A card is given free in every packet of
'Choicest' Edglets and P.G. Tips Tea

also two cards in each ½lb. tin of
Brooke Bond Pure and French Coffee

The seventh set of Brooke Bond cards came in 1960 and featured **Freshwater Fish**. This was another set of fifty cards, with superb illustrations by E. V. Petts, whose colourful renditions of the fish found in Britain's waterways would also find their way into a 1961 book *Fish of Rivers, Lakes & Ponds* by the angler and fishing writer F. J. Taylor.

A SERIES OF 50. No. 37

FRESHWATER FISH
Illustrated by E. V. Petts
Described by A. F. Magri Mac Mahon

BURBOT
(Lota lota)

It resembles a stocky Eel, and is found, not very often, in a few Eastern English rivers. The mouth is mottled brown, the mouth large with three barbels (one on the lower jaw, two near the nostrils); there are two dorsal fins, the first short, the second very long. The Burbot lives in deep water, hidden in weeds, under stones or in the tangled roots of the banks, coming out at night to hunt for small fish, frogs or other aquatic creatures. The average weight is about 1¼ lbs. but may reach 8 lbs. No angling records.

GET A PICTURE CARD ALBUM
FROM YOUR GROCER—Price 6d.

Issued in all packets of
BROOKE BOND TEA
35, Cannon Street, London, E.C.4.

FRESHWATER FISH
Illustrated by E. V. Petts
Described by A. F. Magri Mac Mahon

BROWN TROUT
(Salmo trutta)

Despite its name, it can be of almost every colour from silver (Sea Trout) to black, with a dark back and a lighter belly; the sides are covered with spots and rings of many colours; the tail is not forked. Found all over the British Isles in lakes or rivers, where the water is clean and well aerated. It feeds on insects and larvae, shellfish, worms and small fish. According to the locality adult Trout may weigh from a few ounces to several pounds. The largest Brown Trout angled* was 10 lbs. 6 oz. *up to 1958.

GET A PICTURE CARD ALBUM
FROM YOUR GROCER—Price 6d.

Issued in all packets of
BROOKE BOND TEA
35, Cannon Street, London, E.C.4.

FRESHWATER FISH
Illustrated by E. V. Petts
Described by A. F. Magri Mac Mahon

SEA LAMPREY
(Petromyzon marinus)

It is similar to the Lampern in having a round or sucker-like mouth, seven gill slits behind the eye and no paired fins, but it is much larger (it may reach three feet in length), and its scaleless skin is mottled and spotted with brown, yellow greenish-grey. It comes into the rivers to spawn, and the young spend their larval period buried in the mud like the Prides of the Lampern. When adult it descends to the sea, where, like the Lampern, it lives parasitically on fishes. Excellent to eat. Not angled.

GET A PICTURE CARD ALBUM
FROM YOUR GROCER—Price 6d.

Issued in all packets of
BROOKE BOND TEA
35, Cannon Street, London, E.C.4.

...ERIES OF 50. No. 1

FRESHWATER FISH
Illustrated by E. V. Petts
Described by A. F. Magri Mac Mahon

BARBEL
(Barbus Barbus)

Found in a few Eastern and Southern English rivers, where it favours swift gravelled streams near weirs, or deep fast currents between the pylons of bridges. There shoals of Barbel swim powerfully against the flow, hugging the bottom with their flattened bellies, and feeding on worms, insect larvae, small fish and vegetable matter. The Barbel is olive-green on the back, silvery underneath. It has a crescent-shaped mouth with *four* barbels, and smallish scales. Heaviest specimen angled* was 14 lbs. 6 oz. *up to 1958.

GET A PICTURE CARD ALBUM
FROM YOUR GROCER—Price 6d.

Issued in all packets of
BROOKE BOND TEA
35, Cannon Street, London, E.C.4.

The finely detailed illustrations range from Barbel and Trout to Burbot and Sea Lamprey, showing the fish in a sharp, clean style in their typical environments. Supplementary illustrations in the pages of the album show expanded details of fins, aquatic plants and even the kind of prey on which some fish like to feed.

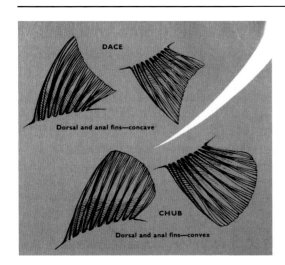

DACE
Dorsal and anal fins—concave
CHUB
Dorsal and anal fins—convex

WATER PLANTS
ON WHICH
FISH LAY EGGS

HORNWORT
Found in quiet waters

WILLOW MOSS
Thrives in fast-moving streams

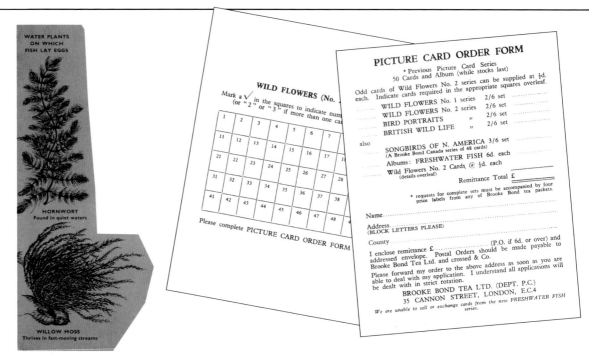

WILD FLOWERS (No.
Mark a ✓ in the squares to indicate num
(or "2" or "3" if more than one ca

Please complete PICTURE CARD ORDER FORM

The album has an introduction and species descriptions by A. F. Magri MacMahon, whose seminal work *Fishlore: British Freshwater Fishes* was first published in 1946. In his introduction MacMahon stated that "Freshwater fish are always attractive. To know more about them will increase your pleasure. That is the purpose of this picture card series." He might well have been talking about Brooke Bond cards themselves. The more that collectors indulged their passion for the cards, the greater that passion became, and so many Brooke Bond cards had been produced by this stage that they were almost as numerous as the fish in our lakes and rivers!

Nowadays, of course, collectors are interested not only in the cards but in anything that makes any one set or album significantly different from another. Slight differences add to the rarity value and desirability of any collectible items, after all. This album was a little different in that it was the first to have removable order forms within the covers of the album. These could be sent off to Brooke Bond to order previously issued cards and albums.

This is another set officially reprinted in 1973 and again the cards can easily be identified from the originals as the card texts are printed in black instead of blue. At the same time the album was also reprinted, again without the price on the cover.

A very rare and highly collectable wallchart can be found which accompanied this set and was only available to schools.

ALBUM FOR

Freshwater Fish

BROOKE BOND PICTURE CARDS

ILLUSTRATED BY E. V. PETTS
DESCRIBED BY A. F. MAGRI MACMAHON

PRICE SIXPENCE

THE world of fish is full of mystery. Rivers, lakes and ponds are of ever-changing beauty. No wonder that people turn to this world of water to enjoy its profound peace and the fascination of its many inhabitants. How different is the stately Carp from the restless silvery Bleak, or the mountain burn, beloved of the Trout, from the still, weedy pond favoured by the Tench! Very soon one wants to know more about fish and their habitat.

Let us make a start. In this album you will find clear descriptions of all our freshwater fish; and the special terms accompanying the drawings will enable you to understand the language of anglers. Freshwater fish are always attractive. To know more about them will increase your pleasure. That is the purpose of this picture card series.

A. F. Magri Mac Mahon.

SOFT-FINNED FISHES

FINS—The paired fins (*pectoral* and *ventral*) assist the fish in its movements. The *caudal* or tail fin and the twisting of the body give speed to the fish. The other fins (*dorsal* and *anal*) act as keels that help the fish in keeping its balance. The *pectoral* fins are close behind the gills. The *ventral* (or *pelvic*) fins are usually on the belly in the Carp and Salmon families. In this group the fins are nearly always supported by soft, branched *rays*.

LATERAL LINE—The majority of fishes have along the sides of their bodies a series of scales with minute holes: this is the *lateral line*, and the number of scales along this line is often an important clue to the identity of the fish. The Shads (Herring family) have no lateral line.

COLOUR—Fish may vary a good deal in colour, from place to place, or according to season or age (the young Bronze Bream is silvery, for instance). Therefore it is wise to consider only those characteristics which do not vary, such as the position of fins and the number of scales or rays.

SOFT-FINNED FISH

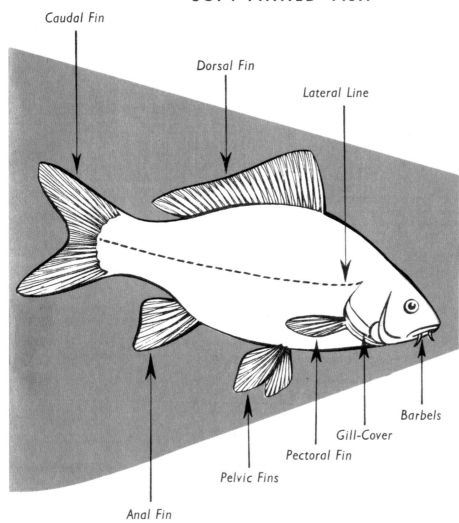

Caudal Fin

Dorsal Fin

Lateral Line

Barbels

Gill-Cover

Pectoral Fin

Pelvic Fins

Anal Fin

BARBEL (*Barbus Barbus*). Found in a few Eastern and Southern English rivers, where it favours swift gravelled streams near weirs, or deep fast currents between the pylons of bridges. There shoals of Barbel swim powerfully against the flow, hugging the bottom with their flattened bellies, and feeding on worms, insect larvae, small fish and vegetable matter. The Barbel is olive-green on the back, silvery underneath. It has a crescent-shaped mouth with *four* barbels, and smallish scales. Heaviest specimen angled*: 14 lbs. 6 oz. **up to 1958.*

GUDGEON (*Gobio gobio*). This small fish is abundant in England, except in the Lake District and in Cornwall, especially over the gravelly stretches of rivers. It keeps to the bottom, grubbing for insect larvae, worms and small shellfish. The body is dark, with a longitudinal row of squarish blue-black blotches on each side. The tail is forked, the scales rather large. It can be distinguished from similar fish because it has only *two* barbels. The largest specimen caught by angling* weighed $4\frac{1}{2}$ oz. **up to 1958.*

COMMON CARP (*Cyprinus carpio*). It grows large in lakes and in the quiet reaches of rivers, but may remain tiny in small ponds. The body is thick and deep, olive-bronze in colour, with large scales; the mouth bears four barbels, two small, two large; the dorsal fin is long and concave, highest at the beginning. The Carp feeds mostly on vegetable matter, but worms, insect larvae and shellfish are also eaten. It has a reputation for caution and cunning. The largest British rod-caught *Carp weighed 44 lbs. *up to 1958.

CRUCIAN CARP (*Carassius carassius*). Found mostly in Eastern and South-Eastern English still waters. It is olive-brown, deeper and thicker than the Common Carp, from which it can be distinguished by its long, convex dorsal fin, highest in the middle, and by having no barbels. The short anal fin and the long dorsal are the most obvious differences from the Bream. A variety of this fish, called the Prussian Carp, is often found in garden ponds. The Crucian is not as large as the Common Carp, and the biggest specimen angled* weighed 4 lbs. 11 oz. *up to 1958.

MIRROR CARP (*Cyprinus carpio var*). The Mirror Carp is merely a variety of the Common Carp, characterised by having only one or two rows of very large and shiny scales on its sides. Another variety, the Leather Carp, has no scales. There is also a golden variety, not to be mistaken for Goldfish. All these varieties have the four barbels, the long dorsal fin (dented, and higher at the beginning) and the mode of life of the Common Carp; all four may be found living together in the same pond, and interbreeding freely.

GOLDFISH (*Carassius auratus*). A fish from the Far East which has been introduced in many ornamental ponds; it often reaches sizes rivalling those of the Crucian Carp, which it closely resembles in the wild state (even in colour). It must not be confused with the golden varieties of the Carp, Tench or Orfe, frequently seen in aquaria and garden ponds. Fish breeders have evolved many varieties of Goldfish with an astonishing assortment of freakish colours and appearances. There are no sporting records, but the Goldfish may reach 4 or 5 lbs. in weight.

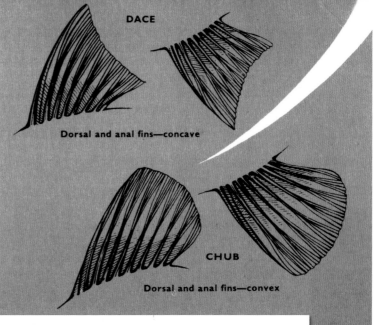

DACE

Dorsal and anal fins—concave

CHUB

Dorsal and anal fins—convex

DACE (*Leuciscus Leuciscus*). This slim and sprightly fish is widespread in England and Wales. It favours fast water, where it can be seen in active pursuit of insects and crustaceans, or rising to flies. The body is silvery, with a dark brownish or blue-green back; the lower fins are yellowish or pale pink; the dorsal and anal fins are concave ("Dented Dace", say fishermen, to distinguish it from "Curved Chub"); the anal fin is short, with 7 to 9 rays. It is usually well under the pound, and the largest angled* was 1 lb. 8½ oz. *up to 1958.

GOLDEN ORFE (*Leuciscus idus*). The Orfe resembles the Dace and is very common in Germany and Russia; a golden variety of it has been introduced in many ornamental ponds, where it is a favourite on account of its golden pink colour and liveliness. It is as slim as a Dace and very active, with a short concave dorsal fin (unlike the Goldfish); it has no barbels, which distinguishes it from the golden varieties of Tench and Carp. The Golden Orfe has not spread to open waters, and in consequence there are no British angling records.

CHUB (*Squalius cephalus*). Common everywhere in Britain except in Northern Scotland, West Wales and Cornwall; not found in Ireland. It likes running water, preferably under trees, where it feeds on insects, small fish and frogs, fruit fallen in the river, worms and shellfish. The back is dark, the sides silvery, usually with a faint brassy tinge; large mouth with whitish lips; tail often with a black edge; the dorsal and anal fins are *convex*, the lower fins bright red. The largest specimen angled* weighed 10½ lbs. *up to 1958.

WATER INSECTS WHICH MAY HARM SMALL FISH

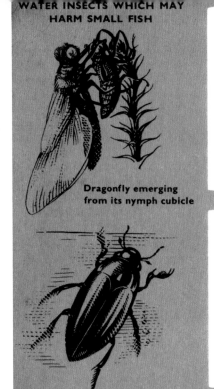

Dragonfly emerging from its nymph cubicle

GREAT SILVER WATER BEETLE

WATER BOATMAN
He swims upside-down and is able to dive and fly

BRONZE BREAM (*Abramis brama*). Body very deep, but narrow and flat, tail fin very forked, anal fin long, with 23 to 29 rays; the colour of the adult fish is bronze-brown, with blackish fins. Very common in quiet, deep waters in Britain and Ireland (except Wales, Northern Scotland and Western England). It goes about in shoals, grubbing in the mud for vegetable matter, worms and shellfish. The young are silvery, and easily mistaken for Silver Bream. The heaviest rod-caught* specimen weighed 13½ lbs. *up to 1958.*

SILVER BREAM (*Blicca bjoernka*). Silvery, with a greenish back, body deep and flat, deserving its nickname of "Tin Plate"; fins whitish tinged with pale pink. It can be distinguished from young Bronze Bream (which are silvery) by counting the rays in the long anal fin (from 19 to 24) and the scales along the lateral line (44 to 50 in the Silver, 49 to 57 in the Bronze). It has the same habits as the Common Bream, but it is not so widespread. It has no sporting or culinary merits. Record specimen angled*: 4½ lbs. *up to 1958.*

BLEAK (*Alburnus lucidus*). Sometimes called the Freshwater Sprat, from its close resemblance to that sea fish, both in size and appearance. In Summer, it dashes here and there near the surface in the slow-flowing rivers of Eastern and Southern England, in pursuit of insects and crustaceans, or following pieces of bread; in Winter it retires to deep water. The body is compressed, green on the back, silvery on the sides and belly, the fins whitish; the anal fin is rather long (having from 15 to 20 rays), unlike that of the Dace (from 7 to 9 rays).

ROACH (*Rutilus rutilus*). The Roach, probably the most popular fish among freshwater anglers, is found in most kinds of water in Britain, except Northern Scotland. The back is dark green, blue or brown, the sides and belly silvery. The concave dorsal fin begins above the base of the ventral fins. The anal fin is concave, short, and bright red. The mouth is small, with a projecting upper lip. It prefers gently flowing weedy water, and feeds on small creatures and vegetable matter. The largest specimen angled* weighed 3 lbs. 14 oz. *up to 1958.

TENCH (*Tinca tinca*). Distributed irregularly over the British Isles. It is very tenacious of life, and easily transported alive in damp moss. It prefers weedy and muddy ponds and meres, where it grubs at night in the mud for shellfish, worms and vegetable matter. The colour varies from olive to blackish; there is also a golden ornamental variety. The eye is small and red, the fins rounded, and there are two little barbels on the side of the mouth. Largest specimen angled*: 8½ lbs. *up to 1958.

RUDD (*Scardinius erythrophthalmus*). Widespread in England, Wales and Ireland (where it is called "Roach"), especially in ponds and lakes, or the quieter reaches of rivers. It resembles the Roach, but a yellow, golden or brownish tinge covers the silvery sides; the dorsal fin is well behind the beginning of the ventral fins, and the lower lip projects (unlike the Roach's). The fins and sometimes even the lips are red. It feeds higher up in the water than the Roach, taking flies and also shellfish, worms and plant material. Largest specimen angled*: 4½ lbs. *up to 1958.

MINNOW (*Phoxinus phoxinus*). This lively, inquisitive little fish is found almost everywhere in the British Isles, provided there is clean water and a sandy or gravelly bottom. Its back is dark green or brown, bordered on the sides with a golden stripe; the rest is silvery grey dappled with dark spots and bars. The scales are very small and numerous. In the Spring the males have a bright red belly. Minnows move about in small shoals, feeding on vegetable matter and minute creatures. It seldom grows to more than four inches in length.

HORNWORT
Found in quiet waters

WILLOW MOSS
Thrives in fast-moving streams

STONE LOACH (*Cobitis barbatula*). This small, slender fish is found in clear water almost everywhere in the British Isles, except Northern Scotland. Usually it hides under stones (whence its name), waiting for the small creatures on which it feeds. Its colour is grey-greenish or brownish, with irregular darker blotches; the belly is white. There are six barbels round its mouth, the two at the corners of the jaws being longer than the other four. The scales and eyes are small, the fins dotted or striped. Average length three to four inches.

SPINY LOACH (*Cobitis taenia*). It has a very local distribution, and is mostly found in small clear rivers in Central England. The body is usually under three inches in length, rather elongated, pale brown with dark blotches in a regular row on its sides. There are six barbels of equal length around the mouth, and a small movable double-pointed spine on the snout just below the eyes. Both Loaches can easily be distinguished from other similar small fishes by the six barbels round the mouth and the rounded tail with a single fluke.

WELS, or EUROPEAN CATFISH
(*Silurus glanis*). This ugly, dark, eel-like fish, with tiny eyes, a ridiculously short dorsal fin and very long anal fin, a wide mouth with six long barbels, grows to enormous sizes in some Continental rivers, especially the Danube. It is found in a few ponds in Bedfordshire and Buckinghamshire, where it was artificially introduced. It is a sluggish fish, usually hidden in the mud or under roots, and feeds on almost anything edible, from fish, frogs and rats to bread. Largest angled* in Britain 37½ lbs.
*up to 1958.

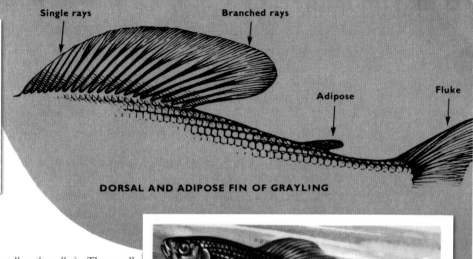

DORSAL AND ADIPOSE FIN OF GRAYLING

Single rays · Branched rays · Adipose · Fluke

HOUTING (*Coregonus oxyrhynchus*). This fish resembles the other members of the Whitefish group, such as the Powan, Skelly and Gwyniad, in being silvery and having a small adipose fin behind the dorsal fin. Unlike the other species, which are found only in freshwater lakes, the Houting is a sea fish, inhabiting Northern waters, which it leaves only to spawn in Danish or German rivers, being found occasionally in a few Eastern English rivers. It can be recognised at once by its peculiar long snout.

GRAYLING (*Thymallus thymallus*). The small adipose fin near the tail shows this fish to be a member of the Salmon family. It is immediately recognisable by the very large striped dorsal fin, and the longitudinal thin grey lines on the sides of the body. It is locally distributed in Britain, in clear streamy rivers with deep pools and swift shallows. It feeds on flies, insect larvae, worms and small crustaceans. It is a Spring spawner, unlike other Salmonids. Largest specimen angled*: 7 lbs. 2 oz. *up to 1958*.

CHAR (*Salvelinus alpinus spp.*). Several forms of this beautiful relative of the Trout inhabit the cold waters of many lakes in the British Isles. Like the Trout, it has a small adipose fin on the back near the tail, but there are no black or brown spots on the sides of the Char, which has often brighter colours, especially on its belly; the spots are red, orange or white, often below the lateral line only. The Char is not usually angled for, and there are no official records of specimen sizes; its maximum weight in British waters is under 3 lbs.

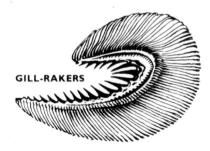

GILL-RAKERS

Anterior branchial arch showing gill-rakers (under gill-cover)

SEA TROUT (*Salmo trutta*). This is not a distinct species, but merely a form of the Brown Trout that, like the Salmon, goes down to the sea and becomes large and silvery. It has more dark spots on its sides than the Salmon, from which it can be distinguished because it has from 8 to 10 rays in the dorsal fin (Salmon from 10 to 12), and from 13 to 16 scales in a line from the back of the adipose fin to the lateral line (Salmon 10 to 13); the 'wrist' of the tail is therefore thicker in the Sea Trout. Largest angled*: 22½ lbs. *up to 1958.*

SEA TROUT SMOLT (*Salmo trutta*). After two or three years in fresh water, the parr of the Salmon and of the Sea trout become silvery and go down to the sea. They are then in the 'smolt' stage of their life. The Sea Trout smolt can be recognised because its pectoral, ventral and anal fins are more or less orange, while in the Salmon smolt the pectoral fins are darkish, and the others pale. Small Sea Trout (called Finnock, Herling, etc.) are more silvery than smolts, and their fins are not orange.

BROWN TROUT (*Salmo trutta*). Despite its name, it can be of almost every colour, from silver (Sea Trout) to black, with a dark back and a lighter belly; the sides are covered with spots and rings of many colours; the tail is not forked. Found all over the British Isles in lakes or rivers, where the water is clean and well aerated. It feeds on insects and larvae, shellfish, worms and small fish. According to the locality, adult Trout may weigh from a few ounces to several pounds. The largest Brown Trout angled* was 10 lbs. 6 oz. *up to 1958.*

YOUNG FISH

CATERPILLARS

EARTHWORMS

5

NY SPECIES

CADDIS WORMS
(larvae of Caddis Fly)

RAINBOW TROUT (*Salmo irideus*). This beautiful species of Trout was introduced in Europe from North America, and is found in a few land-locked clear lakes in several parts of the British Isles. It has not remained in the rivers, and has also disappeared mysteriously from many lakes. It can be distinguished from the Brown Trout by the red 'rainbow' band on its sides, with red blotches; the tail is slightly forked, and covered with many dark spots. The largest angled* in Britain weighed 8½ lbs., but much larger specimens have been caught in Australia. *up to 1958.

BROOK TROUT (*Salvelinus fontinalis*). This American species was introduced years ago in many British waters, but has not prospered. It is really a Char and not a Trout, and can be recognised at once by the peculiar mottled or marbled coloration of its back and sides; the tail is usually barred with blackish streaks, unlike the Trout or British Char. There are no British angling records, but in Britain it seldom weighs more than a pound. It grows much larger in America, where it is called Speckled Trout.

TROUT PARR (*Salmo trutta*). The young Trout and Salmon are similar: they are 3 to 4 inches long, spotted in various colours, and have a row of dark marks on their sides ('Sooty Fingers'). But the Trout parr has more coloured spots, a larger mouth, and pectoral fins pale orange, while the Salmon parr has three dark spots behind the eye (not found in the Trout) on the gill cover, and darkish pectoral fins. The parr of both species snatch at any fly or bait; anglers should take care to unhook and return them to the water.

OVA

ALEVINS

FRY

During the first weeks of life, the Salmon carries underneath it a 'yolk sac' which provides it with sustenance

POWAN (*Coregonus clupeoides spp.*). The Powan of Loch Lomond and neighbouring lochs is a fairly well-known member of the Whitefish group (others are the Skelly, Pollan, Gwyniad and Vendace). These fish have a very local distribution in British and Irish lakes; all are silvery, and resemble Herrings. There is a small adipose fin near the tail, showing membership of the Salmon family and difference from the silvery members of the Carp family. They all feed on minute animal life, and their weight varies from a few ounces to two pounds, according to the locality.

SMELT (*Osmerus eperlanus*). The adipose finlet near the tail shows that this slender sea fish is related to the Salmon family. The back is greenish, the sides silvery, with a very short and incomplete lateral line. The large mouth reveals the Smelt as a voracious fish; it feeds on small fish, worms, prawns and shrimps. It enters estuaries in the Spring, to spawn in fresh or brackish water, provided there is no pollution. Not to be confused with the Sand Smelt (Atherina), with two dorsal fins. No angling records, but the Smelt usually weighs about half a pound.

SALMON (*Salmo salar*). The Salmon may be found in all unpolluted rivers of the British Isles, provided they are connected with the sea. It is silvery, with a dark back and many small black spots on the sides above the lateral line; it has a soft dorsal fin and a small adipose fin near the tail. The Salmon is born in the rivers and usually spends the first two years of its life there; then it descends to the sea where it grows large feeding on fish, returning later to the river to spawn. The largest angled* weighed 64 lbs.
*up to 1958.

TWAITE SHAD (*Alosa finta*). More common than the Allis Shad, with the same appearance and habits, though much smaller. Even when adult it retains a row of dark spots on the upper part of the body. There is no lateral line; the scales are smaller and firmer (58 to 66 in a row from gills to tail), and gillrakers are short and stiff, numbering from 30 to 45; these characteristics distinguish the Twaite from the Allis Shad. Frequent in the River Severn. The largest specimen caught* with rod and line weighed 3 lbs. 2 oz. *up to 1958.*

ALLIS SHAD (*Alosa alosa*). It resembles a very large Herring, silvery with a dark back and a blackish spot on the shoulder. It has no lateral line; there are from 72 to 86 scales from gills to tail, and numerous fine gillrakers (from 60 to 120) visible on lifting the gill-covers. It is a sea fish, coming into large clean rivers to spawn; the year-old fish, which has a row of dark blotches on the upper part of each side of the body, emigrates to the sea. There are no angling records; the maximum length is 2½ feet, maximum weight about 8 lbs.

MOLLUSCA

FRESHWATER WHELK

RAMSHORN SNAIL

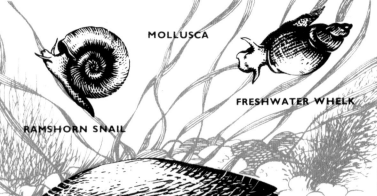

FRESHWATER OR SWAN MUSSEL

PIKE (*Esox lucius*). The "freshwater shark" is found almost everywhere in the British Isles living alone, preferably near weeds, where its immobility and marbled coloration of green and yellow render it almost invisible. It has a large mouth full of sharp teeth, a single dorsal fin set back near the tail, and small-looking scales. It feeds voraciously on fish, frogs, water birds, rats, voles, and also worms and insect larvae. The largest angled* in England weighed 37½ lbs., in Scotland 47 lbs. 11 oz., in Ireland 53 lbs. *up to 1958.*

TEN-SPINED STICKLEBACK (*Pygosteus pungitius*). This species, far less known and widespread than the Three-spined, is not found in Northern Scotland. It is small, seldom reaching three inches in length. It has from 8 to 11 short spines on the back. Its colour is greenish-olive, with many dark dots; in the Spring the male is blue-brown, much less conspicuous than its red-bellied larger brother. The habits of the two species are very similar, but the nest of the Ten-spined is hung on to weeds above the river bottom, unlike that of the Three-spined.

THREE-SPINED STICKLEBACK (*Gasterosteus aculeatus*). Found almost everywhere in fresh, brackish or salt water, the Stickleback or Tiddler is known to everybody. It has three strong spines on its back, followed by a soft fin near the tail; other spines are on the belly. On the sides there is a variable number of small shields. The back is greenish, the sides silvery, shot with blue and pink; in the Spring the male becomes very brightly coloured, with a red belly and dark bands, and builds a nest for the eggs, which it guards jealously. Seldom reaches a length of 4 inches.

BURBOT (*Lota lota*). It resembles a stocky Eel, and is found, not very often, in a few Eastern English rivers. The skin is mottled brown, the mouth large with three barbels (one on the lower jaw, two near the nostrils); there are two dorsal fins, the first short, the second very long. The Burbot lives in deep water, hidden in weeds, under stones or in the tangled roots of the banks, coming out at night to hunt for small fish, frogs or other aquatic creatures. The average weight is about 1½ lbs. but may reach 8 lbs. No angling records.

SEA LAMPREY (*Petromyzon marinus*). It is similar to the Lampern in having a round or sucker-like mouth, seven gill slits behind the eye and no paired fins, but it is much larger (it may reach three feet in length), and its scaleless skin is mottled and spotted with brown, yellow and greenish-grey. It comes into the rivers to spawn, and the young spend their larval period buried in the mud like the Prides of the Lampern. When adult it descends to the sea, where, like the Lampern, it lives parasitically on fishes. Excellent to eat. Not angled.

YELLOW EEL (*Anguilla anguilla*). Born in the depths of the Atlantic, eels reach our rivers in great numbers as very small wriggling elvers. The Eel is common everywhere in the British Isles, and is found even in landlocked ponds. The growing fish is brown and yellow, and lives hidden in the mud, or in holes, coming out mostly at night or when it is thundery, to feed on any animal matter it finds: fish, frogs, insect larvae, worms, shellfish, etc. Very tasty to eat, stewed, grilled or jellied. Largest rod-caught* 8½ lbs. *up to 1958*.

SILVER EEL (*Anguilla anguilla*). After spending at least five or six years in fresh water, the Yellow Eel undergoes a change. Its back becomes almost black, its belly silvery, and there is a bronze stripe along the sides; the snout becomes sharper, the eyes larger. Then in the Autumn, especially when the weather is bad, the Silver Eel descends to the sea and crosses the Atlantic to spawn in deep water near the Bahamas, and never returns.

LAMPERN (*Petromyzon fluviatilis*) This eel-like creature has no jaws or paired fins. The mouth is round and sucker-like, and there are seven little gill slits in a row behind the eye. It is scaleless, uniformly brownish or greenish, with a white belly. It grows buried in the mud in fresh water (it is then called "Pride"), but when adult it usually goes down to the sea (occasionally it remains in lakes or large rivers), returning into fresh water to spawn. It is not angled, but is caught in eel traps. It is usually a foot in length or less.

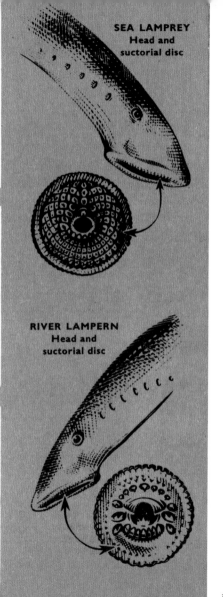

SEA LAMPREY
Head and
suctorial disc

RIVER LAMPERN
Head and
suctorial disc

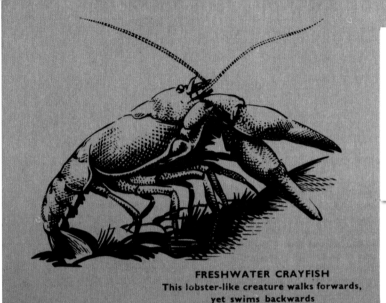

FRESHWATER CRAYFISH
This lobster-like creature walks forwards,
yet swims backwards

BULLHEAD (*Cottus gobio*). The shape of this odd little fish has deserved it the additional name of "Miller's Thumb": it has a large head with wide, spiky gill-covers, wide pectoral fins, a small tapering body, scaleless skin blotched with brown and yellow, and two dorsal fins close together, with dark stripes. It is widespread in British waters, especially in clear streams, where it stays on the bottom, darting occasionally to swallow any creature small enough to enter its capacious mouth. The average length is about 3 or 4 inches, occasionally up to 6 inches.

PIKE-PERCH (*Lucioperca sandra*). The Pike-Perch is widely spread over Europe, and has been introduced in a few British lakes. The back is dark grey, the belly silvery, and there are several broad vertical stripes similar to those of a Perch. The shapes of the body and the large teeth are similar to a Pike's: it has two dorsal fins, the first spiky like a Perch's but without a black spot. It is a distinct species, related to the Perch, not an impossible crossing between Pike and Perch. Largest angled* in Britain 5 lbs.
*up to 1958.

STURGEON (*Acipenser sturio*). A sea fish that enters large rivers to spawn, the Sturgeon is seldom found in British estuaries. The body is grey or brown, with five longitudinal rows of sharp bony shields; the head has a long snout (used to root in the mud for small prey) and a toothless mouth with four barbels in front. It grows to a very large size, up to 18 feet in length, though normally between 7 and 9 feet. It is caught in large numbers in some great rivers of continental Europe. Caviare is obtained from its roes, and isinglass from the swim bladder.

FLOUNDER (*Platichthys flesus*). This smaller relative of the Plaice is common in estuaries, and is often found far upstream from the sea, if the river is not polluted. The upper side varies greatly in colour, from grey to black (according to the bottom on which the fish lives), with small spots and blotches; the lower side is normally white. The lateral line is almost straight (unlike that of the Dab, which makes a half circle above the pectoral fin). Also called Fluke and Butt. The largest specimen angled* weighed 5 lbs. 11½ oz. *up to 1958.

GREY MULLETS (*Mugil chelo and Mugil capito*). Two similar species frequent the estuaries of rivers in the British Isles, and lagoons or ponds near the sea. The Thick-lipped has an upper lip with tiny warts, whereas the Thin-lipped has a smooth upper lip. Both have broad heads and backs of a metallic blue, and silvery sides with numerous longitudinal grey stripes. They feed on soft vegetable matter and small aquatic creatures, and are notoriously difficult to catch by fair angling. Largest rod-caught* specimen: 10 lbs. 1 oz. *up to 1958.

BLACK BASS (Large-mouth) (*Micropterus salmoides*). This species and the closely related Small-mouth (*Micropterus dolomieu*) are well known sporting fish of North America. They have been introduced in a few British waters, but are far from common. They resemble the Perch, but differ from it in having four or five dark transversal stripes on the head, and the second dorsal fin higher than the first; also, the general coloration is considerably darker, and the snout sharper. There are no British sporting records available.

BASS (*Morone Labrax*). Common in the estuaries and on the coasts of Southern and Western Britain and Ireland, ascending the rivers for miles. Though often called 'Salmon Bass' from its resemblance in shape and colour to the Salmon, it can be easily recognised by its large mouth, spiky fins and gill-covers, and by having two true fins (the first spiky) on the back. It feeds voraciously on small fish, crabs, prawns, worms and even offal. A powerful sporting fish, excellent to eat. The largest specimen angled* weighed 18 lbs. 2 oz. *up to 1958.

RUFF (*Acerina cernua*). Also called "Pope", this small cousin of the Perch is common in Central and Eastern England, especially in meres and the quiet reaches of gravelly rivers. It keeps to the bottom, feeding greedily on small animals. The first dorsal fin is spiny, and joined to the second which is soft; there are spines at the beginning of the lower fins, and sharp edges on the gill-covers. The body is olive-grey, with many dark spots and specks; the lower fins yellow and the iris of the eye mauve. Maximum length 7 to 8 inches.

PERCH (*Perca fluviatilis*). This handsome fish is found everywhere in the British Isles in rivers, lakes and ponds. Its skin is rough, olive-green in colour, shading into yellow and white, with from five to seven dark vertical stripes. There are two dorsal fins, the first spiky and with a black spot, the second soft; sharp spines are also present at the beginning of the lower fins, which are bright red. The Perch feeds on small fish, worms, shellfish and aquatic insects. The largest British specimen angled* weighed 5 lbs. $15\frac{1}{2}$ oz. *up to 1958.

SPINY-FINNED FISH

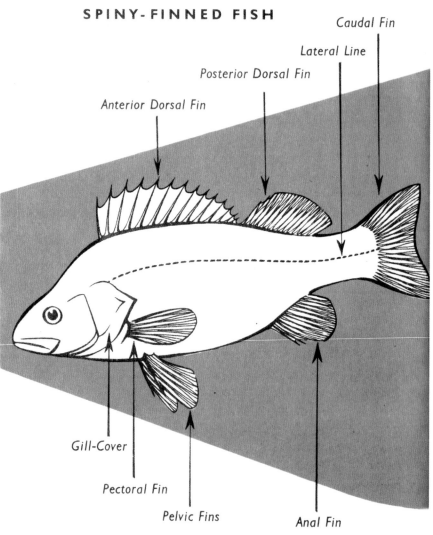

Anterior Dorsal Fin

Posterior Dorsal Fin

Lateral Line

Caudal Fin

Gill-Cover

Pectoral Fin

Pelvic Fins

Anal Fin

SPINY-FINNED FISHES

MUCH of what has been said about the soft-finned fishes applies to the spiny-finned species. The most obvious difference consists in the stiff, sharp *spines* that support the first dorsal fin (or the first part of that fin) and often the beginning of the ventral and anal fins. The ventral (or pelvic) fins are on the chest of the Perch and many other spiny-finned fish. The gill-cover is frequently armed with sharp edges and spines; the scales are as a rule rough and firmly embedded in the skin. Care must be taken when handling a Perch, a Ruff or a Bass, as their needle-like spines and cutting gill-covers may inflict painful wounds.

Certain spiny-finned fish are flattened on one side; they are mostly marine, but one of them, the Flounder, ascends estuaries and rivers for considerable distances.

The spiny-finned fishes have usually a well-marked lateral line; the Grey Mullets are an exception.

The Sturgeon (with rows of bony shields) and the Lampreys (with a round, sucker-like mouth) belong to other and quite distinct groups of rather primitive fishes.

FRESHWATER FISH IN ORDER OF FAMILIES

FAMILY PETROMYZONIDAE
Sea Lamprey
Lampern

FAMILY ACIPENSERIDAE
Sturgeon

FAMILY CLUPEIDAE
Allis Shad
Twaite Shad

FAMILY SALMONIDAE
Salmon   Brown Trout
Sea Trout   Sea Trout smolt
Trout parr   Rainbow Trout
Char   Brook Trout
Powan   Houting
Grayling

FAMILY OSMERIDAE
Smelt

FAMILY ESOCIDAE
Pike

FAMILY CYPRINIDAE
Common Carp   Mirror Carp
Crucian Carp   Goldfish
Barbel   Gudgeon
Tench   Minnow
Chub   Dace
Golden Orfe   Roach
Rudd   Silver Bream
Bronze Bream   Bleak

FAMILY COBITIDAE
Stone Loach
Spined Loach

FAMILY SILURIDAE
The Wels

FAMILY ANGUILLIDAE
Silver Eel
Yellow Eel

FAMILY GADIDAE
Burbot

FAMILY SERRANIDAE
Bass

FAMILY CENTRARCHIDAE
Black Bass

FAMILY PERCIDAE
Perch
Ruff
Pike-Perch

FAMILY MUGILIDAE
Grey Mullet

FAMILY COTTIDAE
Bullhead

FAMILY GASTEROSTEIDAE
Three-spined Stickleback
Ten-spined Stickleback

FAMILY PLEURONECTIDAE
Flounder

In 1961, one of the new sets on offer from Brooke Bond was **African Wild Life**, again with illustrations and text by C.F. Tunnicliffe. In this instance, Tunnicliffe appears to have been given some guidance by the Director of the Royal National Parks of Kenya, Colonel Mervyn H. Cowie, C.B.E., who receives an acknowledgement "for his valuable help in the preparation of this series" on the inside front cover immediately following Tunnicliffe's foreword.

The foreword itself, a full two years ahead of the **Wildlife in Danger** set, provides dire warnings for the future of many species on the African continent. "Children of today," wrote Tunnicliffe, "may live to see the extinction, or near extinction, of some of the animals which haunt the plains, forests and rivers of Africa." That foreword, written almost 50 years ago, carried an enduring message that is still as valid today but, at the time, it put Brooke Bond in the vanguard of the crusade to preserve endangered species.

One of the most famous organisations campaigning on behalf of animals today is the World Wildlife Fund, which was founded in 1961, the same year that this set was issued. Brooke Bond, therefore, can claim some credit for helping to educate the younger generation about the perilous situation faced by some of the world's most extraordinary wild creatures.

Fifty different subjects from the Gorilla and the Chimpanzee (a creature that had been helping to advertise Brooke Bond on television since 1955) to the Nile Crocodile and the Wart Hog were represented in full colour, at a time when some were rarities even in zoos and colour television broadcasts were still some way off.

Included throughout the album are a number of fine black & white line drawings enhancing the details on the cards to show, for example, the difference between Zebras' stripe patterns or the tufts on the ears of a Caracal. Larger scenes decorated the inside front and back covers along with, on the inside back cover, a map of Africa for quick reference.

As had become customary, the album also contained a removable order form for buying previously issued cards and albums.

Collectors will also be interested to know that this is another set officially reprinted in 1973. Again, the cards can easily be identified from the originals as the card texts are printed in black instead of blue. At the same time the album was also reprinted and there are a number of variations in both original and reprinted versions.

A SERIES OF 50. No. 46

AFRICAN WILD LIFE

Illustrated and described by C. F. Tunnicliffe, R.A.

WART HOG

(Phacochoerus aethiopicus)

This grotesque pig is widely distributed through East and Central Africa, and roams about in small family parties of sows and young, the boars preferring a more solitary existence. They live in holes which they invariably enter backwards so that the formidable tusked snout faces outwards. Only rarely will a Wart Hog attack (it has been known to charge) and usually flees from man, galloping away with its tail held vertically. The young are born uniformly coloured and without the white stripes characteristic of the young of many wild swine.

GET A PICTURE CARD ALBUM FROM YOUR GROCER—Price 6d

Issued in all packets of
BROOKE BOND TEA

35 Cannon Street, London, E.C.4

Caracal   (note the tufted ears)

Grant's and Grevy's zebra showing the difference in stripe-patterns

A rare and highly collectable wall chart can be found which accompanied this set and was only available to schools.

The cards were also issued in Southern Rhodesia & East Africa where the card backs were printed in green. A separate album and wall chart were available there, too.

BROOKE BOND PICTURE CARDS

African Wild Life

ILLUSTRATED AND DESCRIBED BY
C. F. TUNNICLIFFE, R.A.
PRICE SIXPENCE

CHILDREN OF TODAY may live to see the extinction, or near extinction, of some of the animals which haunt the plains, forests, and rivers of Africa. The human population of that continent is ever increasing, and more and more virgin land is required for agriculture and large engineering projects. During the last fifty years there has been vast slaughter of big game, chiefly in the interests of agriculture and cattle-rearing, and had it not been for the forming of game reserves the wild animals would have fared even worse. The protection of the law is helping to preserve certain animals, but even so poaching is a serious menace to their numbers. Several species have already been lost, and it will be a sad day when Africa no longer holds the wonderful variety of wild life which may still be found there, and of which the following cards depict but a small section. May that day be long delayed.

C. F. Tunnicliffe

Brooke Bond thanks Colonel Mervyn H. Cowie, C.B.E., Director of the Royal National Parks of Kenya, for his valuable help in the preparation of this series.

A 'plains' scene with giraffe, zebra and wildebeest.

Head of a mountain gorilla

GORILLA (*Gorilla gorilla*) This largest of all the apes lives in the depths of the hot and steamy forests of Equatorial Africa. A fully grown male, when standing erect, may be between six and seven feet high, and his strength is prodigious. Females are smaller. They are vegetarians, and wander about the forest floor in small family groups, feeding during the day. At night the males make a nest of branches often on the ground, while the females and young make platform nests of branches in low trees. On the ground Gorillas progress on all fours. They are shy, and flee from the presence of man, but attack on provocation.

MANTLED BABOON (*Cynocephalus hamadryas*) This dog-faced monkey, with the cape of long hair, inhabits open country and rocky hills in Abyssinia and the Sudan. It is the baboon represented in the carvings and mural paintings of the ancient Egyptians and was held sacred by them, though there are no baboons in Egypt today. They wander about in troops which are dominated and disciplined by the large males, the very young riding on their mothers' backs like jockeys. They are chiefly vegetarians and do much damage to crops. They are bold in their forays and can be dangerous. Their chief enemy is the leopard.

CHIMPANZEE (*Pan troglodytes*) An active, noisy intelligent ape which lives in family groups and communities in the forests of Western and Central Equatorial Africa. They feed on fruits, leaves, shoots and roots, and spend much of the day on the forest floor. However, each night new platform nests are built from leafy boughs among the branches, and none spend the night on the ground. Of all the apes and monkeys the skeleton of the Chimpanzee most nearly resembles that of man. Its powers of reasoning are considerable, and it is very teachable.

Profile of a male mandrill

MANDRILL (*Papio sphinx*) This is the largest and most grotesque of the baboons. The adult male, in addition to the gaudy colouring of his face, has naked red and purple patches on his buttocks. Mandrills, like other baboons, live in troops. The adult males are savage and powerful, and the devilish expression of their countenance is a true indication of their nature. When really in a temper he develops patches of vivid blue on the chest and patches of bright red appear on wrists and ankles. Unlike other baboons Mandrills are forest dwellers, but they often come into the open and search stony places for insects and grubs. In the forest they eat fruit and bulbs. They inhabit the Cameroons, Gabon, and the Congo.

PATAS MONKEY (*Erythrocebus patas*) This monkey which, like Sykes's monkey, belongs to the large family called Guenon is unlike them in that it inhabits open country and semi-desert, and is not a forest dweller. Because of its red coat it is sometimes called the "Hussar" monkey; and because sometimes troops of these monkeys move in ordered formation it is called the "Military" monkey. They live in companies and hunt the grasslands for their food, which consists chiefly of fruit, small animals and insects. They walk and run somewhat like dogs, and their hands and feet are adapted to their terrestrial existence. Their home is West and Central Africa.

COLOBUS MONKEY (*Colobus abyssinicus*) This handsome monkey lives in the high forests of Abyssinia and Central East Africa. Its white cape and tail blend perfectly with the pale lichens which are pendant from the branches of its forest home. It is shy, silent, and aloof, going about its business and ignoring other creatures. In the mid-nineteenth century it was hunted for its "fur", and many thousands were killed and its numbers decreased alarmingly. The black and white Colobus is one of a number belonging to the family called Guereza. "Colobus" is the Greek word for mutilated, and this refers to the fact that this monkey has the merest lump where the thumb should be. It is a vegetarian.

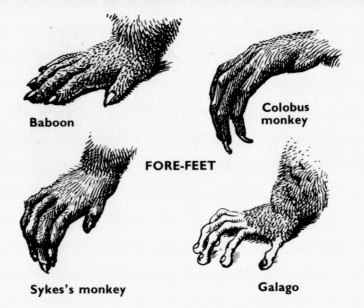

FORE-FEET

Baboon

Colobus monkey

Sykes's monkey

Galago

SYKES'S MONKEY (*Ceropitheous mitis kolbi*) A typical member of the large family called Guenon, a dweller in the high forests of East Africa. The name "Guenon" is French and means "one who grimaces" but it appears that Sykes's monkey is of a grave and sedate disposition, gentle in manner, and not so rowdy and irascible as most members of the Guenon family. It roams the forests in family parties or groups feeding on nuts, leaves, shoots and buds, and also insects. It was first brought to England by Colonel William Henry Sykes in 1831, and was named after him.

BUSHY-TAILED GALAGO (*Galago crassicaudatus*) This galago inhabits East Africa. It is about the size of a small cat, and is nocturnal in its habits, spending the day asleep among the foliage of mangrove and palm forests. It is very agile and makes great leaps from branch to branch. The "fingers" and "thumbs" of all four feet have flattened discs at their tips, these enabling it to grip smooth surfaces with ease. Its food consists of fruit, insects, small birds, and eggs. The large ears are extremely mobile, and can be turned and even folded at will.

RINGED-TAILED LEMUR (*Lemur catta*) The true lemurs are confined to the island of Madagascar and the adjacent Comoro Islands. The Ringed-tailed Lemur lives in south-western Madagascar. It is a ground-living animal, inhabiting dry rocky areas of few trees, and in this differs from other lemurs which are arboreal. It lives in small parties, is noisy, and most active at early morning and in the evening, taking a siesta during the heat of the day, and sleeping with its tail curled round its body at night. This lemur is almost vegetarian, living on fruits and roots, though some animal food such as young birds and reptiles may occasionally be taken. It is very agile and makes an interesting pet.

Lioness

LION (*Panthero leo*) The largest of the cat tribe in Africa. It is unique among cats in that the male grows a large mane. The female has no mane. The young are spotted. Lions are found in many areas of Africa, especially where the animals which are their food abound. Chiefly they live on the plains and prey on antelopes, zebras, wart hogs, etc. They usually hunt at night and in parties, the male circling a herd of zebra or antelope to drive them in the direction of the waiting females. Often it is the female which makes the actual kill.

A lion cub

CHEETAH (*Acinonyx jubatus*) In spite of its superficial resemblance to the leopard the Cheetah is not a true cat. In some ways it resembles a dog—e.g. it cannot fully retract its claws and its powers of speed are far greater than any cat's. It is probably the swiftest of all land animals, for it can run down a gazelle or an antelope. These animals, birds and small rodents are its food. It ranges widely throughout East Africa, and is partial to open hilly country, open tree country, or semi-desert. Like other predators it follows where its food leads.

LEOPARD (*Panthero pardus*) This handsome cat ranges widely in Africa, and when provoked is considered more dangerous than the lion. It is almost as much at home in the trees as on the ground, and two of the principal items in its diet are monkeys and baboons. It is a scourge to African herdsmen, taking goats, calves, and dogs, especially dogs, which it kills at every opportunity. Its strength is amazing, and it will take the body of a victim much heavier than itself up into the branches of a tree with ease. Black leopards are sometimes found in Africa.

Caracal   (note the tufted ears)

SERVAL (*Felis serval*) The Serval is found over a very large part of Africa. Its large ears, small head, long legs and short tail differentiate it from the true cats. It lives in bush country and is chiefly a nocturnal hunter, preying on guinea-fowl, francolins, hares and rats. Sometimes small antelopes are its victims. It stands about nineteen inches high at the shoulder. Its skin was, at one time, much in favour with native chiefs for mantles, and even today its fur is used for that purpose by the European furriers.

CARACAL (*Felis caracal*) This is the nearest approach to a lynx which Africa possesses. It is widely distributed over this continent and into Asia; in fact, the name "Caracal" is of Turkish origin. Like the lynxes it is savage, and possesses great speed. It lives on small mammals and birds, and such is its agility that it can strike down birds even when they have sprung to wing. It is chiefly nocturnal in its hunting but will attack in broad daylight. In size it stands about 17 inches at the shoulder.

GENET (*Genetta*) Genets are of wide distribution throughout Africa, and one species extends northwards into Europe. They are beautiful little animals, and measure, from the tip of their tail to the nose, about thirty-six inches. Genets haunt the jungle and forest and feed on small rodents, birds, and eggs. They are not popular with African farmers for they will raid the chicken pens. They climb well. When stalking their prey they are snake-like with their long thin body and tail pressed close to the ground. They are sometimes tamed, and are expert mouse and rat catchers.

Guinea-fowl   (preyed upon by the smaller cats)

BANDED MONGOOSE (*Crossarchus fasciatus*) This Mongoose is a native of Eastern and Southern Africa, and lives in burrows, or holes under termite nests. Like other species of mongoose it is carnivorous, and hunts its prey on the ground, rarely climbing trees. It is active and bold, and feeds on small mammals, birds, reptiles, insects, eggs, and occasionally fruit. Mongooses are deadly enemies of snakes and, because of their speed and cunning, are usually the victors in their battles with these reptiles. Banded Mongooses live communally, several families occupying the same system of burrows.

ZORILLA (*Zorilla*) Another name for this animal is the Cape Polecat. In appearance it resembles a skunk and, like that animal, can eject an evil-smelling fluid which even the lion respects. Zorillas live in holes. They are rather slow-moving and are quite fearless, knowing full well that their smell is their protection. They feed on mice and rats, birds and their eggs, lizards and frogs, and, in inhabited districts, will destroy poultry. They are nocturnal and are ground hunters, and do not climb trees. If forced to the water they can swim well.

RATEL (*Mellivora capensis capensis*) This sturdy, badger-like animal is found throughout Africa, but more particularly in the south and west of the continent. Its immensely strong fore-legs and claws enable it to dig, partly to house itself (for it lives in holes), and also to tear out the nests of bees. A small bird called the Honey-bird leads the Ratel to the bees and, while the animal is devouring the honey, the bird eats the larvae of the bees. The Ratel also feeds on insects and small mammals. Its courage is as sturdy as its body, and it will stand and fight.

PORCUPINE (*Hystrix galeata ambigua*) A large and powerful rodent whose coat of hair has developed into quills, those on the back being long and stiff, and banded black and white, others are pliable and black. Porcupines are nocturnal, sleeping by day in holes and caves, and foraging for food, which may be of roots, fruit, bark and green vegetation, at night. In defending itself the Porcupine turns its back on its enemy and endeavours to leave some of its easily detachable quills in it. These cause painful and suppurating wounds.

JUMPING HARE (*Pedetes caffer*) This curious rodent, about the size of an English hare, progresses by great leaps on its back legs when travelling fast, but otherwise potters about on all fours. It is a vegetarian, and is entirely nocturnal, lying up during the day in its burrow. Heavy flooding is the only circumstance which will move it from its burrow in the daytime. It lives in family groups, sometimes in colonies, in a labyrinth of burrows, usually made in arid and semi-desert ground. It is distributed through South Africa and northwards to Angola and Kenya.

GROUND SQUIRREL (*Euxerus erythropus fulvior*) This squirrel is widely distributed through tropical Africa, and inhabits a variety of country from the forest edge to the margins of desert. Unlike its tree-haunting cousins it lives in burrows. Its food is mainly vegetarian and consists of roots, grass-seeds, etc., although some insects are taken. It is diurnal in its hunting, and may often be seen running across roads. Its total length is about seventeen inches, of which eight inches is tail.

ROCK HYRAX (*Heterohyrax*) This curious little animal is in a class alone, and its nearest relative is, of all animals, the elephant! It lives in holes in rocky outcrops, hills and mountains, and usually in colonies. It is well adapted to its life among rocks, especially in the structure of its feet, which enables it to grip almost vertical surfaces. Hyraxes are vegetarians, are shy and retiring in their habits, but will turn and bite anything which molests them. They are very noisy, chattering and screaming loudly among themselves. They are the "Coneys" of the Bible.

FENNEC FOX (*Fennecus zerda*) This pretty fox lives in the deserts of North and East Africa. It spends the daytime asleep in its burrow which it lines with feathers, hair, and soft vegetable material. At dusk it makes for the nearest waterhole, and, having quenched its thirst, begins to hunt for food which may be mice, insects, small birds, lizards, or fruits. The burrows are often linked together by passages. As might be expected in an animal with such large ears, it is ever wary and alert, and, when the need arises, it can burrow at prodigious speed, and often escapes the hunter by this stratagem.

Marabou storks.

(scavengers)

AFRICAN HUNTING DOG (*Lycaon pictus*) From Somaliland to the Cape the hunting dog may be found wherever there is game. It is dreaded by all the antelope tribe. It hunts in packs, and captures its victim by sheer relentless running, biting at haunches and flanks, and then at the throat before its prey goes down. Once the hunt is on it rarely abandons its chosen victim. Its colour is very variable, and no two are identical, though different localities tend to produce dogs of differing colour. As a rule it is nocturnal, but not invariably so. It has a peculiar un-dog-like call.

SPOTTED HYENA (*Crocuta crocuta*) This hyena is found over most of Africa south of the Sahara. It is an uncouth beast of great strength, and can crack and demolish large bones with its powerful jaws. It is cowardly yet dangerous, and will attack anything that is weak or wounded, and it is also a scavenger. It has a peculiar gait which looks clumsy, but which is, in reality, very fast. Hyenas are noisy, and give voice to the most hair-raising howls ending in a maniacal laugh. They travel in packs. They give birth to pups which are jet black in colour.

BLACK-BACKED JACKAL (*Thos aureus bea*) The Black-backed Jackal is widely distributed through East and South Africa. It is a shy and wary creature and has many ways of obtaining food. Often it will wait on until the lion has finished his meal, and will then move in with the vultures and take his fill. When hunting for itself it preys on small antelopes, rats, mice, and insects. Sometimes jackals will hunt in packs, but are usually seen single or in pairs. They are chiefly nocturnal and, when on the prowl, they give vent to the most appalling and hair-raising cries.

Vultures   (scavengers)

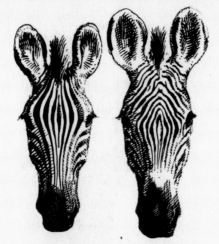

Grant's and Grevy's zebra showing the difference in stripe-patterns

ZEBRA (*Equusquagga granti*) Zebras still roam the plains of Africa in large numbers. There are several species between which there is a marked difference in the pattern and arrangement of the stripes. These stripes are a very effective camouflage when the animals are grazing on the grassy plains for they tend to break up the beast's contours. Zebras and wildebeest are the chief food of lions. No wonder then that they are such nervous creatures and will suddenly stampede for no apparent reason. This is especially so at their drinking places where enemies may lurk. The Zebra depicted is known as Grant's Zebra.

A Barbary lamb

BUFFALO (*Syncerus caffer*) The Cape Buffalo (depicted) is distributed from the southern Sudan to South Africa. It is a large and powerful member of the ox tribe, and, by some hunters, is considered to be the most dangerous of animals to hunt. It lives in herds, and its preference is for swampy ground, though it often grazes on the drier plains. In South Africa the calves are born in the African summer —January to March, and, for some weeks after the birth, the mother separates from the herd and tends her calf, which she hides in long herbage. Often solitary old bulls, which have been banished from the herd by a master bull, are encountered.

BARBARY SHEEP (*Ammotragus lervia*) This is the only true wild sheep found in Africa and its distribution is limited to the southern slopes of the Atlas Mountains. It is adept at concealment, its colour admirably matching its arid surroundings. Possibly its chief enemies are the wandering Arabs who use all its drinking places to water their own flocks and herds; and, had the Barbary Sheep been less expert at concealing itself, it would no doubt have become extinct by now. The rams are distinguished by great fringes of hair which hang from neck and fore-legs. In the females the hair is much shorter. They are agile rock climbers.

BRINDLED GNU or WILDEBEEST (*Connochaetes taurinus*) A grotesque animal resembling a buffalo in front, and a horse behind, but which is really classed with the antelopes. It is an animal of the open plains of East Africa, and is often seen in large herds grazing in the company of zebras. In spite of its morose appearance it is capable of performing the most hilarious antics, rearing, bucking, leaping, and kicking in a most spirited manner, then suddenly lining up to face the intruder as if to charge, which they never do. Both sexes are horned. They are preyed upon by lions.

The long tongue of a giraffe

Profile of a gnu

COKE'S HARTEBEEST (*Alcelaphus buselaphus cokii*) Although the Hartebeest looks ungainly it is reputed to be the swiftest of the antelopes. Its melancholy long face is an indication of its sober disposition, and it does not indulge in the mad gambols and capers so characteristic of the gnu. It is the commonest species of hartebeest in East Africa, and is distributed widely on the open plains and scattered bush. When they graze they always place a sentry on some adjacent high ground. If danger is seen or sensed a snort from the sentry puts the whole herd to the gallop. It is called Kongoni in East Africa.

GIRAFFE (*Giraffa*) This strange and beautiful animal feeds solely on leaves and shoots of trees, chiefly acacia. It does not graze on grass or other ground herbage as its head cannot reach the ground when standing normally. When drinking it is forced to spread its fore-legs widely to enable its head to reach the water. Its tongue is long and its upper lip prehensile, both adaptations for tree-grazing. Wherever the thorn acacia thrives giraffe may be found, especially in East Africa. They usually live in small herds of twenty or thirty. There are several species, each varying in the pattern of its marking. That shown is the reticulated giraffe.

126

Head of female okapi

ELAND (*Taurotragus*) Eland are the largest of all the antelopes, an average sized bull measuring almost six feet at the shoulders. They are found in large herds in a wide variety of country from forest edge to semi-desert in East Africa. As well as being grass eaters they also browse on young leaves. They are timid and difficult to approach, being often accompanied by tick-birds, which give the alarm at the approach of an enemy. (Tick-birds search the hides of various African animals for parasites.) In spite of their size eland are speedy, and are surprisingly good jumpers. Both sexes are horned.

OKAPI (*Okapia johnsoni*) Before 1901 this animal was unknown to science. It inhabits the deep forests of Central Africa, and is related to the giraffe. Like it is a leaf grazer. Okapis are timid, inoffensive animals, living either in pairs or alone. Secluded as they are in the deepest recesses of the forest little is known of their habits. Their peculiar colouring and markings are admirable camouflage in their dark homes. Only a few have appeared in zoos. The males have short stubby horns, the females none, thus differing from the giraffe in which both sexes are horned; and whereas the giraffe is almost mute the Okapi is said to have a cow-like call.

BONGO (*Boocercus isaaci*) This large antelope is essentially a forest animal. Its rich red, white striped colouring helps to camouflage it, and its large ears enable it to pick up the slightest sounds. It is shy and nocturnal in its habits, and is normally solitary or in pairs. Both sexes have horns, those of the male being markedly larger than those of the female. The Bongo inhabits the dense forests of West, Central, and East Africa. Few Europeans have seen it, and only occasionally has it appeared in zoos.

Tick-birds clinging to an animal

An adult Sable antelope

KUDU (*Strepsiceros*) A large and handsome antelope, and a coveted trophy of the hunter. Only the male is horned, and it is said that the longer the horns the more wary the animal. Kudu are partial to bush country and forested hill-country, and, in spite of their size and long horns, the males dash through dense woodland with ease, keeping their heads horizontal to the ground and their horns flat along their necks. They are found in pairs or in small parties, and their distribution extends through East Africa where country is suitable. That illustrated is the Greater Kudu; the Lesser Kudu is much smaller.

SABLE ANTELOPE (*Egocerus niger*) The Sable Antelope is found across Africa south of the equator. The name "sable" really refers to the old males of this handsome species. They alone are black. Young males are reddish, and the females are more rufous. Both males and females are horned. They inhabit country of scattered trees and bush, and are found in small herds. They have the reputation of being very courageous, and will attack if sufficiently provoked. Their horns are deadly weapons, and an adult sable bull is considered a match for a lion.

ORYX (*Oryx beisa annectens*) There are several species of oryx in Africa, the one depicted being the Beisa Oryx of East Africa. It is an animal of the dry bush and the semi-desert country. Oryx live in herds. Both sexes are horned, the males being quarrelsome and often indulging in fierce fights. The females have longer, thinner horns than the males, but in both they are very deadly weapons, especially against dogs, which poaching natives employ to hunt the oryx. Probably as a protection the skin on their necks and shoulders is nearly an inch thick.

THOMSON'S GAZELLE (*Gazella thomsoni*) "Tommies" as they are called in Africa, are the commonest, as well as one of the handsomest, of the small antelopes. Hunters frequently describe seeing them in countless thousands on the plains of Kenya and Tanganyika. They graze on short grass. When the grass grows tall the Tommies move away to younger, shorter pastures, for tall grass will hide lurking enemies such as leopards and jackals. Like other gazelles they appear to glory in their agility, turning, twisting, and leaping when at play. Both sexes are horned.

IMPALA (*Aepycerus malampus*) A graceful, agile antelope inhabiting scrub-land and sandy plains near rivers. Their presence is an indication that water is in the vicinity for they are seldom seen far from it. They are very fleet of foot, and amazing leapers. When a herd panics the animals leap in all directions, one over the other, this way and that, with little forward progression. When they are really going away they indulge in effortless bounds of twenty to thirty feet. Only the males are horned. Impala are found in South, East, and Central Africa.

Impala panic

GRANT'S GAZELLE (*Gazella granti*) This handsome gazelle measures about three feet at the shoulders. It is perhaps the most beautiful of the gazelles, especially the male which has slender graceful horns. It is found in parties (usually consisting of a male with a number of females) on the plains of East Africa, where it grazes and also browses on shrubs. The fawns, as soon as they are born, are hidden under a bush or a canopy of long grass, while its mother feeds near it. Grant's Gazelle has many enemies, hunting dogs and leopards probably being the most deadly.

KLIPSPRINGER (*Oreotragus*) This little antelope measures only twenty-two inches at the shoulder. It inhabits rocky hills and outcrops, and is widely distributed through South and East Africa. It has hoofs which are adapted to its rocky home, and only the tips make contact with the ground. It can climb up almost vertical rock faces. In its often arid surroundings it appears to be able to do without water. The Klipspringer lives as a family, a male, a female and a fawn, and does not herd. It is covered with a peculiarly thick and brittle coat of which the hairs are hollow.

The huge ears of the African elephant

The jaws of a hippo

HIPPOPOTAMUS (*Hippopotamus*) An adult male hippo weighs about 2¼ tons. It is entirely vegetarian in its diet, and spends the night feeding. Leaving its river home after dusk it often travels several miles for food. Being so heavy much damage is done to native crops for as much is trampled as is eaten. The daytime is spent almost completely submerged in a favourite pool or mud wallow, exposing only the eyes and nostrils. It has a prodigious mouth and huge teeth, and can bite a crocodile completely in two. Usually it lives in herds, and is found in most of the rivers and lakes of West, Central and East Africa.

ELEPHANT (*Loxodonta africana*) An adult male African Elephant may weigh six tons and measure eleven feet at the shoulder. In spite of its size it can move through bush and forest amazingly quietly. Elephants have acute senses of smell and hearing but their eyes are not so efficient. The trunk is a versatile fifth limb; it is a scenting organ, a hand for tearing away leaves and branches, a squirt for spraying water when bathing, and a duster for blowing sand over the body. The tusks are used as digging implements for obtaining roots in addition to being weapons of defence. Elephants are entirely vegetarian, and their tempers are unpredictable.

White rhino

(note the square muzzle)

RED RIVER-HOG (*Potamochoerus*) If the Wart Hog is the most grotesque of pigs then the Red River-Hog is surely the most handsome. It lives in herds in the moist forests and swampy river banks of West Africa. Like other bush-pigs the Red River-Hog, with its strong elongated snout, is a forager of the forest floor, rooting for its food which may be roots, tubers, grubs and snails. It is nocturnal in its feeding. The female makes a deep nest of dry grass and leaves in which the young are born.

BLACK RHINOCEROS (*Diceros bicornis*) There are two species of rhino in Africa—Black and White. Both are shades of grey, the chief difference lying in their anatomy. The Black is a nervous, even timid beast, uncertain in its temper and liable to charge any moving thing. It is a vegetarian, a browser of leaves and fruit, and usually inhabits open tree and bush country. For so heavy a beast it is fleet of foot. Its horns are not really horn but are consolidated hair, and are not attached to the bone of the skull but to the tough skin of the head. Rhinos rely on their senses of smell and hearing to give warning of approaching danger. They are also aided in this by the tick-birds which accompany them.

Warts and tusks of a wart hog

WART HOG (*Phacochoerus aethiopicus*) This grotesque pig is widely distributed through East and Central Africa, and roams about in small family parties of sows and young, the boars preferring a more solitary existence. They live in holes which they invariably enter backwards so that the formidable tusked snout faces outwards. Only rarely will a Wart Hog attack (it has been known to charge) and usually flees from man, galloping away with its tail held vertically. The young are born uniformly coloured and without the white stripes characteristic of the young of many wild swine.

AARDVARK (*Orycteropus*) The Boers of the Cape named this animal Aardvark which means "earth pig". However this curious creature is no pig but is in a class by itself in the animal kingdom. Aardvarks feed on the nests of ants and termites, their tremendously strong legs and claws enabling them to dig rapidly in even the hardest ground. They are nocturnal in their feeding, and by day they sleep in holes, excavated by themselves, at the base of ant-hills. They are not common but their distribution extends from the Cape to Somaliland.

GIANT PANGOLIN (*Manis giantea*) "Scaly ant-eater" is another name for the Pangolin. Of the four species of African pangolin this is the largest. Several of these are arboreal in their habits, but the Giant Pangolin is a ground species and does not climb trees. It feeds on ants and termites, digging out their nests with its immensely strong front limbs. The ants exposed, it flicks out a very long, sticky, worm-like tongue to which the ants adhere and are swallowed. It sleeps in holes, curling up on its side, encircled by its tail for protection. When thus curled up no human is strong enough to uncurl it.

NILE CROCODILE (*Crocodylus niloticus*) These fierce reptiles infest many African rivers and lakes, but only the upper reaches of the Nile. They are flesh eaters and feed on fish, animals, and, too often, humans; grabbing them at the water's edge and drowning them. They will also knock animals into the water with their immensely powerful tails. Crocodiles are fond of basking on sand-banks, usually with their mouths wide open. Females lay their eggs in the sand, covering them, and leaving them to be incubated by the sun's heat. When the young are ready to hatch, the nests are uncovered by the females.

Termite nests and an aardvark

ATLAS MTS.

SAHARA DESERT

EGYPT

R. SENEGAL

SENEGAL

R. NIGER

SUDAN

R. NILE

ABYSSINIA

SOMALILAND

L. RUDOLF

CAMEROONS

KENYA

EQUATOR

GABON

R. CONGO

L. VICTORIA

ATLANTIC

L. TANGANYIKA

OCEAN

ANGOLA

L. NYASA

R. ZAMBEZI

MADAGASCAR

KALAHARI DESERT

R. LIMPOPO

ORANGE R.

N

CAPE OF GOOD HOPE

INDIAN OCEAN

THE BERKSHIRE PRINTING CO. LTD. READING. ENGLAND.

THIS SERIES OF
PICTURE CARDS IS OFFERED
IN THE INTERESTS OF EDUCATION BY

Brooke Bond

A card is given free in all packets of Brooke Bond tea
also two cards in each $\frac{1}{2}$ lb. tin of
Brooke Bond Pure and French Coffee

The front cover image from **Asian Wildlife** is undoubtedly one of the most striking ever seen on a Brooke Bond album. It engages you immediately through the vivid colours of the Tiger's coat, the detail and contrasting green of the foliage and, most of all, those "burning bright" tiger eyes that follow you around the room no matter how you try to dodge them – almost as if this tiger is actually stalking you!

This 50-card set from 1962 was once again illustrated by C.F. Tunnicliffe, who also wrote the texts that accompanied the cards. In his foreword he delivered another warning about the animals facing extinction across Asia, making specific reference to the Dugong, the Indian Rhinoceros, the Mongolian Wild Horse and the Indian Lion. "Soon, unless man becomes suddenly more intelligent," wrote Tunnicliffe, "we shall have to face the fact that where he lives and works, animal life will continue to suffer, and where he is in complete control the animals must disappear completely."

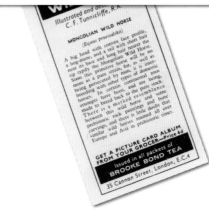

It is also interesting to note that, immediately following Tunnicliffe's foreword, there was a footnote encouraging readers to write to the World Wildlife Fund to find out about what was being done to preserve endangered species. On the same page (the inside front cover) was a highly detailed line drawing of two Blackbuck locked in combat while on the facing page there was a map of the entire continent of Asia.

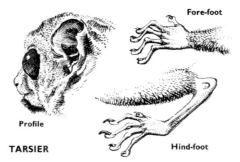

Fore-foot

Profile

TARSIER

Hind-foot

Few of Brooke Bond's albums would achieve the splendour of *Asian Wild Life*, making it a highly desirable addition to any card fan's collection.

A wall chart was available to schools which is highly collectable today. The cards and album were also printed in Southern Rhodesia and East Africa, where the card backs were printed in magenta.

OTHER ASIAN CATS

Leopard Cat of S.E. Asia

Manul Cat of Tibet and Mongolia

Indian Jungle Cat—link between Cats and Lynxes

Tibetan Lynx

Supplementary illustrations abounded in this album with details, such as those showing the Tarsier's hands and feet, appearing as we had come to expect but there were also entire pages devoted to, for example, the different types of Asian big cats. All of these extra illustrations, beautifully displayed, meant that this album stretched to 32 pages, twice the length of the African Wildlife album, although they housed exactly the same number and size of cards.

ASIA is a vast and varied continent stretching from the Arctic Circle in the north to the Equator in the south. Within its boundaries are some of the most thickly populated areas in the world, and some of the most desolate, empty spaces of desert, mountain and steppe. It has the highest mountains in the world, and some of the deepest tropical jungles. All this variety maintains a corresponding variety of wild life, except in those places where humans are dominant. Thus, in India, the lion and the rhinoceros are reduced to a remnant, the Mongolian wild horse will soon be extinct, if it is not already so, and the dugong has been hunted to a shadow of its former numbers. Soon, unless man becomes suddenly more intelligent, we shall have to face the fact that where he lives and works, animal life will continue to suffer, and where he is in complete control the animals must disappear completely.

C. F. Tunnicliffe

If you are interested in the work being done to preserve wild life, write to The World Wildlife Fund, 2 Caxton Street, London, S.W.1, who will gladly give you an account of what is being achieved.

Blackbuck fighting

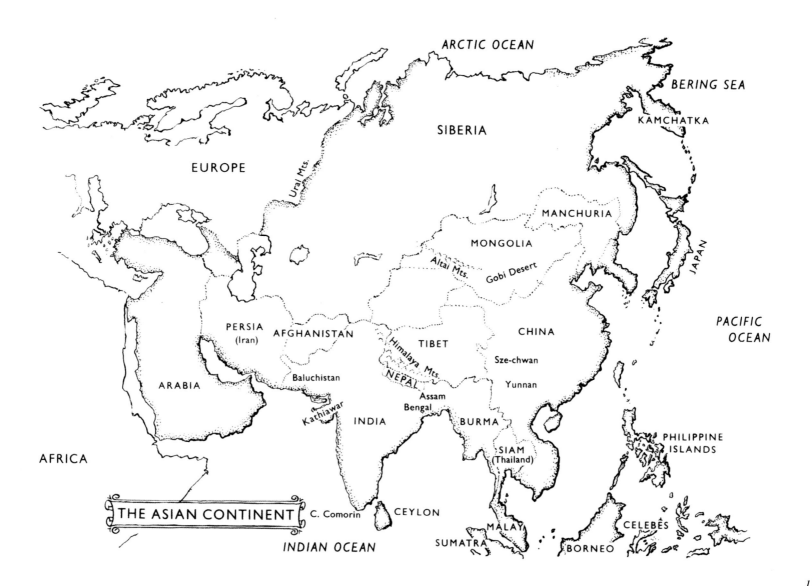

ARCTIC OCEAN

BERING SEA

SIBERIA

KAMCHATKA

EUROPE

Ural Mts.

MANCHURIA

MONGOLIA

Altai Mts.   Gobi Desert

JAPAN

PACIFIC
OCEAN

PERSIA
(Iran)   AFGHANISTAN

CHINA

TIBET

Himalaya Mts.

Sze-chwan

Baluchistan

NEPAL

Yunnan

ARABIA

Assam
Bengal

Kathiawar

INDIA

BURMA

PHILIPPINE
ISLANDS

AFRICA

SIAM
(Thailand)

THE ASIAN CONTINENT   C. Comorin   CEYLON

CELEBES

MALAY

SUMATRA   BORNEO

INDIAN OCEAN

TUPAI or TREE SHREW (*Tupaia glis*) Anthropologists state that a tupai-like animal was the probable ancient source from which sprang the later ancestors of lemurs, monkeys, apes and man. Be that as it may, there are several forms of tupai in the world today. They are squirrel-sized creatures and much resemble those animals in their ways, in fact the name 'Tupai' is a Malay word applied to both the smaller squirrels and the tupais. They hunt their food—fruit and insects—both in trees and on the ground. Their range extends from India, through Burma, into Malaya, to Borneo and the Philippines.

Old male
Orang-utan
with cheek pouches

ORANG-UTAN (*Pongo pygmaeus*) This large red ape lives in the forests of Borneo and Sumatra, where it feeds chiefly on fruit, shoots and leaves. It is at home in the trees, its long powerful arms enabling it to swing through the canopy with ease. Orang-utans wander in small parties, feeding during the day, and spending the night in tree nests made of branches. Adult males develop large pads on the cheeks, and both sexes have an inflatable throat pouch connected with the windpipe, perhaps associated with voice production. Orang-utans, if cornered, can be very dangerous, especially the males which have powerful teeth.

AGILE GIBBON (*Hylobates agilis*) In the Malay Peninsula and the island of Sumatra the Agile Gibbon may be found. This gibbon (though all gibbons are agile) is reputed to be so acrobatic and fast that it has been known to catch birds on the wing. On the ground it walks upright, often with arms held high above the head. Gibbons are small slender apes with very long arms. They spend their lives in the tree branches among which they swing and leap at great speed. Their food consists of fruit, nuts, shoots, birds' eggs, young birds and insects, and one tribe will fight another for possession of feeding grounds. They are often very noisy.

Orang-utans at home

Profile of an adult male Proboscis monkey

PROBOSCIS MONKEY (*Nasalis larvatus*) The young Proboscis Monkey has a snub nose, the adult female has a small proboscis, and it is only in the adult male that the nose becomes large and pendulous. Why it develops this caricature of a nose is not known. It is difficult to see what useful purpose it serves. This large monkey is found only in Borneo. In the forests it moves about in large groups and is never far from water, for it loves to swim. It indulges in bouts of great activity, alternating with periods of complete inactivity during which it resents any intrusion either of other monkeys or of noise. In the wild they are almost exclusively leaf-eaters.

SLENDER LORIS (*Loris tardigradus*). The forest lands of southern India and Ceylon are the homes of the Slender Loris. This small creature, not more than ten inches long, feeds on leaves, nuts, flowers, insects, eggs and any small animal it can catch. It is completely nocturnal in its foraging, and spends the daylight hours asleep, curled up in a ball with its head between its thighs and one hand grasping the branch on which it is resting. Hands and feet are especially adapted for grasping branches. Its normal progress is very deliberate, but it can move fairly fast when the need arises and when capturing food.

HANUMAN MONKEY (*Semnopithecus entellus*) This is an Indian monkey common in the central portion of the peninsula. Dedicated to the god Hanuman, they are held sacred and are strictly protected wherever the Hindu faith exists. These monkeys are well aware of their privileged state, and are regularly fed by priests in some Hindu temples, where they can hardly be called wild. Their food consists of leaves, shoots and grain. Usually they roam in groups, the females carrying their young clasped to their breasts for some considerable time after they are born. Hanuman Monkeys belong to the group called Langurs.

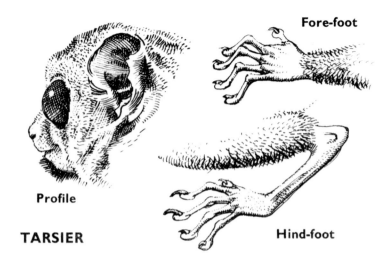

Fore-foot

Profile

TARSIER

Hind-foot

TARSIER (*Tarsius bancanus*) This fascinating little animal, no bigger than a small rat, lives in the islands of Sumatra and Borneo. There are other races in Celebes and the Philippines. It lives in the forests, and its hands and feet have discs at the end of the toes to increase the grip on twigs and branches as it leaps from one to the other. Nocturnal in its hunting, it lives on insects and tree frogs which it stalks, and captures with a final leap; it holds its prey in its 'hands' like a squirrel. Tarsiers sleep clinging to upright branches and, as well as gripping with hands and feet, they use their tails as supports. Their remarkable ears are very mobile and can be folded at will.

COBEGO (*Cynocephalus volans*) This strange animal has always been a puzzle to zoologists, so much so that it has had to be placed alone with no strong connections with any other animal. The Malay Cobego is found in Sumatra, Borneo, Java, and the Malay Peninsula. It lives among trees and feeds on flowers and leaves and, because of the web of skin which stretches between limbs, from head to tail, is able to glide very efficiently from tree to tree. On the trunks and branches its progress is laboured and jerky. It has a single young, born quite helpless, which spends a long period after birth clinging to its mother's underside; she glides with the young in this position.

MALAY FRUIT BAT (*Pteropus vampyrus*) This, the largest of the fruit bats, has a wing span of four feet, and inhabits the Malay Peninsula. Fruit bats, sometimes called Flying Foxes, feed exclusively on fruit. They feed at night and are a great pest in areas where fruit is cultivated. During the hours of daylight they roost in some secluded spot, hanging in thousands to the tree branches; at sundown they rouse and, in vast numbers, make their way to their chosen feeding ground which may be as much as twenty miles from their roosts. Near dawn they return to the roost and, with much bad tempered quarrelling and biting, settle in the upside-down position, hanging by their feet, to sleep.

Part of a Fruit Bat roost

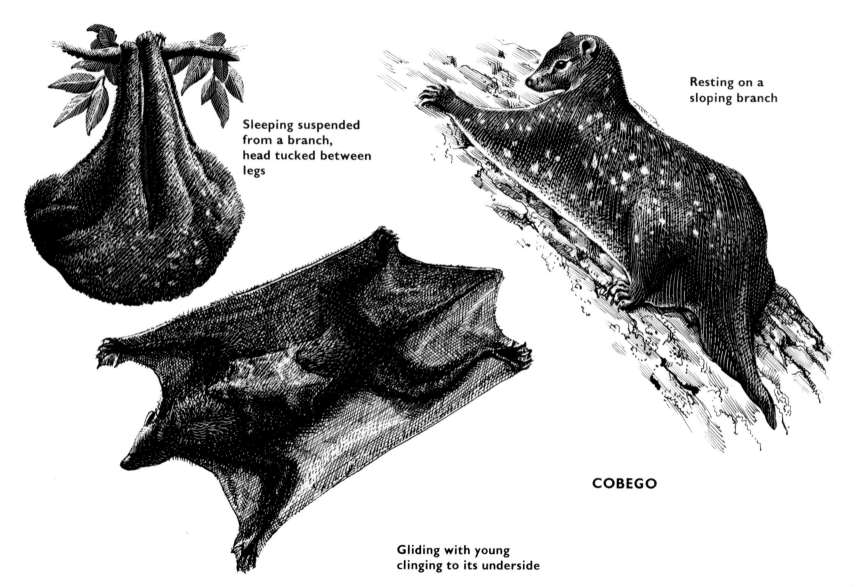

Sleeping suspended
from a branch,
head tucked between
legs

Resting on a
sloping branch

Gliding with young
clinging to its underside

COBEGO

The yawn of a Tiger

INDIAN LION (*Panthera leo*) The lion in Asia is almost extinct except for a small remnant in the Gir forest in Kathiawar, India, which now receives protection. A few years ago a count there revealed a total of approximately 220. Compared with the African lion the Indian is reputed to be slightly smaller and the mane is not so full. It is interesting to note that in certain Indian manuscript paintings male lions are sometimes depicted with very scanty manes which scarcely hide the anatomy of necks and shoulders. In habits the Indian lion is very like its African brother. Its prey consists of Nilgai, Blackbuck, Chital Deer, Sambar and the like.

Lion copied from a 16th cent. Indian painting. Note the scanty mane

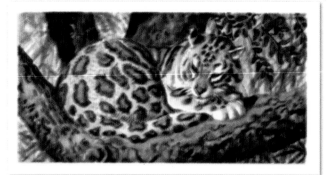

CLOUDED LEOPARD (*Neofelis nebulosa*) This beautifully marked cat, somewhat smaller than the common leopard, and having a longer tail, shorter legs, and a longer face than the leopard, ranges from the eastern Himalayas, Assam, Burma, South China and Malaya, into the islands of Borneo and Sumatra. It is a forest animal and spends most of its life in the trees, where it hunts birds and small mammals; it also sleeps in the trees. Little appears to be known of its life in the wild state. Examination of its skull reveals that it has canine teeth in the upper jaw proportionately larger than those of any other cat.

TIGER (*Panthera tigris*) The tiger is widely distributed in Asia, and is found from Manchuria and Siberia, through India and Burma to Malaya. This savage, powerful, handsome cat haunts the jungles and forests of these countries, and takes its toll of deer and antelopes, wild swine, monkeys and peafowl. Domestic cattle and humans are also its prey, and when a tiger becomes a man-eater it can play havoc with the human population of a district. Tigers are usually solitary and nocturnal in their activities. They are not so noisy as lions and their roar has none of the earth-shaking quality of that beast's, but in all other respects they are as formidable, and even more savage.

CLOUDED LEOPARD

Note the length of
the upper canine teeth

MARBLED CAT of Assam, Burma and Malaya. This cat is almost a miniature Clouded Leopard, and has the same tree-haunting habit

Snow Leopard

SNOW LEOPARD (*Uncia uncia*) At elevations between 6,000 and 20,000 feet, in the mountain ranges of central Asia, the Snow Leopard may be found. The beautiful coat, composed of long outer fur and a close inner fur, is the animal's protection against the intense cold of these altitudes. In such unpromising surroundings it preys on wild sheep and goats, marmots and small rodents. Besides differing from the common leopard in the length and colour of its coat it has a rounder, more arched skull. As it lives in treeless areas it is doubtful if it can climb, but little is known of its habits in the wild.

PANTHER (*Panthera pardus*) 'Panther' was the name given to a large type of leopard which was at one time thought to be a separate species. Black phases, like the one depicted, are often called panthers, but these too are leopards, and interbreed with the spotted variety. The leopard is widely distributed in Asia, and is found in India, Burma and Malaya, etc. It preys on deer and antelopes, domestic cattle, monkeys and dogs. Leopards like to rest in tree branches, and often capture their prey from such a vantage point. They have astonishing strength and ferocity, and will drag prey heavier than themselves up into the tree branches to be devoured at leisure.

INDIAN CIVET (*Viverra zibetha*) Civets are cat-like creatures, but differ from the cats in the long shape of the head, in the long and flattened body, and in long claws which are only partly retractile. They have a crest of hair along the spine which they can erect at will. The Indian Civet is a nocturnal hunter and kills any bird or small mammal it can capture. It also feeds on frogs, snakes and insects, and will raid domestic poultry. It is very destructive. From the secretion of a gland of the civet many perfumes and cosmetics are made. The Indian Civet ranges through eastern India, Burma, Thailand, Malaya and southern China.

Indian Civet

OTHER ASIAN CATS

Leopard Cat of
S.E. Asia

Manul Cat of Tibet
and Mongolia

Indian Jungle Cat—link between Cats and Lynxes

Tibetan Lynx

149

SIBERIAN CHIPMUNK (*Eutamias sibiricus*) This ground squirrel is found over the whole of northern Asia. It feeds on nuts and beech mast, grain and roots, insect larvæ, and sometimes young birds. It differs from the true squirrels in having cheek pouches in which it carries food. In the northerly parts of its range it hibernates in winter, gathering great quantities of food against this season. It lives in a hole in the ground or among the spreading roots of trees. This hole serves as a retreat, a place to hibernate in, and a principal storehouse. For the most part it spends its life on the ground but will sometimes take to the tree branches.

YARKAND JERBOA (*Euchoreutes naso*) Sometimes called the Long-eared Jerboa, this little animal inhabits the desert and steppe regions of Yarkand in north-west China. It differs from other jerboas in its longer nose and its enormous ears, and is similar to them in the smallness of the forelegs and the development of the hind legs. Jerboas progress in great leaps and are very fast; the hind legs only are used in these leaps. They live in burrows, and are nocturnal in their feeding. Their food consists chiefly of vegetable matter, though they will take birds' eggs and insects. During the winter cold they hibernate in their burrows in which they live in small colonies. Their burrows consist of a central chamber with several branching tunnels leading from it.

INDIAN MONGOOSE (*Herpestes edwardsi*) This mongoose occurs throughout India. Like other mongooses it is savage for its size, and lives on rats and mice, snakes and lizards, birds, eggs and insects. It lives in a hole in hedgerows, stream banks and rough scrubland, but is not normally a forest dweller. It often approaches houses and can play havoc among domestic poultry and rabbits. When excited it erects its long stiff hair, and this may be some protection in its encounters with venomous snakes; it is not immune from the effects of snake venom, but is so agile that, as a rule, it is the victor in such battles. It can be tamed, and makes an interesting and useful pet for it is death to all rats.

INDIAN GIANT SQUIRREL (*Ratufa indica*) This handsome squirrel can attain a length of 30 inches. It is confined to the forest land of India and is strictly a tree dweller, feeding by day on nuts, fruit, buds and young shoots. In its passage through the trees it reveals remarkable powers of leaping, bridging gaps of almost 20 feet. As a rule, except in the breeding season, it is solitary, each individual having its own territory in which it constructs several globular nests of twigs and leaves. In these it sleeps, and the females give birth to their young in them. Other giant squirrels are found in Ceylon, Indo-China, the Malay Peninsula and Borneo.

MONGOOSE v COBRA

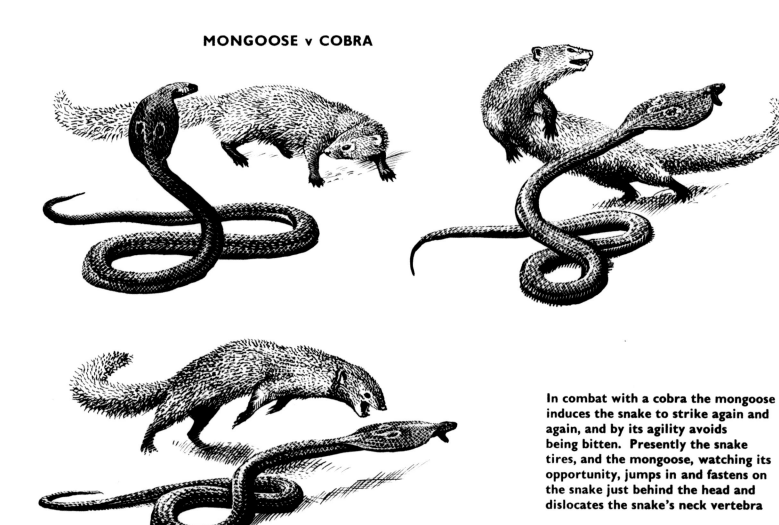

In combat with a cobra the mongoose induces the snake to strike again and again, and by its agility avoids being bitten. Presently the snake tires, and the mongoose, watching its opportunity, jumps in and fastens on the snake just behind the head and dislocates the snake's neck vertebra

GIANT PANDA (*Ailuropoda melanoleuca*) Not really a panda, and certainly not a bear, the Giant Panda occupies a niche of its own in zoology. Its range is restricted to the bamboo jungles of central and western Szechwan, and its food is exclusively bamboo shoots and stems. To grasp these the panda's forefeet are especially adapted, there being a swollen pad which acts almost like a thumb on the underside. When a stem is grasped this pad is opposite to the first toe, and between them a good grip of the bamboo is obtained. When not feeding the Giant Panda lies up in caves, and sometimes in the forks of trees. It is said to hibernate, but this is not invariable.

RED PANDA (*Ailurus fulgens*) This handsome animal inhabits the mountain forests from Nepal eastwards through Assam to Yunnan and Szechwan in China. It is sometimes called the 'cat-bear'. Its sharp claws are partially retractile and are used chiefly for tree climbing and not for defence, for it appears to be rather slow and dull in temperament. Very much a creature of the trees and a vegetarian, it feeds on fruit, acorns, bamboo shoots and roots. The Red Panda feeds in the morning and the evening and sleeps much during the day, though it is not entirely nocturnal. When sleeping it curls up on its side completely covering its head with its long bushy tail. The undersides of the feet are covered with hair which hides the pads.

SLOTH BEAR (*Melursus ursinus*) This bear lives in India and Ceylon and, though it has been exterminated from some of its haunts, is still fairly common. Chiefly nocturnal, but is sometimes seen abroad on cloudy days. It passes the day in caves or concealed among trees and bushes. The tongue is exceptionally long which enables it to scoop up termites and ants, and its claws are prodigiously strong, efficient tools for digging out the nests of bees, for this bear loves honey. Fruit, leaves, and carrion are also eaten, and it is known to climb the date palms in which natives hang pots to catch the exuding juice which, when fermented, makes a drink called 'Toddy'. The bear sometimes drinks so much of this as to become quite drunk.

STRIPED HYENA (*Hyaena hyaena*) In Asia the Striped Hyena ranges through India, Baluchistan, Persia and Arabia, inhabiting open sandy desert country or woodland, and is chiefly nocturnal. Any hole or cave serves for its daytime retreat. Usually solitary in hunting, this hyena feeds on the carcase remnants of animals killed by other beasts of prey, and even when a skeleton has been picked clean by jackals and vultures, the bones themselves are a meal for the strong-jawed hyena. In inhabited districts it is particularly dreaded for its grave-robbing habits. It will carry off sheep, goats and dogs. Compared with the Spotted Hyena of Africa it is a much more silent animal.

Giant Panda at home

**HIMALAYAN
BLACK BEAR**
Found from E.
Persia, through the
Himalayas, into
Assam and Burma

MALAY BEAR or
BRUANG.
Found in the Malay
Peninsula, Sumatra,
Java and Borneo

WOLF (*Canis lupus*) The wolf ranges across Asia from the Ural Mountains in the west across Siberia to Kamchatka in the east, and is also found in Tibet and India. Wolves inhabit both forest and open country and, as a rule, they are either solitary or in pairs, though in winter they may congregate in large packs. Any living thing is food for a wolf and, with its strong jaws and tireless speedy running, it is a formidable hunter, though it will not attack man unless it is frantic with hunger and is hunting in a pack. The cry is a prolonged howl.

Indian fox at its burrow

Wolf cub

INDIAN WILD DOG or DHOLE (*Cuon alpinus*) The Dhole inhabits a variety of country from the large forests of southern India to the forest-clad portions of the Himalayas. It hunts, both by night and day, in small packs of from six to ten. Following the scent of their prey until it is in view, and pursuing relentlessly until they can spring at their victim, they eventually drag it down. In India they hunt blackbuck, gazelles, deer and wild pig, and, in the Himalayas, wild sheep, goats and antelopes. They are capable of bringing down such large animals as nilgai and buffalo. They shun the neighbourhood of man.

INDIAN FOX (*Vulpes bengalensis*) This is one of the smallest of the true foxes, and is common throughout India. It feeds on rats, land crabs, grasshoppers, beetles and the like, and may hunt at all hours of the day or night. It lives in a burrow which has several openings converging towards the centre, some blind, others leading towards a large central space where the animal breeds, and which may be 2 or 3 feet below the ground surface. This burrow is often in the open plain. This slender, pretty fox is easily tamed and is more suitable than other foxes for this purpose owing to the absence of odour.

OTHER
ASIAN
CANINES

ASIATIC JACKAL ranges through India and Ceylon, into Assam and Burma. It is a scavenger

SIBERIAN WILD DOG ranges through Eastern and Northern Siberia and south to the Altai mountains. It hunts in the manner of the Indian Dhole

RACOON DOG inhabits Japan, China and Amurland. It feeds on small rodents and fish, and is a nocturnal hunter. In certain parts of its range it is said to hibernate

Indian Buffalo

INDIAN BUFFALO (*Bubalus bubalis*) This buffalo, in its domesticated form, is widespread throughout the oriental regions, but as a truly wild animal it is becoming rare. In India the haunts of the wild buffalo are the tall grass jungles of the plains and river valleys. They love swamps. They are found in herds of about 50, and feed chiefly on grass in the evening, at night, and in the early morning, spending the heat of the day lying in high grass. They can play havoc among growing crops. Large bulls are said to attain a height of 6 feet at the shoulder.

GAUR (*Bos gaurus*) This largest of all the ox tribe inhabits the hill forests of India, Assam and Burma. The bull Gaur may be 6 feet tall at the shoulder and is massively built. They roam the forests in small herds of a dozen or so and these herds are dominated by a master bull. Sometimes solitary old bulls are encountered which have been banished from the herd by a stronger bull; these outcast bulls usually bear many scars of battle on their horns, ears and flanks. They are often dangerous beasts. As cultivation in India spreads Gaur are decreasing in numbers for they are apt to be infected with the diseases of domestic cattle.

TAKIN (*Budorcas taxicolor*) Among the bamboo and rhododendron forests of the hills, from the eastern Himalayas, through Assam and northern Burma into western China, the Takin may be found. These grotesque beasts, which look like a mixture of sheep and ox, roam their mountain homes in herds of anything from 5 to 50, and at altitudes up to 10,000 feet. Males and females are usually in separate herds, the males ranging higher than the females which have young to tend. They move about their precipitous homes with ease, and men find them difficult to hunt.

Profile of a Takin

A Gaur Calf

A Bull Gaur. Note the shoulder ridge caused by the great elongation of the spines of the vertebrae

An Argali ewe

ARGALI (*Ovis ammon*) This is the largest of the wild sheep, the adult rams being as large as a medium sized donkey. Argalis are widespread across central Asia and are invariably mountain animals. There is a variety of races, the one depicted being the Siberian, of the type found in the Altai mountains. Here these sheep spend their lives and, unless disturbed, remain on the same mountain always. Except in the breeding season rams and ewes remain separate, the former in small groups of 3 to 5, the latter singly. The ewes have much smaller horns than the rams, and are quite different in appearance.

TAHR (*Hemitragus jemlahicus*) There are three varieties of Tahr, one inhabiting the Himalayas, another the Nilgiri Hills in India, and another in Arabia. The Himalayan Tahr is depicted. Tahr differ from other goats in that they have no beard, the extremity of the muzzle is naked, and the females have four teats instead of two. The females have horns which are almost as large as those of the males. In the Himalayas Tahr frequent the precipitous forest regions. Except in the breeding season the males herd separately from the females. Kids are born in June and July, a single one only being produced at a birth.

MARKHOR (*Capra falconeri*) 'Markhor' is a native name meaning 'snake eater', but whether this is one of the habits of this fine goat is not known. Markhor are mountain animals and they range from Kashmir and Afghanistan to Baluchistan, where they haunt the precipitous mountain forests and pastures, feeding on grass and tree shoots. They are extremely agile on the rock faces. There are several races inhabiting various mountainous countries, and the horns are extremely varied, one race having the horns in the form of a tight screw, and another extreme having horns of a very open spiral. Between these extremes there is a variety of twisted horns.

Variations in the shape of Markhor horns

Type of country inhabited by the Himalayan Tahr

Male and female Blackbuck

BLACKBUCK (*Antilope cervicapra*) In India, from the northern plains to Cape Comorin, the Blackbuck may be found where the country is suitable—grassy districts or cultivated areas being its choice. It wanders about in herds of from 10 to 50, though it has, at times, been observed in hundreds. Only the males have the long spiral horns, and only fully adult males have the black-brown and white coat. Young males and all females are yellowish-fawn and white. Blackbuck are immensely fast and have great stamina. Few animals can overtake them on good ground. The males are quarrelsome in the rutting season and fight much among themselves.

SAIGA (*Saiga tatarica*) This grotesque, swollen-nosed antelope inhabits the great steppes of western Asia. It lives in herds, sometimes of several hundreds, and wanders far. In summer it may be found far enough north to mix with reindeer, while in winter it may be south enough to have the Goitred Gazelle for company. In winter the herds split up into smaller numbers. While the majority of the herd sleeps there are always several members alert and watchful. Over a short distance Saigas are speedy, but soon become blown. When captured young they can be easily tamed, and follow their owners like dogs.

NILGAI (*Boselaphus tragocamelus*) This is the largest of the Indian antelopes, and the name means 'blue bull'. This refers to the male which is indeed blue-grey. The females and young males are brown, and the females are hornless. They are distributed in certain areas in India and nowhere else. Nilgai both graze and browse and prefer thin bush with scattered trees, and sometimes wander on to cultivated ground when they do much damage; they feed at any time of the day. The bulls are usually separated from the females and young, and are often solitary.

NILGAI

Head of female Nilgai

Nilgai Bull

**Goitred
Gazelle**

**Note the
swelling
on the neck**

GOITRED GAZELLE (*Gazella subgutturosa*) As a rule the females of the gazelle family have horns, but in the case of the Goitred Gazelles they are hornless. They have a peculiar swelling in front of the neck which, in the males, becomes much enlarged in the mating season, hence the name 'goitred'. This gazelle is found in the highlands of Persia (now Iran), and a larger relative ranges across the Mongolian steppes. They are animals of the bleak plains, over which they wander in large herds grazing on the scanty herbage. Wolves and cheetahs prey upon them, but when put to flight they can be very speedy.

Indian Chevrotain

INDIAN CHEVROTAIN (*Tragulus meminna*) This little animal lives in southern India and Ceylon. It is related to the deer and, but for one African species, is the smallest of the ruminants. The males have canine teeth which are elongated into tusks. Chevrotains appear to walk on their hoof points, and have a peculiar, mincing stiff-legged gait. They are shy and retiring and come out to feed only at dawn and dusk. During daylight they hide away in rock crevices or thick jungle cover, and it is in such a place that the female gives birth to her one, or two, young. Except in the mating season the adults are solitary.

CHITAL (*Axis axis*) This handsome species is found over much of India, especially where there are trees and water, or bush and bamboo cover. Chital are never far from water, and wander about in herds, sometimes of several hundreds. They feed for a few hours after sunrise, and again before sunset; they both graze and browse. During the heat of the day they retire to cover. From northern India to the south, Chital vary much in size, in the time they cast their antlers, and in the time they have their young. They are white-spotted at all ages and at all times, unlike our own Fallow Deer, which are spotted in spring and summer only.

OTHER ASIAN DEER

MUSK DEER. A small, hornless deer of the Himalaya and Central Asia. From it the musk of perfume-makers is obtained

SAMBAR DEER. A large deer of India and Burma, dark red in colour, a forest animal, and a night feeder.

SIKA DEER. This deer is widely distributed in Manchuria and Japan. Escaped zoo Sika are now wild in certain parts of Britain

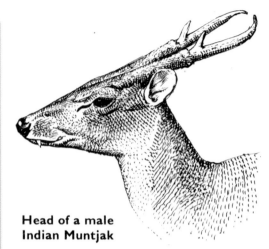

**Head of a male
Indian Muntjak**

MONGOLIAN WILD HORSE (*Equus przewalskii*) A big head with convex face profile, a hog-mane, and a tail with short hair near its base and long hair nearer the tip typify the Mongolian Wild Horse. Soon this primitive horse will be no more as a pure strain, for, as well as being persecuted by man, it is interbreeding with other types of domestic horses. In certain continental zoos attempts have been, and are being, made to breed back to the pure stock. There is a marked resemblance between this wild horse and some prehistoric rock paintings and bone carvings, and there is little doubt that similar wild horses roamed all over Europe and Asia in prehistoric times.

MUNTJAK (*Muntiacus muntjak*) Muntjak are widely distributed through the oriental regions, from India to China, Sumatra, Java and Borneo. They are small, not more than 20 inches high at the shoulder, and have peculiar horns which spring from long hair-covered pedicles. The females are hornless. The males have long canine teeth or tusks which show outside the lower lip. When attacked by dogs they have been known to use their tusks as weapons, inflicting quite deep gashes. Muntjak are solitary forest dwellers, shy and retiring, and diurnal in their feeding.

KIANG (*Equus kiang*) The Kiang, or Tibetan Wild Ass, is a fine animal living on the plains and river valleys of Tibet at altitudes up to 16,000 feet above sea level. It is a powerfully built animal standing about 13 hands high with small, horse-like ears, strong legs and broad hoofs. They live in herds and whilst they are grazing a sentinel keeps watch at a point some distance from the herd. Any alarm signal sends the whole herd away at a speedy canter, interrupted when it wheels about and stops to watch the intruder from a safe distance. As a rule Kiangs are silent animals, but sometimes they utter a bray-like sound. In winter they grow a long coat and are paler in colour.

**The tail of a
Mongolian
Wild Horse**

A painting on a cave wall at Font-de-Gaume

Prehistoric rock paintings of wild horses, discovered in France. Note their resemblance to the Mongolian wild horse

Part of a painting on cave walls at Lascaux

165

Young Malay Tapir

MALAY TAPIR (*Tapirus indicus*) This tapir is found in Burma, Thailand, the Malay Peninsula, and Sumatra. It is a vegetarian and feeds on aquatic plants and other succulent greenery, and is nocturnal and very shy. When it enters deep water it is said to walk along the bottom. Although in a zoo it appears very conspicuous, it is camouflaged almost to invisibility in its natural forest habitat, especially in bright moonlight. Tapirs give birth to one, sometimes two, young which are dark brown, spotted and striped with yellow. They are thick-skinned beasts, and have few enemies except leopards and tigers. They have tusk-like canine teeth and can inflict terrible bites when necessary.

**Hind-foot and
fore-foot of Malay Tapir**

INDIAN RHINOCEROS (*Rhinoceros unicornis*) In 1956 there were only about 300-350 Indian Rhinos left in the world, and of these the greatest number were in Assam. A few remained in West Bengal, a few in Nepal. Unfortunately these rhinos carry a fortune on their noses, 2,500 dollars regularly being offered by Chinese traders for a single horn which is sold in China as a medicine for even more fantastic prices. This rhino stands $5\frac{1}{2}$ feet at the shoulders, is a vegetarian, likes swampy ground and is fond of a mud wallow. It has two tusk-like teeth in its lower jaw as well as the single horn, all of which it may use as weapons. It is as temperamental as its black cousin in Africa, and will attack elephants without hesitation.

ASIATIC ELEPHANT (*Elephas maximus*) India, Ceylon, Assam, Burma, Thailand, Sumatra and Borneo are the countries of the wild Asiatic Elephant. In undulating forest country, particularly where bamboos flourish, they live in herds, keeping to the dense forest near water during the hot period of the year, but venturing into more open land in the rainy season to feed on the young grass. Elephants are entirely vegetarian in their food. They are fond of water and are excellent swimmers. At all times they are temperamental and are usually shy, but old solitary bulls, and females with calves are often dangerous. An adult male will weigh between $2\frac{1}{2}$ and 3 tons and average a height of 9 feet at the shoulders.

The Javan Rhino is smaller than the Indian, and has a less-rough hide. It is single horned

OTHER ASIAN RHINOCEROSES

The Sumatran Rhino is the smallest and hairiest of the Asian rhinos, and has two horns

Young Wild Pig

INDIAN WILD PIG (*Sus cristatus*) This wild pig is similar to the European species, except that it is rather taller, has a thinner covering of hair, and no under fur. It also has a crest of long black bristles running along the spine. It is distributed throughout India, Ceylon and Burma. Away from human haunts these wild swine live chiefly on roots, but in areas of cultivation they are devastating, for the herds destroy as much by trampling as by eating. They will also feed on carrion and animal carcasses. They feed at dusk and dawn and lie up in the heat of the day. The young may number 6 to 10 at a birth and are striped. Adult boars, in their prime, are considered a match for a tiger.

BACTRIAN CAMEL (*Camelus bactrianus*) Though this camel has been domesticated for many centuries, wild remnants may still wander the great expanses of the Gobi Desert in Mongolia. In build and constitution they are adapted to a much colder and harsher habitat than the Arabian Camel. They are two-humped, have short sturdy legs, and are protected with great masses of hair. They need no shelter, but sleep in deep snow, and can cross mountainous country, as well as deserts, with ease. They can stand the greatest extremes of temperature. The bitter and saline plants of the steppes are their food and they drink freely from the salt lakes which occur in their terrain.

BABIRUSA (*Babyrousa babyrussa*) The Malay word 'babirusa' means 'pig deer', and no doubt it was the fantastic development of the tusks of the male which gave this pig that name. Babirusas inhabit the Celebes and Boru. Moist forest, bamboo canes, and the banks of lakes and rivers are their favoured places, for they feed on roots and water plants. They are nocturnal in their feeding and are excellent swimmers, crossing lakes and even narrow channels of the sea. The sow has only one, or two, at a birth, and these are very tiny and without the stripes which characterise the young of wild swine.

Young Babirusa

BABIRUSA

It is difficult to imagine what useful purpose the tusks of the male Babirusa can serve

—whereas those of the Wild Pig are formidable weapons always kept razor sharp by their contact with tusks on the upper jaw

WILD PIG

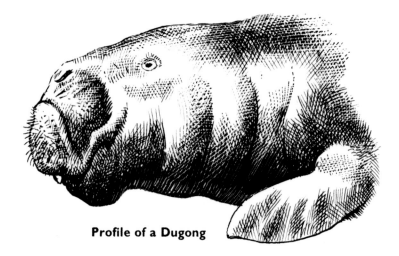

Profile of a Dugong

DUGONG (*Dugong dugon*) Around the shores of the Indian Ocean, for about 15 degrees each side of the Equator, Dugongs may be found. They are strange leisurely creatures, browsing on seaweeds and marine grasses. They do not enter fresh water. In days gone by they were numerous, but they have been so hunted and persecuted for their oil and their flesh that they are now scarce and shy. It was the Dugong that was supposedly responsible for the sailors' stories of mermaids, but anything less like a mermaid would be difficult to imagine. Dugongs may measure up to 10 feet in length.

INDIAN GHARIAL (*Gavialis gangeticus*) This peculiar thin-jawed crocodile is found mainly in the rivers Indus, Ganges and Brahmaputra. It is a fish-eater and its long jaws, armed with numerous, long curved teeth, are adapted for this purpose. It rarely attacks mammals and, because of its fish diet, is more aquatic than other crocodiles. The female lays her eggs in the sand of the river bank, depositing them in two layers, and covering them with a considerable depth of sand. Fully grown Gharials may reach a length of at least 20 feet. They are held sacred by the Hindus.

STARRED TORTOISE (*Testudo elegans*) This species of Starred Tortoise inhabits India and Ceylon. It is common in dry hilly districts and is found in the grass jungles at the foot of the hills. Against these grassy, rocky surroundings its starred shell is difficult to see. In the heat of the day they conceal themselves beneath shrubs or grass tussocks. In the rainy season they become much more active, and feed during all hours of the day, but in the cold season they thrust themselves into some protected cavity, and become almost torpid until the hot season. They lay their eggs in a hole which they excavate in the ground, then push the earth back over the eggs and flatten it with their own weight so that no trace of disturbance is to be seen.

Indian Crocodiles on a river-bank

With its display album rivalling that of **Asian Wildlife** in terms of the amount of information and supplementary illustrations it provided, the **British Butterflies** set was truly spectacular. The eleventh set issued by Brooke Bond, it first appeared in 1963 and, again like Asian Wildlife, stretched to 32 pages.

The texts accompanying the cards were written by Richard Ward, the artist who also created the magnificent illustrations. Ward was a highly respected wildlife artist, although he also painted trains, ships and aircraft, aeroplanes featuring prominently in his work as he had served in the RAF during the Second World War.

While some of the album text focussed on catching and collecting butterflies, Ward did point out in his foreword that the habitats vital to the survival of our butterflies were under increasing pressure from farming, industry and urbanisation. He advised that "Would-be butterfly collectors should always be mindful of the threat to our native varieties and be discriminating and careful when collecting." Nowadays, of course, collecting butterflies to be killed and mounted in display cases is greatly frowned upon.

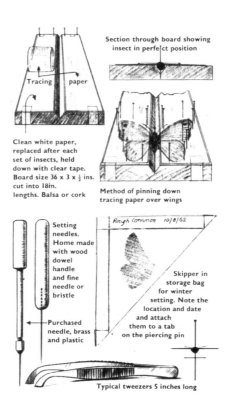

Section through board showing insect in perfect position

Tracing   paper

Clean white paper, replaced after each set of insects, held down with clear tape. Board size 36 x 3 x ½ ins. cut into 18in. lengths. Balsa or cork

Method of pinning down tracing paper over wings

Setting needles. Home made with wood dowel handle and fine needle or bristle

Purchased needle, brass and plastic

Rough Common   10/8/62

Skipper in storage bag for winter setting. Note the location and date and attach them to a tab on the piercing pin

Typical tweezers 5 inches long

Fifty different subjects show the butterflies in full colour and intricate detail, although one slight criticism would be that, while the illustrations on other cards such as the **Asian Wildlife** series showed the subject in its natural habitat, in British Butterflies, the subjects all appeared with wings open, as though pinned to a board in a display case. Ward obviously wanted to be able to show the intricacy of the markings on the creatures' wings, and the habitats are there as backgrounds to the illustrations, but the cards do tend to look a little repetitive, the butterflies always framed in the same "pose". Nevertheless, the cards are wonderfully colourful and very pleasing to study.

BRITISH BUTTERFLIES

Illustrated and described by Richard Ward

SPECKLED WOOD ♀
(Pararge aegeria)
SATYRIDAE

This fairly common butterfly is found over most of England and Ireland. It may be seen on the wing, mainly in woods, from April to October, its flight appearing erratic and uncertain. There is little difference between the male and female, though the latter is slightly larger, and sometimes the male may have bigger spots than the female. The caterpillar is bright green with darker stripes slightly edged with yellow, and is covered with white hairs. It feeds on a number of grasses such as Couch Grass and Annual Meadow Grass. Wingspan approx. 1¼—1½ inches.

GET A PICTURE CARD ALBUM
FROM YOUR GROCER—Price 6d

Issued with
BROOKE BOND TEA
Crown Cup Instant Coffee
35 Cannon Street, London, E.C.4

Illustrated and described by
Richard Ward

MARSH FRITILLARY ♀
(*Euphydryas aurinia*)
NYMPHALIDAE

Distributed very locally over most of the British Isles this butterfly may be seen from May to early July flying over marshy ground and other open sunny places. It may vary a great deal in size though the female is usually larger and has more rounded wings. Its colour varies from pale yellow to deep reddish brown and the markings range from deep brown to black. The blackish caterpillar has a white stripe and short spines and feeds on Devil's Bit Scabious on which the butterfly is depicted. Wingspan approx. 1⅜—1½ inches.

GET A PICTURE CARD ALBUM FROM YOUR GROCER—Price 6d
Issued with

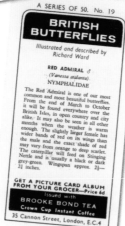

A SERIES OF 50. No. 19

BRITISH BUTTERFLIES

Illustrated and described by
Richard Ward

RED ADMIRAL ♂
(*Vanessa atalanta*)
NYMPHALIDAE

The Red Admiral is one of our most common and most beautiful butterflies. From the end of March to October it will be found everywhere over the British Isles, in open country and city alike. It may also be seen in all other months when the weather is warm enough. The slightly larger female has wider bands of red on its wings than the male and the exact shade of red may vary from orange to deep scarlet. The caterpillar will feed on Stinging Nettle and is usually a black or dark grey-green. Wingspan approx. 2½—2¼ inches.

GET A PICTURE CARD ALBUM FROM YOUR GROCER—Price 6d
Issued with

BROOKE BOND TEA
Crown Cup Instant Coffee
35 Cannon Street, London, E.C.4

GRIZZLED SKIPPER ♀
(*Pyrgus malvae*)
HESPERIIDAE

The Grizzled Skipper is common in the south and midlands of England but may be found only in scattered localities in the north. On the wing during April, May and June, it may be seen flying over rough ground and open woodlands. The female is the larger and generally darker in colour of both sexes. However the colour grey to black, may vary from dark that, again, will vary in intensity. The caterpillar is very pale green covered with white hair and has the pale-edged dark brown line along the back and sides. It feeds on Wild Strawberry. Wingspan approx. ⅞—1⅛ inches.

GET A PICTURE CARD ALBUM FROM YOUR GROCER—Price 6d
Issued with

BROOKE BOND TEA
Crown Cup Instant Coffee
35 Cannon Street, London, E.C.4

The albums contained a removable order form for buying previously issued cards and albums and this is another set officially reprinted in 1973. Again the cards can easily be identified from the originals as the card texts are printed in black instead of blue. At the same time the album was also reprinted and there are a number of variations in both original and reprinted albums.

SILVER-WASHED FRITILLARY var. *negraina* Undersides

HIGH BROWN FRITILLARY albino

SOME FRITILLARY VARIETIES

SMALL PEARL-BORDERED FRITILLARY var. *flavo-pallidus*

Varieties (va occurowing! difference d insect, thou there is the occur due temperatu one throu occur in a

DARK GREEN FRITILLARY var. *ater-discus*

HIGH BROWN FRITILLARY var. *bronzea*

MARSH FRITILLARY albo-fasciata

Bred specimen

Enlarged egg

Chrysalis

The many line illustrations that adorn the pages of the album do show the butterflies in different poses and also help to explain the anatomy of the creatures as well as providing a study of their eggs, caterpillars and complete life cycle.

A rare and highly collectable wall chart accompanied this set and was only available to schools.

BROOKE BOND PICTURE CARDS **British Butterflies**

ILLUSTRATED AND DESCRIBED BY RICHARD WARD · PRICE SIXPENCE

The butterflies of the British Isles are slowly decreasing in number and variety, mainly owing to the widespread and often pointless use of chemical sprays which, though ridding crops of harmful pests, destroy caterpillars and butterflies' natural food plants. Similarly the ever-expanding growth of towns and factories eats into large tracts of rough and tilled land where many butterflies breed. Would-be butterfly collectors should always be mindful of the threat to our native varieties and be discriminating and careful when collecting.

Most British butterflies are depicted in this series but some of them will be seen in this country only on rare occasions. Overseas, where there is often a much wider variety, they may be quite commonplace. The Camberwell Beauty, a rare immigrant here, is common in Europe and North America where it is called Mourning Cloak. The Small Blue, our smallest butterfly, ranges from here to Japan, so that an exactly similar butterfly to the Small Blue you may observe flitting about on the South Downs, could be seen on the lower slopes of Fujiyama.

Richard Ward

SYMBOL OF THE PLANET VENUS DENOTES FEMALE ♀   SYMBOL OF THE PLANET MARS DENOTES MALE ♂

COLLECTING

Here are a few tips and a list of items required to do the job properly. First of all decide what to collect. Begin with one or two family groups, not an aimless collection of any species which come your way. Take care not to kill insects which are of no use to you. The way to ensure this is to make an inspection box. Purchase a round pill box and replace the top with a sheet of acetate or any thick transparent material. When you have netted a specimen, put it in the box. If you do not want it, set it free. Remember, the females lay the eggs for next year's butterflies, so be careful not to collect too many.

EQUIPMENT

The inspection box is your first item. Others, which may be bought or made at home, are:

Storage case: Purchase the best one you can afford, new or second-hand.

Net: The handle, long or short, can be made from any piece of wood. Nylon curtain material makes a very good net, with a plastic clothes line for a hoop.

Setting boards and pins: The board should be grooved, as illustrated, to a width and depth sufficient to take the body of the butterfly, and can be made from $\frac{1}{2}$-inch balsa plank. Entomological pins must be bought from a dealer.

Setting needles: Make these from small pieces of wood dowel fitted with a needle or strong bristle at one end.

Killing bottle: Get a large tin with an airtight lid. Place inside it screwed-up blotting paper. Pour on a teaspoonful of ammonia, and cover with a flat piece of blotting paper. On this you place your box with butterfly inside, and replace the tin lid for only a few minutes. Be careful of ammonia. It is poison. Never lean over the tin when opening.

SETTING A BUTTERFLY

Firstly, fit the grooves of the setting board snugly with a strip of white paper, cellotaped at either end. Then pierce your butterfly with a pin at a right angle to the thorax. Push the pin down into the groove until the body fits snugly and the wings lie evenly on the board surface. Next, cut strips of tracing paper or thick cellophane to the size of the board-halves, and attach them to the top of the board. Gently flatten down one side of the wings with a setting needle. Hold this wing down lightly with your finger and place the point of the setting needle under the vein of the forewing. Move the forewing up until the inner margin is at a right angle to the body, and pin it down at the side. Then bring up the hind wing into position and pin it down also. Cover this wing with the tracing paper and repeat the whole process for the wing on the other side. Be certain to arrange the antennae neatly *above* the tracing paper. Always allow an inch between specimens on the same board, and leave them there for at least ten days.

REMOVAL FROM THE SETTING BOARD

Hold down the tracing paper as you remove the needles. Then, with great care, take off the tracing paper. Use a pair of tweezers to hold the pin when you move your butterfly from the board.

PRESERVING YOUR BUTTERFLY BEFORE SETTING

You may prefer to wait until winter before setting. If so, place each butterfly in a paper envelope, which should in turn be put into a stout box. Add a few crystals of Paradichlor-benzene, obtainable from your local chemist. This will protect your butterflies from the ravages of mites.

When the time comes to set, you will require relaxing fluid which is obtainable from your dealer. Get a large airtight tin. Cover the bottom with sand and pour on the fluid. Place crumpled blotting paper on the sand and cover with a sheet of grease-proof paper. On to this place your specimen and leave for 24 hours, at the end of which the wings should be quite limp. Then begin the setting process. Leave the specimen on the board for at least ten days, until the wings are dried out.

DAMAGE TO SPECIMENS

Broken-off antennae can be stuck back with a tiny drop of seccotine applied to the head. Support them until set with a small block of wood. Repair torn wings with gum obtainable from dealers, using patches taken from badly damaged specimens.

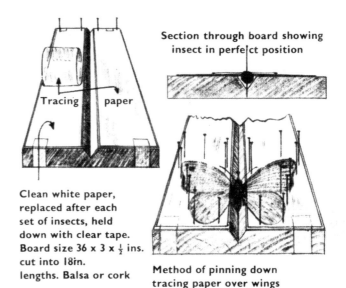

Section through board showing insect in perfect position

Tracing paper

Clean white paper, replaced after each set of insects, held down with clear tape. Board size 36 x 3 x $\frac{1}{2}$ ins. cut into 18in. lengths. Balsa or cork

Method of pinning down tracing paper over wings

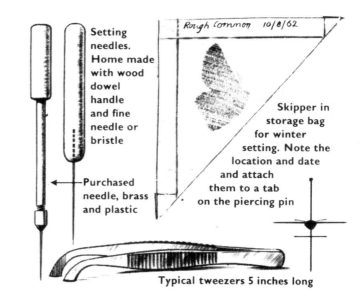

Setting needles. Home made with wood dowel handle and fine needle or bristle

Purchased needle, brass and plastic

Rough Common 10/8/62

Skipper in storage bag for winter setting. Note the location and date and attach them to a tab on the piercing pin

Typical tweezers 5 inches long

SPECKLED WOOD ♀ (*Pararge aegeria*) **SATYRIDAE** This fairly common butterfly is found over most of England and Ireland. It may be seen on the wing, mainly in woods, from April to October, its flight appearing erratic and uncertain. There is little difference between the male and female, though the latter is slightly larger, and sometimes the male may have bigger spots than the female. The caterpillar is bright green with darker stripes slightly edged with yellow, and is covered with white hairs. It feeds on a number of grasses such as Couch Grass and Annual Meadow Grass. Wingspan approx. $1\frac{3}{8}$–$1\frac{9}{8}$ inches.

WALL ♀ (*Pararge megera*) **SATYRIDAE** The Wall is very common in England, Wales, Ireland and the southern counties of Scotland. There is a small difference between the male and female wing shapes, the fore wings of the latter being more rounded. The female is also slightly larger. The wing 'eyes' may vary in size; sometimes they lack the white pupil in the fourth dot on the hind wing; occasionally a small dot appears alongside the fore wing 'eye'. The caterpillar is bright green and feeds on grass. The butterfly is on the wing in April to October and favours bright sunlight. Wingspan approx. $1\frac{1}{2}$–$1\frac{7}{8}$ inches.

SPECKLED WOOD ♂
and caterpillar

WALL ♂ and caterpillar

SMALL MOUNTAIN RINGLET
The 'eye' markings vary greatly in size, and in Scotland are usually more clearly marked than in northern England

♀

♀

SCOTCH ARGUS
Male and female undersides

♀

♂

♀

Caterpillar

SMALL MOUNTAIN RINGLET ♂ *(Erebia epiphron)* **SATYRIDAE** This small butterfly is found locally in the English Lake District and in parts of the Grampian Highlands of Argyll, Perth and Inverness. Its markings may be very indistinct or disappear altogether, and they also may vary quite a lot; sometimes the black dots are separately outlined and sometimes the outline colour forms a continuous band as illustrated. The caterpillar is green with darker green and white lines and feeds on grasses, chiefly Mat Grass. On the wing in June and July. The female is slightly larger than the male. Wingspan approx. $1\frac{1}{4}$–$1\frac{3}{8}$ inches.

SCOTCH ARGUS ♂ *(Erebia aethiops)* **SATYRIDAE** This butterfly is found only in the north of England and Scotland and in the isles of Skye, Mull and Arran. There is little difference between the males and females though the former may be generally darker in colour and the latter slightly larger. The wing 'eyes' are larger on the female especially on the fore wing. From July to September it can be seen in valleys and woodsides that face the sun. The caterpillar is pale grey-brown with lighter and darker markings and is covered with small white hairs. It feeds mainly on Blue Moor Grass. Wingspan approx. $1\frac{5}{8}$–$1\frac{3}{4}$ inches.

MARBLED WHITE ♂ (*Melanargia galathea*) **SATYRIDAE** In July and August the Marbled White is found mostly in the south of England but extends into southern Wales and up the east coast as far as Yorkshire. It often lives in colonies, sometimes in large numbers, where it prefers rough ground in and near woods, cliff tops and hill sides. It is a slow flier and easily caught. The colour varies from white to a bright pale yellow, and the usually creamy underside has bright olive green markings. The caterpillar is a pale pinky-green with darker stripes and feeds on grasses, mainly Sheep's Fescue Grass. The female is larger than the male. Wingspan approx. 1⅞–2¼ inches.

GRAYLING ♀ (*Eumenis semele*) **SATYRIDAE** From July to September, the Grayling is fairly common in the British Isles, and may be seen flying over rough waste ground, cliffs and heaths. The female is larger than the male and has much clearer markings on the wings, whilst the male is darker brown in colour. The undersides of both sexes show interesting markings which make very efficient camouflage when the butterfly is at rest on the ground or tree trunks. The caterpillar is pale ochre-yellow with dark lines and feeds on a variety of grasses including Annual Meadow Grass and Tufted Hair Grass. Wingspan approx. 2–2¾ inches.

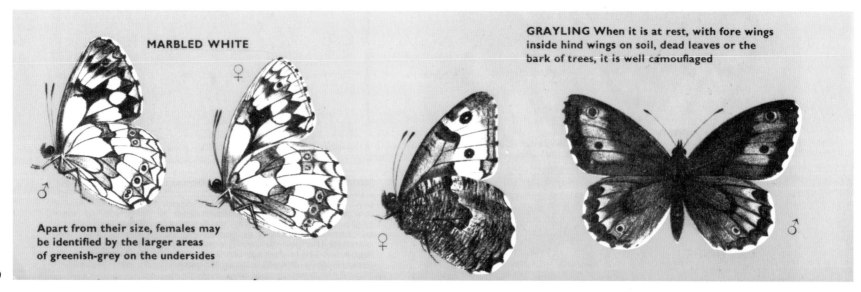

MARBLED WHITE

GRAYLING When it is at rest, with fore wings inside hind wings on soil, dead leaves or the bark of trees, it is well camouflaged

Apart from their size, females may be identified by the larger areas of greenish-grey on the undersides

MEADOW BROWN ♀ (*Maniola jurtina*) **SATYRIDAE** One of the commonest butterflies found in the British Isles the Meadow Brown may be seen flying everywhere except on very high ground. The female is larger than the male and is marked quite differently. The female has patches of light orange-brown on the wings whilst the male is a more uniform colour, usually a darker brown. The wing 'eyes' may be double-pupilled on the fore wing and sometimes there is a small spot on the hind wing. The caterpillar is green and feeds on grasses such as Annual Meadow Grass. On the wing from June to September. Wingspan approx. 1¾–2 inches.

HEDGE BROWN ♀ (*Maniola tithonus*) **SATYRIDAE** In July, August and September the Hedge Brown may be found more or less all over England particularly along the south coast. As its name suggests it favours hedges but may also be found in rough ground and along the cliffs. The larger female is usually slightly lighter in colour. Her fore wing 'eyes' vary—sometimes they are double pupilled and sometimes there are up to three further 'eyes'. The hind wing may also vary in the same way. The caterpillar is a pale yellowish-green and feeds on various grasses such as Annual Meadow Grass. Wingspan approx. 1⅜–1⅝ inches.

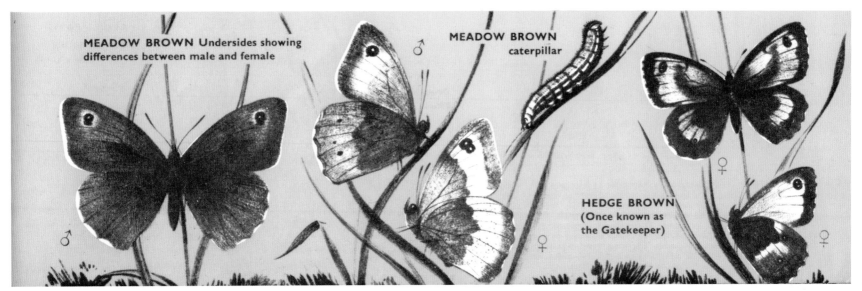

MEADOW BROWN Undersides showing differences between male and female

♂

MEADOW BROWN caterpillar

♀

♂

♀

HEDGE BROWN (Once known as the Gatekeeper)

♀

SMALL HEATH ♂ (*Coenonympha pamphilus*) **SATYRIDAE** Except in the far north of Scotland, is widely distributed over the British Isles and may be seen from May to September. The female is slightly larger than the male and does not always have the dark grey band round the edge of wing. The 'eyes' on the fore wings vary in size and may be absent altogether. It looks like the Large Heath except that its wings have a somewhat blunter shape. The caterpillar is a medium green colour with light and dark lines and feeds on grasses such as Mat Grass and Annual Meadow Grass. Wingspan approx. $1\frac{3}{16}$–$1\frac{9}{16}$ inches.

LARGE HEATH ♀ (*Coenonympha tullia*) **SATYRIDAE** In June and July, to be found on moors and hillsides mainly in the north of England and Scotland. It is larger, but similar in appearance to the Small Heath. There is little difference in size between male and female, the male is usually somewhat darker in colour. The butterfly illustrated is a light-coloured one caught in Scotland, but the colour may vary from this to a medium brown, from north to south. The wing 'eyes' may differ in size or be absent altogether. The caterpillar is a medium green with light stripes and feeds on grass. Wingspan approx. $1\frac{7}{16}$ inches.

SMALL HEATH
showing undersides
and caterpillar

LARGE HEATH
Local variations
of markings

Broughton
Moor

Kildonan

Forres

Kendal

Stanton upon Hine Heath

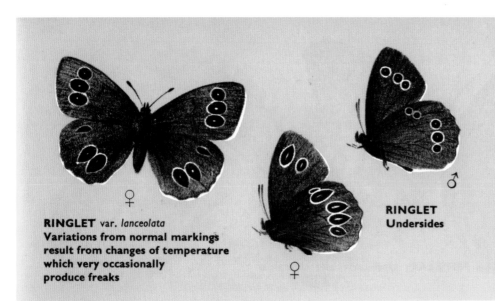

RINGLET var. *lanceolata*
Variations from normal markings
result from changes of temperature
which very occasionally
produce freaks

♀

RINGLET
Undersides

♂

♀

RINGLET ♀ (*Aphantopus hyperanthus*) **SATYRIDAE** Fairly common in wood-lands and hedges over most of the British Isles. The female is slightly larger than the male which is usually a darker colour, often nearly black. The size and number of the wing 'eyes' vary, with usually two or three on each upper wing, up to three on the underside of the fore wing, and as many as five on the hind wing. On the wing from June to August, it has a slow fluttering flight. The yellowish-pink caterpillar is slug-shaped and feeds on various grasses. Wingspan approx. $1\frac{3}{8}-1\frac{7}{8}$ inches.

PEARL-BORDERED FRITILLARY
Found near woods and damp ground in
Great Britain, though it is rare in places

♂

♂

SMALL
PEARL-
BORDERED
FRITILLARY
Undersides

♂

♀

DARK GREEN FRITILLARY Undersides and caterpillar

♂

♂

SMALL PEARL-BORDERED FRITILLARY ♂ (*Argynnis selene*) **NYMPHALIDAE**
Though not common this Fritillary is found in most parts of England
and Wales and more frequently in Scotland. It is easily confused with
the Pearl-bordered Fritillary which is slightly larger, and only the
underside markings will tell them apart. From June to early August it
may be found flying fast and gracefully in woodlands, over marshy
ground and beside sea cliffs. The caterpillar is brown with light spots
and yellowish spines, of which the first two are largest. The food plant
is Dog Violet. Wingspan approx. 1⅝–1¾ inches.

DARK GREEN FRITILLARY ♀ (*Argynnis aglaia*) **NYMPHALIDAE** One of the
fastest flying butterflies to be found in the British Isles the Dark Green
Fritillary may be seen on the wing in most counties during July and
August, usually on heaths, cliffs and open forest land. The female is
slightly larger than the male and is usually paler in colour. The underside of the hind wing is green and pale yellow marked with silver and
green spots, and the fore wing is a darker yellow marked with near
black and silver. The caterpillar is a reddish colour with white and
orange spots and black spines. It feeds on Dog Violet. Wingspan
approx. 2⅛–2¾ inches.

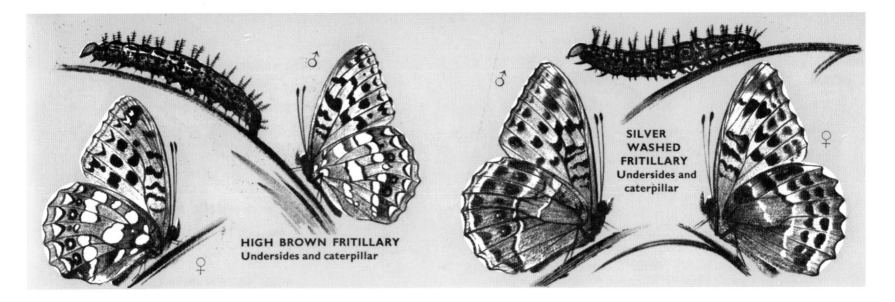

HIGH BROWN FRITILLARY
Undersides and caterpillar ♀

SILVER
WASHED
FRITILLARY
Undersides and
caterpillar ♀

HIGH BROWN FRITILLARY ♀ (*Argynnis cydippe*) **NYMPHALIDAE** Not a common butterfly it is found in many districts from the Midlands to the south coast, and may be seen flying during July and August in and near forest and woodlands. The female is substantially larger than the male and is a paler colour, with very large silver markings on the underside of the hind wing. The caterpillar, similar in appearance to the Dark Green Fritillary, is drab brown with black marks and red spines, and feeds on Dog Violet. Wingspan approx. $2\frac{1}{2}-2\frac{3}{4}$ inches.

SILVER-WASHED FRITILLARY ♀ (*Argynnis paphia*) **NYMPHALIDAE** Found mostly in the southern half of England this butterfly may also be found in certain areas in the north and in Scotland. From June to September it will be seen in woods, and lanes, sometimes basking on thistles. It is easily distinguished from other large Fritillaries by the silver underneath the hind wing which is 'washed' on and does not form definite patches. The caterpillar is brown with paler and black marks. The food plant is Dog Violet. Wingspan approx. $2\frac{3}{8}-2\frac{5}{8}$ inches.

SILVER-WASHED FRITILLARY var. *negrizina* **Undersides**

HIGH BROWN FRITILLARY albino

SOME FRITILLARY VARIETIES

SMALL PEARL-BORDERED FRITILLARY var. *flavus-pallidus*

DARK GREEN FRITILLARY var. *ater-discus*

HIGH BROWN FRITILLARY var. *bronzus*

Varieties (var.) or Aberrations usually occur owing to some great temperature difference during the pupa stage of the insect, though with certain butterflies there is the possibility that aberrations occur due to hereditary reasons. The temperature change may be a general one throughout the country or may occur in a very local sense

QUEEN OF SPAIN FRITILLARY

♂

♀

A once rare immigrant from the Continent; may be considered extinct, if indeed it ever was a true British butterfly

Eggs

Caterpillar

MARSH FRITILLARY
alba-fasciata

♀

♂

Bred specimen

♂

Enlarged egg

Chrysalis

♀

♂

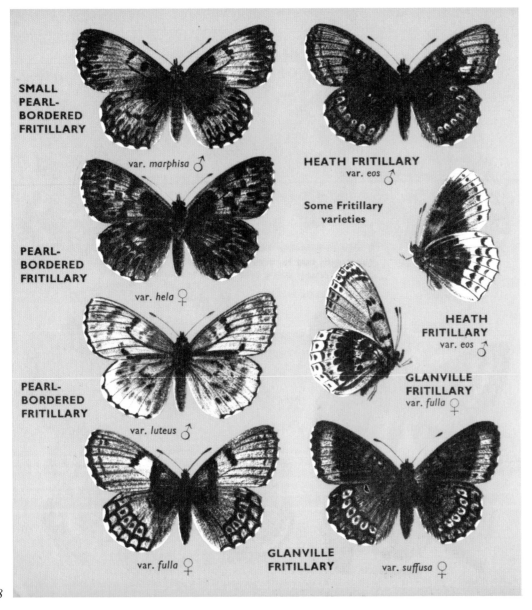

SMALL PEARL-BORDERED FRITILLARY

PEARL-BORDERED FRITILLARY

var. *marphisa* ♂

PEARL-BORDERED FRITILLARY

var. *hela* ♀

var. *luteus* ♂

var. *fulla* ♀

HEATH FRITILLARY
var. *eos* ♂

Some Fritillary varieties

HEATH FRITILLARY
var. *eos* ♂

GLANVILLE FRITILLARY
var. *fulla* ♀

GLANVILLE FRITILLARY

var. *suffusa* ♀

HEATH FRITILLARY

♂

♂

♀

Caterpillar

Cluster of eggs

Enlarged eggs

Chrysalis

188

MARSH FRITILLARY ♀ (*Euphydryas aurinia*) **NYMPHALIDAE** Distributed very locally over most of the British Isles this butterfly may be seen from May to early July flying over marshy ground and other open sunny places. It may vary a great deal in size though the female is usually larger and has more rounded wings. Its colour varies from pale yellow to deep reddish brown and the markings range from deep brown to black. The blackish caterpillar has a white stripe and short spines and feeds on Devil's Bit Scabious on which the butterfly is depicted. Wingspan approx. $1\frac{7}{16}-1\frac{3}{4}$ inches.

HEATH FRITILLARY ♀ (*Melitaea athalia*) **NYMPHALIDAE** Very rare, this butterfly is found only locally in a few southern English counties. It is on the wing from June to early August in and near woodlands where there is a minimum of undergrowth. It is easily identified by the curious markings on the fore wing which look like the numerals 08 8o. The female is slightly larger than the male which is a darker colour with heavier black markings. The caterpillar is black with white spots and black hairs and feeds on Cow Wheat, Wood Sage and Plantain. Wingspan approx. $1\frac{3}{8}-1\frac{9}{16}$ inches.

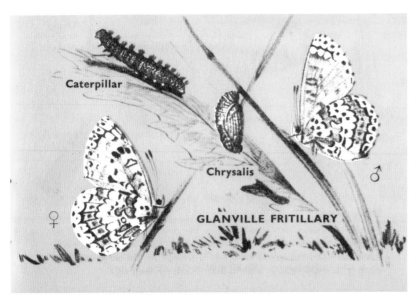

Caterpillar

Chrysalis

♂

♀

GLANVILLE FRITILLARY

GLANVILLE FRITILLARY ♀ (*Melitaea cinxia*) **NYMPHALIDAE** A very rare butterfly found only in the Isle of Wight. It is very similar to the Heath Fritillary except that the markings on the fore wings look like the figures oB 8o not the Heath's o8 8o. The female is considerably larger than the male and is paler, usually with somewhat heavier brown markings. The butterfly is on the wing from May to the end of June. The caterpillar is black with white spots and dark green spines, and eats Sea and Ribwort Plantain. Wingspan approx. $1\frac{1}{2}-1\frac{3}{4}$ inches.

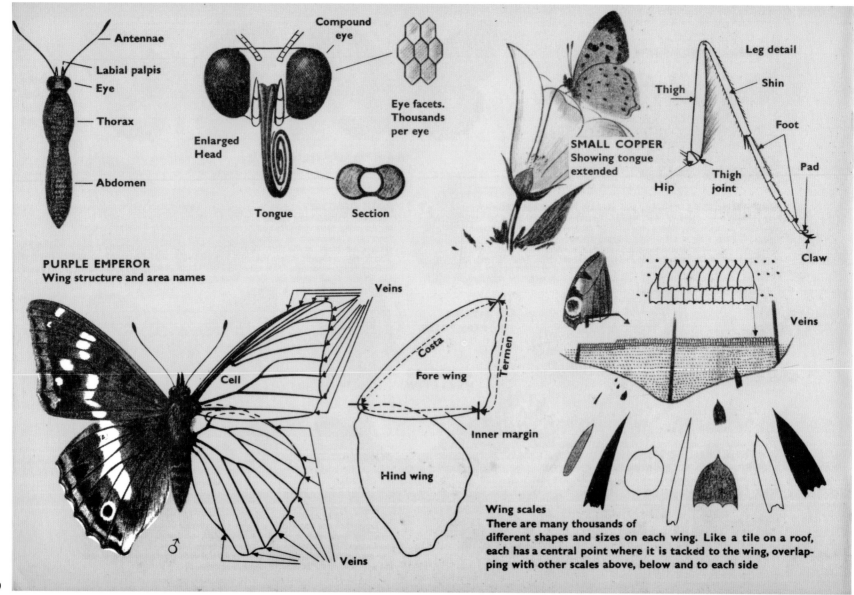

Antennae

Labial palpis

Eye

Thorax

Abdomen

Compound eye

Eye facets.
Thousands
per eye

Enlarged Head

Tongue

Section

SMALL COPPER
Showing tongue extended

Leg detail

Thigh

Shin

Foot

Pad

Hip

Thigh joint

Claw

PURPLE EMPEROR
Wing structure and area names

Veins

Cell

Costa

Fore wing

Termen

Inner margin

Hind wing

Veins

Veins

Wing scales
There are many thousands of
different shapes and sizes on each wing. Like a tile on a roof,
each has a central point where it is tacked to the wing, overlap-
ping with other scales above, below and to each side

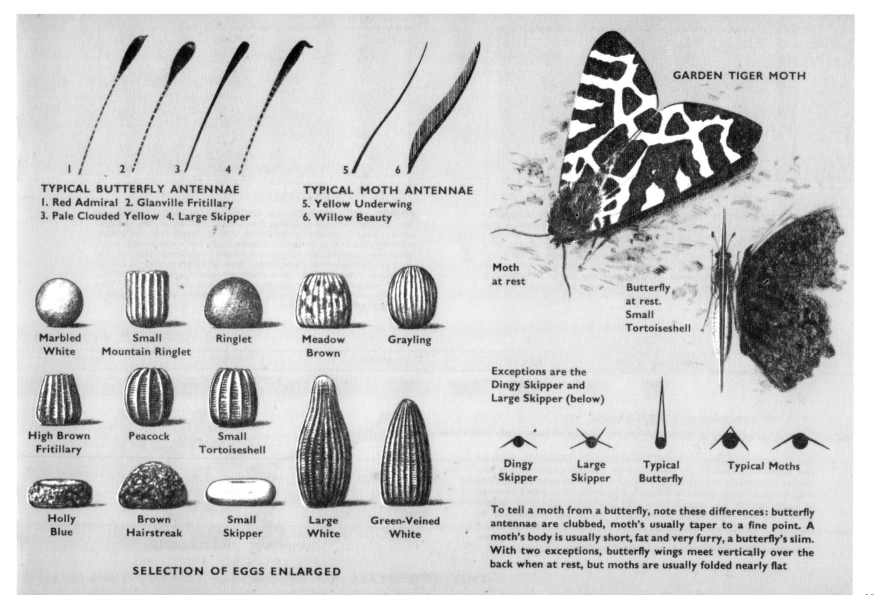

TYPICAL BUTTERFLY ANTENNAE
1. Red Admiral 2. Glanville Fritillary
3. Pale Clouded Yellow 4. Large Skipper

TYPICAL MOTH ANTENNAE
5. Yellow Underwing
6. Willow Beauty

GARDEN TIGER MOTH

Moth at rest

Butterfly at rest. Small Tortoiseshell

Marbled White

Small Mountain Ringlet

Ringlet

Meadow Brown

Grayling

High Brown Fritillary

Peacock

Small Tortoiseshell

Holly Blue

Brown Hairstreak

Small Skipper

Large White

Green-Veined White

Exceptions are the Dingy Skipper and Large Skipper (below)

Dingy Skipper

Large Skipper

Typical Butterfly

Typical Moths

To tell a moth from a butterfly, note these differences: butterfly antennae are clubbed, moth's usually taper to a fine point. A moth's body is usually short, fat and very furry, a butterfly's slim. With two exceptions, butterfly wings meet vertically over the back when at rest, but moths are usually folded nearly flat

SELECTION OF EGGS ENLARGED

191

RED ADMIRAL ♂ (*Vanessa atalanta*) **NYMPHALIDAE** The Red Admiral is one of our most common and most beautiful butterflies. From the end of March to October it will be found everywhere over the British Isles, in open country and city alike. It may also be seen in all other months when the weather is warm enough. The slightly larger female has wider bands of red on its wings than the male and the exact shade of red may vary from orange to deep scarlet. The caterpillar will feed on Stinging Nettle and is usually a black or dark grey-green. Wingspan approx. 2½–2¾ inches.

PAINTED LADY ♂ (*Vanessa cardui*) **NYMPHALIDAE** An early immigrant from the Continent which breeds soon after arrival, this butterfly may be seen on the wing from May to as late as October, some years in greater numbers than others. It has a particular liking for rough ground where thistles are plentiful, but will be found nearly everywhere flying fast and strongly. The female is slightly larger than the male and there is a small difference in wing shape. Colour may vary from a salmon pink to rich tawny orange and other variations are known but very rare. The caterpillar feeds on thistle and is black with yellow marks and spines. Wingspan approx. 2–2¼ inches.

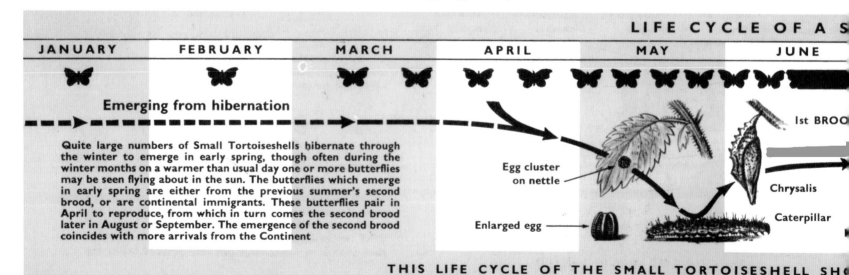

LIFE CYCLE OF A S

| JANUARY | FEBRUARY | MARCH | APRIL | MAY | JUNE |

Emerging from hibernation

Quite large numbers of Small Tortoiseshells hibernate through the winter to emerge in early spring, though often during the winter months on a warmer than usual day one or more butterflies may be seen flying about in the sun. The butterflies which emerge in early spring are either from the previous summer's second brood, or are continental immigrants. These butterflies pair in April to reproduce, from which in turn comes the second brood later in August or September. The emergence of the second brood coincides with more arrivals from the Continent

Egg cluster on nettle

Enlarged egg

1st BROO

Chrysalis

Caterpillar

THIS LIFE CYCLE OF THE SMALL TORTOISESHELL SHO

SMALL TORTOISESHELL ♂ (*Aglais urticae*) **NYMPHALIDAE** One of the most common and brilliantly coloured butterflies in the British Isles the Small Tortoiseshell will be found in city garden and open country alike, mainly from May to November, though any warm spell during the year will bring out the occasional winter hibernator. It is very fond of thistles and of basking in the sun with wings wide open. The colour and markings may vary, the slightly larger female from orange to deep red. The caterpillar is black with yellow markings, and feeds on Stinging Nettle. Wingspan approx. 2–2¼ inches.

LARGE TORTOISESHELL ♂ (*Nymphalis polychloros*) **NYMPHALIDAE** Once fairly common this butterfly is now but rarely found over most of England and Wales. On the wing from late June to September, some hibernate through the winter when they may be discovered in old sheds and barns. The sexes vary little although the female is slightly larger. They will be seen flying strongly and swiftly up and down over the same piece of ground in country lanes or open ground alongside hills. The caterpillar is black with yellow marks and spines and feeds on various trees such as Elm and Sallow. Wingspan approx. 2¼–2½ inches.

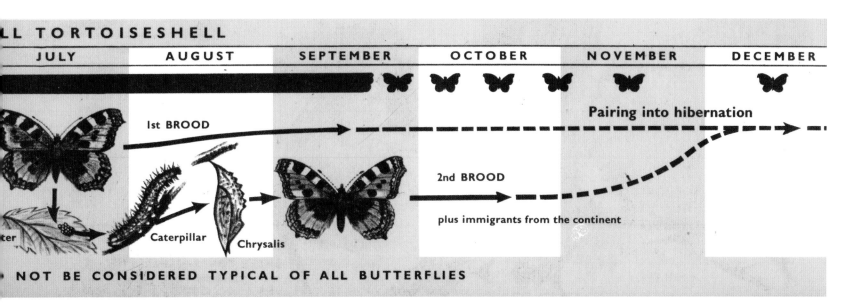

LL TORTOISESHELL

JULY	AUGUST	SEPTEMBER	OCTOBER	NOVEMBER	DECEMBER

Pairing into hibernation

1st BROOD

Caterpillar Chrysalis

2nd BROOD

plus immigrants from the continent

NOT BE CONSIDERED TYPICAL OF ALL BUTTERFLIES

193

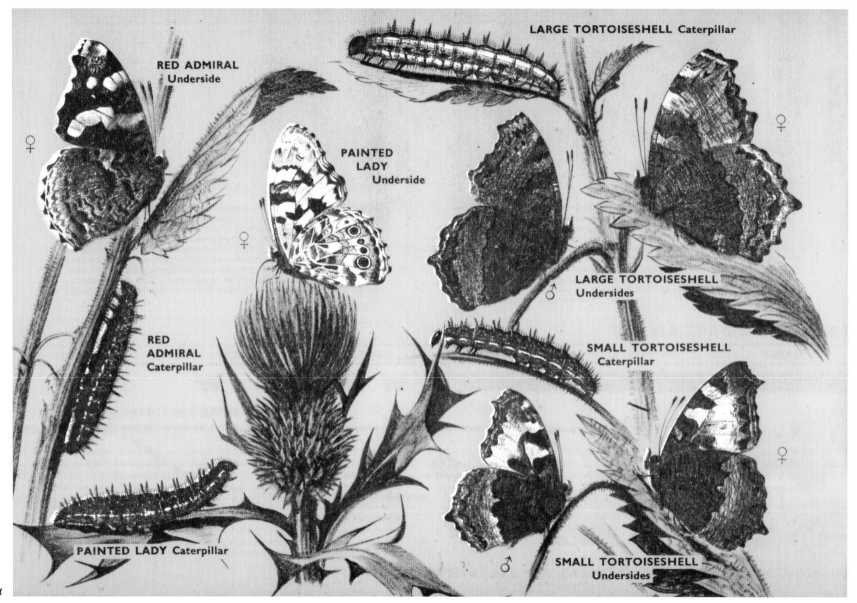

RED ADMIRAL
Underside

♀

LARGE TORTOISESHELL Caterpillar

PAINTED
LADY
Underside

♀

LARGE TORTOISESHELL
Undersides

♂

RED
ADMIRAL
Caterpillar

SMALL TORTOISESHELL
Caterpillar

PAINTED LADY Caterpillar

♀

♂

SMALL TORTOISESHELL
Undersides

Caterpillar

PURPLE EMPEROR
var. *iole* ♂

♀

♂

PURPLE EMPEROR
Undersides

PAINTED LADY var. *inornata*

♀

Underside

♀

♀

PURPLE EMPEROR
Life size

PEACOCK ♀ (*Nymphalis io*) **NYMPHALIDAE** This butterfly, unmistakable with its large peacock 'eyes' on the wings, is found over most of the British Isles except in the north of Scotland, and most commonly in the south of England. Though the female is slightly larger, the markings of both sexes are the same. On the wing in July to late October, some hibernate and may be seen as early as March when the weather is warm enough. The caterpillar is black with black spines and feeds on Stinging Nettle. Wingspan approx. 2¼–2⅝ inches.

COMMA ♀ (*Polygonia c-album*) **NYMPHALIDAE** A rare butterfly found locally in the south of England, it may be thought at first glance to be a tatty Small Tortoiseshell, but close inspection will reveal one of the most unusual and interesting looking English butterflies. The slightly larger female has flat brown undersides, unlike those of the male which are variegated. When at rest with wings closed on a tree trunk or amongst dead leaves, they are nearly impossible to detect. On the wing from May to September, the Comma hibernates during the winter. Wingspan approx. 1⅞–2⅛ inches.

CAMBERWELL BEAUTY ♀ (*Nymphalis antiopa*) **NYMPHALIDAE** Though common in Europe, the Camberwell is a rare and beautiful immigrant in this country where it has usually been seen in the eastern counties, though it has been recorded in the past in Scotland and Ireland. It is thought to come from Norway and does not breed here; possibly because of the dampness of the English winter as opposed to the dry cold of Scandinavia. The butterfly is shown at rest on Larger Bindweed. Wingspan approx. 2⅜–2¾ inches.

PEACOCK   CAMBERWELL BEAUTY

PURPLE EMPEROR ♂ (*Apatura iris*) **NYMPHALIDAE** One of our largest butterflies, the Purple Emperor is found in the midland, western and southern counties and Wales, during July, August and September. Only the male has the purple sheen on the wings, the female being darker, brown and larger. Found in Oak woods, the male stays mainly in the tree tops, while the female flies lower near the ground. Eggs are laid singly on Sallow leaves which are the main food. The caterpillars are blue-green marked with thin white stripes, and flat in shape like young Sallow leaves. Wingspan approx. 2½–3 inches.

WHITE ADMIRAL ♀ (*Limenitis camilla*) **NYMPHALIDAE** This fast flying butterfly of the large woods of the midland and southern counties, is on the wing from the end of May to early September. There is little difference between male and female, though the latter is slightly larger and a darker brown. The underside of the wings is brilliant orange-brown with white markings. May often be found at rest on Bramble flowers, though it lays its eggs on Honeysuckle, the caterpillar's main food. The caterpillar is green with a white line along the body and tufts of yellowish spines on its back. Wingspan approx. 1⅞–2 3/16 inches.

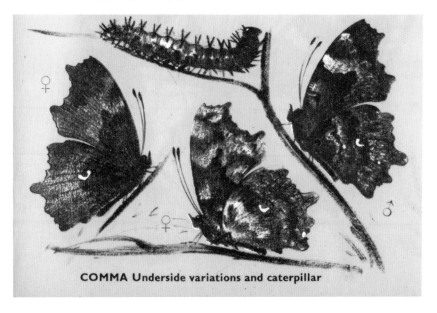

COMMA Underside variations and caterpillar

SWALLOW TAIL ♂ (*Papilio machaon*) **PAPILIONIDAE** The only Swallow-tail found in England is restricted to very local areas of the Norfolk and Cambridgeshire fens. The female is larger than the male, which often has heavier black markings. The underside of the wings is much paler but similarly marked to the upperside. It has a slow and uncertain flight and may be seen on the wing from June to October. The caterpillar is green with black and orange markings, and has two orange horns over the head. It feeds on Milk Parsley. Wingspan approx. 2⅛–2⅞ inches.

WHITE ADMIRAL

WHITE ADMIRAL undersides

♂

♀

WHITE ADMIRAL undersides

♂

♀

♀

Underside

WHITE ADMIRAL var. *nigrina*

♂

Caterpillar

SWALLOW TAIL Underside

♀

SWALLOW TAIL Life size

198

SMALL BLUE *Cupido minimus* LYCAENIDAE
Upper wing surfaces are dingy brown, with a little blue on male. Undersides are very pale blue, female inclined to be yellowish

SILVER-STUDDED BLUE
Plebejus argus
LYCAENIDAE
Found during July and August over most of the British Isles where heather and furse grow thickly

COMMON BLUE
Polyommatus icarus
LYCAENIDAE
The female is rich dark brown with red-orange markings and may also be found with much blue on the upper wings

WHITE LETTER HAIR-STREAK
Strymonidia w-album
LYCAENIDAE
A dusky brown colour somewhat lighter on the undersides. The female is the more heavily marked

DUKE OF
BURGUNDY
FRITILLARY

BROWN ARGUS

Undersides

HOLLY BLUE

Spring
brood

DUKE OF BURGUNDY FRITILLARY ♀ (*Hamearis lucina*) **RIODINIDAE** Fairly common in the south of England, this small, pretty butterfly is scarcer in the north and found only very locally in one part of Scotland. On the wing in May and June, it is seen in open woodlands where it flits about over paths and open spaces. Though much smaller it is similar in appearance to the Marsh Fritillary. The female is larger and more brightly coloured than the male. The caterpillar looks like a pale brown hairy wood-louse and feeds on Cowslip. Wingspan approx. I 1/16–1 3/16 inches.

BROWN ARGUS ♀ (*Aricia agestis*) **LYCAENIDAE** This small butterfly, found over all England, Wales and southern Scotland, is fairly common except in Scotland. On the wing from May to September, it may be seen flitting about over open grassland, often in a small group and sometimes in company with other Blues. The female is slightly larger than the male and has more red-orange colour on the upperside and underneath. The small, black-headed caterpillar is wood-louse shaped, pale green with dark green and purple stripes and white hairs. It feeds on Stork's-bill. Wingspan approx. I 1/16–1 1/8 inches.

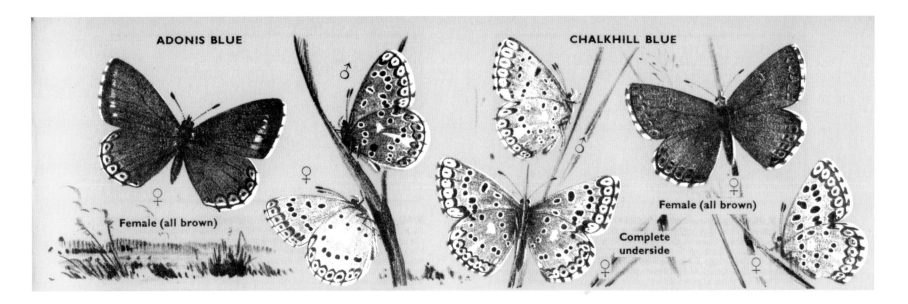

ADONIS BLUE

CHALKHILL BLUE

♂

♀

Female (all brown)

Female (all brown)

Complete underside

♀

♂

♀

CHALKHILL BLUE ♂ (*Lysandra coridon*) **LYCAENIDAE** Only the male is blue, the female being a rather drab brown colour, and the size of both sexes varies quite a lot. Fairly common in the south of England in Hunts., Herts. and Oxfordshire, it is also found in Lancashire. From July to September it may be seen flying quickly and strongly, often in a group over open grasslands and rolling hillsides. The caterpillar is bright green with yellow marks and is covered with white hairs. It feeds on Horseshoe Vetch. Wingspan approx. $1\frac{3}{16}$–$1\frac{1}{2}$ inches.

ADONIS BLUE ♂ (*Lysandra bellargus*) **LYCAENIDAE** The Adonis Blue is found only in the south of England, and even there very locally. The male may vary from a greenish to pale purple tint of blue, but the female is brown. It is a strong, swift flier and may be seen, singly or in a pack, on grassy rides and hillsides. There are two broods between May and September. The caterpillar is dark olive green marked with yellow and has white hairs. It feeds on Horseshoe Vetch. Wingspan approx. $1\frac{1}{4}$–$1\frac{3}{8}$ inches.

HOLLY BLUE♀ (*Celastrina argiolus*) **LYCAENIDAE** Found in Britain the Holly Blue is rarer in the north than the south where it is quite common. It may be seen flying quite early in the year from March till October. The male and female are more or less the same size, but the male has no black border on the fore wings. This black border on the female varies in thickness between the spring and summer brood; the illustration shows the latter. The caterpillar is greenish-yellow with pink or red markings and feeds on Holly. Wingspan approx. 1 3/16-1 9/16 inches.

SMALL COPPER♀ (*Lycaena phlaeas*) **LYCAENIDAE** One of the commonest butterflies in the British Isles, except for the north of Scotland, the Small Copper is unmistakable by the brilliant copper-red of its wings. The slightly larger female has small tails and a wider band of colour on the hind wings, and sometimes its colour varies to light coppery-orange. It will be seen from May to October in all sorts of country and gardens. A swift flier, and seldom inactive. The caterpillar is yellowish-green covered with short pinkish hairs, and feeds on Sheep Sorrel. Wingspan approx. 1 3/8-1 9/16 inches.

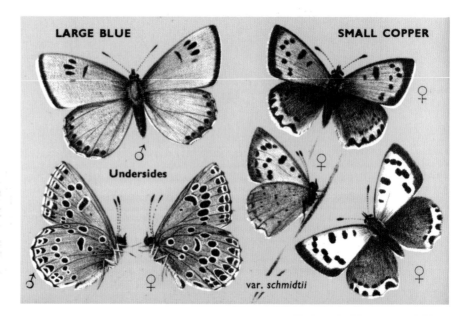

LARGE BLUE

SMALL COPPER

♂

Undersides

♀

♀

♂

♀

var. schmidtii

♀

LARGE BLUE♀ (*Maculinea arion*) **LYCAENIDAE** Found only in the southwest of England, mainly in Devon and Cornwall, the Large Blue is the only blue butterfly with black markings on both wings of both sexes. The female is slightly larger and has much darker markings both on the upper and under surfaces of the wings. On the wing from May to July it is found mostly in hilly grasslands. The yellowish caterpillar looks like a fat maggot, and feeds on Wild Thyme. Wingspan approx. 1 1/16-1 9/16 inches.

GREEN HAIRSTREAK ♂ (*Callophrys rubi*) **LYCAENIDAE** The Green Hairstreak is widely distributed over Great Britain, but is not so common in Ireland. During May, June and early July it may be found on rough bushy ground and in and near woodlands. It is the only British butterfly with a solid green colour, which gives excellent camouflage when at rest among leaves. Sometimes the single white dot on the underside of the hind wing becomes a row joined together to form a 'hairstreak'. The caterpillar is green with yellow markings and feeds on Buckthorn, and numerous other plants. Wingspan approx. 1–1⅛ inches.

BROWN HAIRSTREAK ♀ (*Thecla betulae*) **LYCAENIDAE** This, the largest of the English Hairstreaks, is found only locally in the southern half of the country. The larger female, unlike the male, has a big patch of reddish-orange on the fore wings. The undersides of both sexes are white. During August and September it will be seen in thinly wooded ground, mainly in coastal districts. The caterpillar is green with purplish markings and feeds on Blackthorn. Wingspan approx. 1½ inches.

PURPLE HAIRSTREAK

BLACK HAIRSTREAK

BROWN HAIRSTREAK

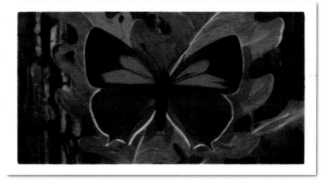

PURPLE HAIRSTREAK ♀ (*Thecla quercus*) **LYCAENIDAE** On the wing over most parts of Great Britain, from July to early September this Hairstreak is seldom seen as it spends most of its time among the tops of Oak trees, the food plant of the caterpillar. The male is often larger than the female and though it has more purple on its wings, this can be seen only at a certain angle. The undersides of both sexes are a warm grey marked with black, white and dark brown. The pale, ochreous-brown caterpillar is similarly marked. Wingspan approx. 1 9/16–1⅜ inches.

WOOD WHITE ♂ (*Leptidea sinapis*) **PIERIDAE** A delicate looking butterfly of woodland clearings and tracks, it is on the wing from May to August mostly in the western counties of England and Wales and in Lincolnshire. It is the slowest and most fluttering flier of all British butterflies. The fore wing marking varies in size and in colour from near black to pale grey, and there is a difference in wing shape between the sexes. The caterpillar is bright green with yellow marks along the side, and feeds mainly on Bird's-foot Trefoil. Wingspan approx. 1½ inches.

LARGE WHITE ♀ (*Pieris brassicae*) **PIERIDAE** By its popular name, 'Cabbage White', it is known as the most destructive of all British butterflies. From early May to October it may be found everywhere in town and country alike, its numbers being increased by quite large immigrations from the Continent. The female is much larger than the male and has more black markings on the wings. Much damage is done to cabbage crops by the caterpillar which is greenish-yellow with yellow lines, and is covered with white hairs. Wingspan approx. 2⅛–2½ inches.

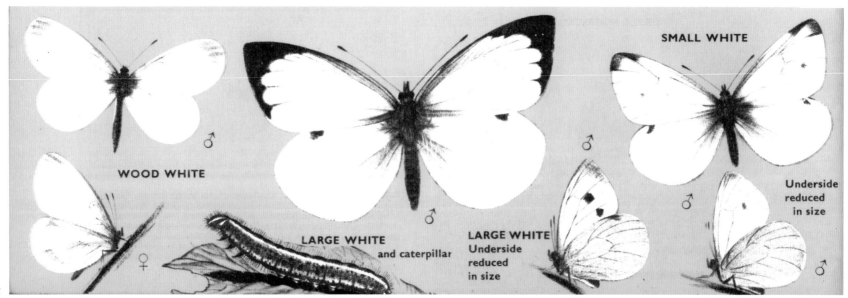

WOOD WHITE ♂

SMALL WHITE ♂

WOOD WHITE ♀

LARGE WHITE and caterpillar ♂

LARGE WHITE Underside reduced in size

Underside reduced in size ♂

SMALL WHITE ♂ (*Pieris rapae*) **PIERIDAE** This butterfly is possibly just as common as the Large White in town and country alike. It is on the wing from early May to late Autumn during which time native numbers are increased by immigration from the Continent. The larger female has big black markings on the fore wing which vary in size and degree of blackness. The caterpillar is green with black dots and has a yellow line along the back and a row of yellow dots forming a line along the sides. It is covered with black hairs and feeds on cabbage and some garden plants such as Nasturtium. Wingspan approx. 1¾–2 inches.

GREEN VEINED WHITE ♀ (*Pieris napi*) **PIERIDAE** Common over the British Isles except the north of Scotland. On the wing from June to September over fields, lanes and meadows, but seldom in gardens or towns. The slightly larger female has more fore wing markings which vary in size and in colour from pale grey to black. Like on all Whites, the undersides, especially the hind wing, are tinted with yellow to a greater or lesser degree. The caterpillar is green with a yellow line along the sides and is covered with white and black hairs. It feeds on Cuckoo Flower, Hedge Mustard and similar plants. Wingspan approx. 1¾–2 inches.

GREEN-VEINED WHITE ♂ ♀

ORANGE TIP ♀

CLOUDED YELLOW ♀ ♂

NEW CLOUDED YELLOW ♀

ORANGE TIP ♂ (*Anthocharis cardamines*) **PIERIDAE** Common over all England and Wales but rare in Scotland. It will be seen during May and June in sunny lanes, hedges and woodsides. Only the male has the orange tip which may vary on the fore wings from pale yellow to deep orange. The underside of the hind wings is generally mottled green though somewhat yellowish on the female. The size of this butterfly varies considerably in both sexes. The caterpillar is a bluish-green covered with white and black hairs. It feeds on Cuckoo Flowers, Hedge Mustard and similar plants. Wingspan approx. 1⅝ inches.

PALE CLOUDED YELLOW ♀ (*Colias hyale*) **PIERIDAE** The Pale Clouded Yellow is a rare immigrant from the Continent where it is found on the shores of the Mediterranean. In appearance and markings it is very similar to the Clouded Yellow. The female is very pale cream approaching white and the male a pale yellow. The wings are only lightly marked with black—less than on the Clouded Yellow. Usually found in fields of Clover, the food plant of the caterpillar. Wingspan approx. 1⅝ inches.

CLOUDED YELLOW ♀ (*Colias croceus*) **PIERIDAE** The Clouded Yellow usually immigrates from the Continent but has been known to breed here. It is often found in Clover fields, Clover being the food plant of the caterpillar. The butterfly varies considerably from pale yellow to deep orange and may have more or less dark areas on the upper surface of the wings. The underside is inclined to be greenish, usually more so in the male. The caterpillar is dark blue-green covered with small dots and fine hairs, and has a yellow line, marked with pink, along the sides. Wingspan approx. 2–2¼ inches.

DINGY SKIPPER
Rare in Central and North Scotland. The female is usually lighter and not so heavily marked

ESSEX SKIPPER
Slightly larger and darker than Small Skipper. Has black area below antennae tips: S. Skipper's are orange

BRIMSTONE ♂ (*Gonepteryx rhamni*) **PIERIDAE** A winter hibernator, the Brimstone emerges as early as March, if the weather is warm, and will be seen until late July in open woods and Clover fields all over southern England and the midlands. It is the only British butterfly with the curved and pointed wing shape, the female is a paler yellow often tinted with green. The caterpillar is bluish-green covered with small black spots with a pale line along the sides. The food plant is Buckthorn. Wingspan approx. 2⅛ inches.

SMALL SKIPPER ♂ (*Thymelicus sylvestris*) **HESPERIIDAE** This little butterfly is common from the midlands of England southwards. It may be seen from June to early September flitting from flower to flower on rough ground, sand hills and woodland clearings. When at rest it has the curious habit of arching its fore wings over its back, with hind wings wide open and flat. The caterpillar is pale grass green shaded with darker green, and has one light stripe, giving it excellent camouflage amongst the grasses upon which it feeds. Wingspan approx. 1 1/16 inches.

LULWORTH SKIPPER
♂ Local to coastal areas of Devon, Dorset and Cornwall

LARGE SKIPPER
Note the unusual position of the wings at rest. Common to England and Wales but rare in Scotland

CHEQUERED SKIPPER ♂ (*Carterocephalus palaemon*) **HESPERIIDAE** A rare butterfly found only in some east Midland counties in scattered localities, from late May until July, when it may be seen over wide tracks through woodlands. It has a liking for the flowers of the Bugle and darts from one to the next with great rapidity. The slightly larger female has paler, more yellow markings than the male, and the wing undersides of both sexes are a bright yellow, inclined to be green on the hind wings. The caterpillar is a pale yellowish-white with darker stripes and feeds on grasses such as False Brome Grass. Wingspan approx. 1–1⅛ inches.

SILVER-SPOTTED SKIPPER ♀ (*Hesperia comma*) **HESPERIIDAE** During late July and August this butterfly may be found over the hills and downs of southern England, where the caterpillar feeds on grasses such as Sheep's Fescue. The females are usually larger and somewhat darker, their yellow markings showing up more clearly. The male may also be distinguished from the female by the black line of scent scales on the fore wing. The white spots on the underside of both sexes do not appear on any other Skippers. Wingspan approx. 1 3/16–1 1/4 inches.

GRIZZLED SKIPPER ♀ (*Pyrgus malvae*) **HESPERIIDAE** The Grizzled Skipper is common in the south and midlands of England, but may be found only in scattered localities in the north. On the wing during April, May and June, it may be seen flying over rough ground and open woodlands. The female is the larger and generally darker in colour than the male. However the colour of both sexes may vary from dark grey to black, with white markings that, again, will vary in intensity. The caterpillar is very pale green covered with white hair and has pale-edged dark brown lines along the back and sides. It feeds on Wild Strawberry. Wingspan approx. 7/8–1 1/16 inches.

SMALL SKIPPER

SILVER SPOTTED SKIPPER

GRIZZLED SKIPPER

CHEQUERED SKIPPER

THE BERKSHIRE PRINTING CO. LTD., READING

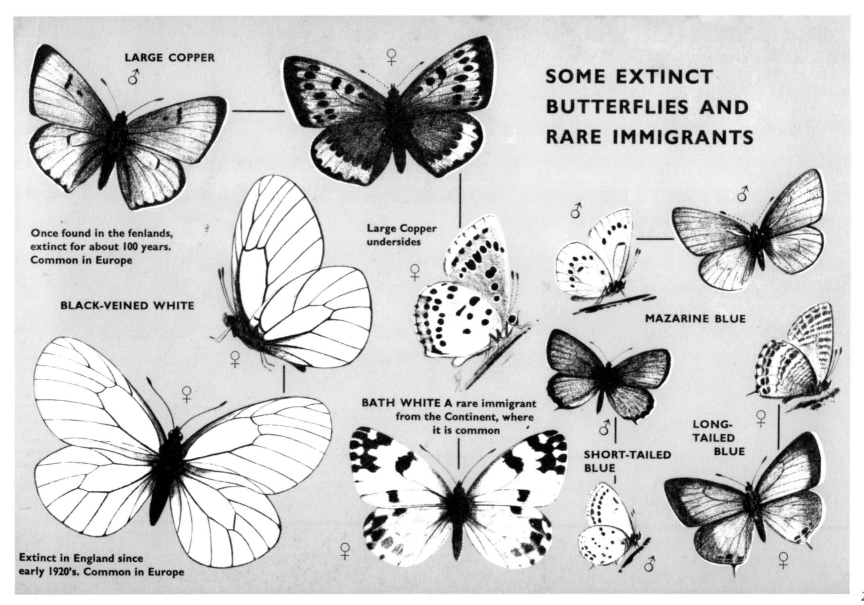

LARGE COPPER ♂

♀

SOME EXTINCT BUTTERFLIES AND RARE IMMIGRANTS

Once found in the fenlands, extinct for about 100 years. Common in Europe

Large Copper undersides

♂

♂

BLACK-VEINED WHITE

♀

MAZARINE BLUE

♀

♀

BATH WHITE A rare immigrant from the Continent, where it is common

♂

LONG-TAILED BLUE

SHORT-TAILED BLUE

♀

♂

Extinct in England since early 1920's. Common in Europe

♀

209

THIS SERIES OF PICTURE CARDS
IS OFFERED IN THE INTERESTS OF EDUCATION BY

Brooke Bond

A card is given free in all packets of Brooke Bond tea.
Cards are also given in ½ lb. tins of Brooke Bond Pure and French coffee
and in jars of Crown Cup Instant Coffee.

As C. F. Tunnicliffe pointed out in his foreword to the **Wild Birds in Britain** display album, we have over 400 species of birds in our countryside which "For a small area of land such as Britain this is a goodly collection, and one which is providing an absorbing interest for an ever increasing number of people." His overriding message, however, was one of foreboding, continuing his campaign for wildlife preservation and protection as he described how the birds' habitats were being eroded by man's incursion. "Will many of our birds be but a memory in a few years to come?" he wrote. "Some are already just that."

This 15th set of Tea Cards from the Brooke Bond stable included only 50 of Britain's bird species and the album was once again only 16 pages, although it included an abundance of supplementary illustrations printed on the pages. Details of plumage, nesting habits and anatomy were presented in masterful line drawings, with the entire inside back cover devoted to extra images of the Guillemot, the last card in the collection.

**Nest of a
Long-tailed Tit**

The fifty cards added a wealth of colour to the black-and-white pages of the album with subjects varying from the Waxwing and the Redstart to the Hoopoe and the Red-legged Partridge. Each card depicted the birds in their natural habitat in full colour, sometimes showing both the male and female birds to highlight the differences in their plumage.

Once again the backgrounds of Tunnicliffe's paintings brought an extra dimension with at least three showing full landscapes within the borders of the picture.

First issued in 1965, this is another

set officially reprinted in 1973, again with the card backs in black instead of blue.

The album also contained a removable order form for buying previously issued cards and albums, and when reprinted at the same time as the cards, there were variations of note to collectors.

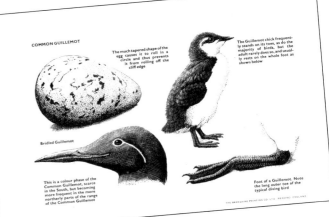

COMMON GUILLEMOT

The much tapered shape of the egg causes it to roll in a circle and thus prevents it from rolling off the cliff edge

The Guillemot chick frequently stands on its toes, as do the majority of birds, but the adult rarely does so, and usually rests on the whole foot as shown below

Bridled Guillemot

This is a colour phase of the Common Guillemot, scarce in the South, but becoming more frequent in the more northerly parts of the range of the Common Guillemot

Foot of a Guillemot. Note the long outer toe of the typical diving bird

THE BERKSHIRE PRINTING CO. LTD. READING. ENGLAND

A SERIES OF 50. No. 1

WILD BIRDS IN BRITAIN

Illustrated and described
by C. F. Tunnicliffe R. A.

WAXWING

(*Bombycilla garrulus garrulus*)

The Waxwing is an irregular winter visitor to Britain, its summer home being in arctic Norway, Sweden, Finland, Russia and Siberia. Hard winters and the shortage of food bring it south, and its numbers in Britain vary considerably—sometimes there is a great influx while in other winters it is scarce. It feeds on berries such as hips and haws, rowan, etc., and when hunting its food is quite acrobatic, often hanging upside down. Male and female are alike in their plumage colour, and the peculiar sealing-wax-like tips of the secondaries give the bird its name. Length 7 ins.

GET A PICTURE CARD ALBUM
FROM YOUR GROCER—Price 6d

Issued with

BROOKE BOND TEA
Crown Cup Instant Coffee

35 Cannon Street, London, E.C.4

A SERIES OF 50. No. 18

WILD BIRDS IN BRITAIN

Illustrated and described
by C. F. Tunnicliffe R. A.

HOOPOE

(*Upupa epops epops*)

This striking bird comes to Britain in small numbers every year and, were it unmolested, would probably nest with us more frequently. The bird from which the painting was made came to the paved ground near the studio, and hunted for ants. It had frequented neighbouring lawns for some time, feeding on ants and grubs. Usually the nest is in a hole in a tree or in a wall or rock crevice, and is a very smelly affair. The crest is usually depressed and is only raised when the bird is excited or alarmed. It winters in tropical Africa, Arabia and S. India. Length 11½ ins.

GET A PICTURE CARD ALBUM
FROM YOUR GROCER—Price 6d

Issued with

BROOKE BOND TEA
Crown Cup Instant Coffee

35 Cannon Street, London, E.C.4

SERIES OF 50. No. 23

WILD BIRDS IN BRITAIN

Illustrated and described
by C. F. Tunnicliffe R. A.

RED-LEGGED PARTRIDGE

(*Alectoris rufa rufa*)

First introduced into Suffolk about 1770 the Red-leg has spread to many parts of England and North Wales. The Red-leg likes the chalk downs and sandy heaths, and I have often seen it on plough-land in East Anglia. Its nest is on the ground, protected by herbage, and is sometimes lined with grass and dead leaves. Food consists of grain, leaves of grasses and clovers, peas and beans, and some insects and spiders. Like the Common Partridge, they move about in coveys after the nesting season, and split up into breeding pairs in the early spring. Length 13¼ ins.

GET A PICTURE CARD ALBUM
FROM YOUR GROCER—Price 6d

Issued with

BROOKE BOND TEA
Crown Cup Instant Coffee

35 Cannon Street, London, E.C.4

A SERIES OF 50. No. 10

WILD BIRDS IN BRITAIN

Illustrated and described
by C. F. Tunnicliffe R. A.

REDSTART

(*Phoenicurus phoenicurus phoenicurus*)

In Britain the Redstart is a summer resident only, arriving about the first week in April and leaving the south coasts in September to winter in Africa and S.W. Asia. It is chiefly a bird of the woods, and the usual situation of the nest is a hole in a tree, though the bird depicted had its nest in the ruined timber roof of an old summer house. All day long he and his mate hunted for insects and caterpillars among the woodland foliage. The female, though she has the same coloured tail as the male, is much duller in her general colour. Length 5½ ins.

GET A PICTURE CARD ALBUM
FROM YOUR GROCER—Price 6d

Issued with

BROOKE BOND TEA
Crown Cup Instant Coffee

35 Cannon Street, London, E.C.4

Schools were able to order a wallchart to accompany the series and this, as with other Brooke Bond wall charts, has also now become a rare and highly desirable item for collectors.

WILD BIRDS in BRITAIN

ILLUSTRATED AND DESCRIBED BY C. F. TUNNICLIFFE R.A.

PRICE SIXPENCE

213

WILD BIRDS in BRITAIN

HERE are fifty bird portraits, fifty of the over four hundred species contained in the British List. For a small area of land such as Britain this is a goodly collection, and one which is providing an absorbing interest for an ever increasing number of people. Perhaps its chief attraction lies in the fact that, as a study, it is inexhaustible—there is always something new to be discovered about birds. Also we must not forget their beauty—a difficult quality to define, but one which is made up of form and colour, balance and movement—a quality to which all sensitive and alert people respond, and which birds have in abundance. Surely, then, these valuable creatures are worthy of our care and protection. But alas! modern man's activities are, on the whole, against their survival. Towns increase in size, land is drained, harmful chemicals are used in the cultivation of the soil, more and more people shoot birds, and so the destruction goes on. Will many of our birds be but a memory in a few years to come? Some are already just that.

C. F. Tunnicliffe

THE 50 PICTURE CARDS ILLUSTRATED

1. Waxwing
2. Hooded Crow
3. Chough
4. Ring Ouzel
5. Mistle Thrush
6. Dipper
7. Reed Bunting
8. Chaffinch
9. Hawfinch
10. Redstart
11. Whinchat
12. Robin
13. Long-tailed Tit
14. Yellow Wagtail
15. Goldcrest
16. Wood Warbler
17. Skylark
18. Hoopoe
19. Nightjar
20. Turtle Dove
21. Red-backed Shrike
22. Black Grouse
23. Red-legged Partridge
24. Dunlin
25. Woodcock
26. Curlew
27. Golden Plover
28. Turnstone
29. Moorhen
30. Sparrow Hawk
31. Montagu's Harrier
32. Kestrel
33. Snowy Owl
34. Long-eared Owl
35. Bittern
36. Goosander
37. Pintail
38. Eider
39. Mallard
40. Barnacle Goose
41. Canada Goose
42. Whooper Swan
43. Cormorant
44. Herring Gull
45. Common Gull
46. Arctic Skua
47. Common Tern
48. Manx Shearwater
49. Black-throated Diver
50. Guillemot

HOODED CROWS

From studies made on the Isle of Iona

These bright
red wax-like
terminals
give the bird
its name

Wing of a Waxwing

2 HOODED CROW *Corvus cornix cornix.* To England this crow is usually a winter visitor though it is resident and plentiful in Scotland, particularly north and west, and in the Hebrides. In winter England has immigrants from the Continent, usually in the eastern half of the country. Like its relative, the Carrion Crow, it nests in trees, on rocks, in bushes, and even on the ground. The nest is made of sticks and fine twigs with a lining of wool. The Hoodie's taste in food is catholic —carrion, eggs, small mammals, fish and refuse—nothing comes amiss. Length 18½ ins.

1 WAXWING *Bombycilla garrulus, garrulus.* The Waxwing is an irregular winter visitor to Britain, its summer home being in arctic Norway, Sweden, Finland, Russia and Siberia. Hard winters and the shortage of food bring it south, and its numbers in Britain vary considerably—sometimes there is a great influx while in other winters it is scarce. It feeds on berries such as hips and haws, rowan, etc., and when hunting its food is quite acrobatic, often hanging upside down. Male and female are alike in their plumage colour, and the peculiar sealing-wax-like tips of the secondaries give the bird its name. Length 7 ins.

3 CHOUGH *Pyrrhocorax pyrrhocorax pyrrhocorax.* This elegant bird is not common. Only a few cliffs, quarries and rocky hills know it. Chiefly it is a western sea-cliff bird, and about these its flight, and acrobatics on the wing, are graceful and vivacious. Usually it nests in deep fissures or in caves, and the nest is made of furze and bracken, stems, sticks or heather stalks, and lined with wool. It was thought to be on the verge of extinction in Britain, but has been holding its own and, lately, there may have been a slight increase. It feeds chiefly on insects and larvae. Length 15 ins.

The curved bill of a Chough

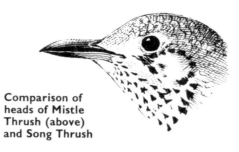

Comparison of heads of Mistle Thrush (above) and Song Thrush

4 RING OUZEL *Turdus torquatus torquatus.* The Ring Ouzel belongs to the thrush family and is unique in being our only migratory breeding thrush, for it winters in the Mediterranean and N.W. Africa. It is a thrush of the hills and the mountains and, in summer, may be found from Cornwall to the north of Scotland. Its nest is placed in heather clumps, on rock ledges, or in the banks of moorland streams. Ring Ouzels feed on insects, worms, and such berries as bilberry and mountain ash. The male is depicted. The female is paler and browner, and the light band across the chest is narrower and duller. Length 9½ ins.

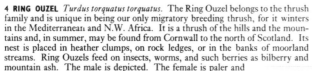

Dipper walking into the water

6 DIPPER *Cinclus cinclus gularis.* A bird of character, a haunter of swiftly flowing streams, and a thorough stay-at-home, for it owns its own length of stream. The Dipper spends much time perched on mid-stream stones and boulders and, when feeding, goes deliberately under the water, walking submerged on the stream bed and moving pebbles in its search for larvae etc. The cup-shaped nest is of moss, dry grasses and dead leaves, over which is built a hood of moss. It may be placed on a rock face, under a waterfall, under a bridge, or on a stream-side tree bole. Length 7 ins.

5 MISTLE THRUSH *Turdus viscivorus viscivorus.* This wild impetuous bird deserves its other name—'Storm Cock'. It begins nesting activities while winter is still with us —early March in the north—and is fearless in protecting its nest. Jackdaws, Magpies and crows do not stay to argue when it attacks. The nest is usually placed in the fork of a tree, and has a foundation of grass, roots, moss and mud with a lining of dry grass and wool. As its name implies it will feed on the berries of mistletoe, but more often of yew, mountain ash, hawthorn and ivy, as well as snails, earthworms and insects. Length 10½ ins.

7 REED BUNTING *Emberiza schoeniclus schoeniclus*. In summer you may often see the Reed Bunting perched on some waterside branch or reed, singing his monotonous little song, while his wife attends to nesting duties in some bushy cover nearby. They are an unobtrusive pair, especially the hen which, in her sober browns and fawns, is often overlooked. The nest is placed in a rush clump, in young willows, often in bank herbage, and is constructed of moss, dry grass and bents. The summer food consists largely of insects and small freshwater crustacea, but in winter seed and grain are also taken. Length 6 ins.

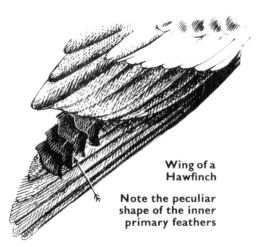

Wing of a Hawfinch

Note the peculiar shape of the inner primary feathers

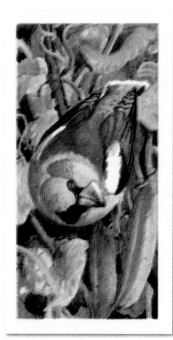

A female Reed Bunting

8 CHAFFINCH *Fringilla coelebs gengleri*. The Chaffinch is one of our commonest birds. In summer it haunts the hedgerows, gardens, orchards, and little copses throughout Britain, and in winter it flocks and frequents the stackyards, the stubble and arable fields. It feeds on both insects and a variety of seeds according to the season of the year. The nest is an exquisite structure of grasses, roots and moss, decorated on the outside with lichens and spiders' webs. A favourite nest position is on a side branch against a small trunk. The male is depicted. The female has no pink on the breast, nor russet on the face. Length 6 ins.

9 HAWFINCH *Coccothraustes coccothraustes*. The enormous bill of this finch is for the purpose of penetrating to the kernels of such fruits as plums, cherries, sloes, and hawthorn. Green peas, beechnuts, a variety of seeds and certain caterpillars are also much liked. The Hawfinch is a shy bird and spends much time in the tops of high trees. It nests in woods and orchards on some horizontal branch on which it places a small platform of twigs as a foundation. The nest is a shallow construction of fine roots with lichen, and is lined with hair. In winter Hawfinches flock. Length 6½ ins.

A young Robin in spotted juvenile plumage

11 **WHINCHAT** *Saxicola rubetra*. The spritely Whinchat is a summer visitor to Britain, appearing about mid-April and leaving us again in September or early October to winter in tropical Africa. It is a haunter of heaths and rough lands, and is often seen on pastures and in railway cuttings as it hunts for beetles, wireworms, flies and other insects. The nest is placed close to the ground, in low herbage or low shrubs. It is loosely constructed of dry grass and moss and is lined with hair and fine fibres. Only the hen builds the nest while the male accompanies her. The male is depicted. Length 5 ins.

10 **REDSTART** *Phoenicurus phoenicurus phoenicurus*. In Britain the Redstart is a summer resident only, arriving about the first week in April and leaving the south coasts in September to winter in Africa and S.W. Asia. It is chiefly a bird of the woods, and the usual situation of the nest is a hole in a tree, though the bird depicted had its nest in the ruined timber roof of an old summer house. All day long he and his mate hunted for insects and caterpillars among the woodland foliage. The female, though she has the same coloured tail as the male, is much duller in her general colour. Length 5¼ ins.

12 **ROBIN** *Erithacus rubecula melophilus*. This familiar solitary bird which seems to enjoy the company of humans, is aggressive towards its own kind and to other birds. The male has a 'territory' which he defends against all other male robins. The nest is placed usually in earth banks sometimes in stone walls, in ivy or in a tree stump, in old tin cans and old kettles. The young in their first plumage are brown and speckled, and have no red breast. The Robin's food ranges from earthworms, wireworms, larvae, ants, spiders, centipedes to grain, soft fruit and berries. Length 5½ ins.

13 LONG-TAILED TIT *Aegithalos caudatus rosaceus*. This little charmer likes the tall hedgerows, the scrub-land of small trees, and the copses and small woods of Britain. In winter family parties may be seen flickering along the hedges. It nests mostly in thorn or furze bushes. The nest is oval-shaped with the entrance near the top. It is made of moss, wool, lichen and spiders' webs and lined with many feathers. The brooding bird sits with her tail bent forward so that its end often protrudes from the nest above the bird's head. There may be as many as twelve nestlings in the one nest. Length 5½ ins.

Nest of a
Long-tailed Tit

Young
Yellow
Wagtail
catching
flies

14 YELLOW WAGTAIL *Motacilla flava flavissima*. The Yellow Wagtail comes to Britain in April and leaves in September. It winters in tropical W. Africa. During the summer months it haunts our pastures and low-lying marshy fields, where it may be seen running hither and thither as it chases insects. The nest is often placed in a ground depression, or in low thick herbage, and is made of root fibres and bents and lined with a mat of cow-hair and some feathers. Except when the bird is asleep the tail is in constant up-and-down motion. This wagtail though not common, is widely distributed in Britain. Length 6½ ins.

15 GOLDCREST *Regulus regulus anglorum*. This, our smallest British bird, is difficult to find for it haunts thick conifers and ever-greens, and usually remains fairly high in the branches. Once found, however, it is indifferent to the observer and goes about its hunting of spiders, insects and their larvae quite unconcerned by his presence. It is almost as acrobatic as the tits and is often seen with them. The nest is usually suspended beneath the thick foliage of cypress, spruce or yew. It is constructed of moss and spiders' webs and lined with feathers. The family is large, seven to ten as a rule. Length 3½ ins.

Hoopoe with crest lowered

16 WOOD WARBLER *Phylloscopus sibilatrix*. The Wood Warbler is well named for it is partial to beech and oak woods. Very spruce in its appearance, and brightly coloured, it is a delight to watch as it hunts the leaves for its insect food, or sings with bill wide open and throat throbbing. The nest is on the ground in undergrowth, and is made of dead leaves, grasses and bracken lined with fine fibres and hair, with the entrance at the side. Wood Warblers arrive in Britain in April and May and leave in July and August for their winter home in Central Africa. Length 5 ins.

17 SKYLARK *Alauda arvensis arvensis*. In spring, in open country, the male Skylark sings as he climbs above his nesting place, fluttering higher and higher until, at the zenith of his flight, he hovers for a time before his slow fluttering descent to a point a few yards above the ground where he raises his wings and drops suddenly to earth. That is his display song to his mate on the ground. The nest is on the ground and is made of grasses lined with finer grasses and hair. Skylarks feed on seeds and grains, insects, worms and spiders. Length 7 ins.

18 HOOPOE *Upupa epops epops*. This striking bird comes to Britain in small numbers every year and, were it unmolested, would probably nest with us more frequently. The bird from which the painting was made came to the paved ground near the studio, and hunted for ants. It had frequented neighbouring lawns for some time, feeding on ants and grubs. Usually the nest is in a hole in a tree or in a wall or rock crevice, and is a very smelly affair. The crest is usually depressed and is only raised when the bird is excited or alarmed. It winters in tropical Africa, Arabia and S. India. Length 11½ ins.

19 NIGHTJAR *Caprimulgus europaeus europaeus.* Nightjars arrive in Britain in May and leave in September. Open heather or woodland, rough ground, woodland margins and sand dunes are their haunts and nesting places. The nest is in a hollow on the bare ground. The Nightjar is most active at twilight when it hunts flying insects, such as moths and beetles, its enormous mouth being a particular development for this purpose. When resting on a branch it usually perches lengthwise, though it will perch crosswise on occasions. The male has white areas on the outer primaries and outer tail feathers. Nightjars winter in Africa as far south as the Cape. Length 10½ ins.

20 TURTLE DOVE *Streptopelia turtur turtur.* A summer pigeon arriving in Britain in May and leaving in August and September to winter in tropical Africa. It prefers open woods, plantations and parkland, and areas where there are bushes or high hedges and its food is almost entirely vegetable. The nest is built in high hedges, bushes and orchard trees, and is a meagre platform of twigs, sometimes lined with finer roots. Usually the Turtle Dove is seen singly or in pairs, but small flocks may be seen in late summer. Its smaller size, warmer colour, and striking tail pattern differentiate it from our other wild pigeons. Length 10¾ ins.

The wide gape of the Nightjar

21 RED-BACKED SHRIKE *Lanius collurio collurio.* This predatory bird with a hooked bill and trim figure comes to Britain in May, takes up its residence in bushy areas, and leaves between August and October to winter in tropical and S. Africa and S.W. Asia. It feeds on beetles, moths, grasshoppers, small birds and their young, worms, frogs and lizards. Sometimes it makes 'larders' of surplus food, impaling this on thorns. It nests in thickets of bramble and thorn. The nest is rather large and made of moss, bents and green leaves, lined with fibre and hair, and sometimes wool. The male is depicted. The female is not so striking in her plumage. Length 6¾ ins.

The tail of
the male
Black Grouse

22 BLACK GROUSE *Lyrurus tetrix britannicus*. This fine grouse is now confined to a few areas in Devon, Wales, north Midlands and Scotland. They are not such high moorland birds as the Red Grouse, but prefer lower grounds in the proximity of trees. They are polygamous, and in early spring the males gather in a chosen spot, called a 'lek' and there posture and display, and sometimes fight for mates. The nest is a hollow in the ground sheltered by grass or heather. Black Grouse feed on heather shoots and leaves, bilberry, raspberry, and wild strawberry, buds of conifers and other plants, with some insect life. Male is known as Blackcock and female as as Greyhen. Length 22 ins.

Dunlin in winter plumage

23 RED-LEGGED PARTRIDGE *Alectoris rufa rufa*. First introduced into Suffolk about 1770 the Red-leg has spread to many parts of England and North Wales. The Red-leg likes the chalk downs and sandy heaths, and I have often seen it on ploughland in East Anglia. Its nest is on the ground, protected by herbage, and is sometimes lined with grass and dead leaves. Food consists of grain, leaves of grasses and clovers, peas and beans, and some insects and spiders. Like the Common Partridge, they move about in coveys after the nesting season, and split up into breeding pairs in the early spring. Length 13½ ins.

24 DUNLIN *Calidris alpina alpina*. The Dunlin is our commonest bird of the shore. There are two races, the Northern and the Southern, but they are much alike. It is the northern race which is depicted. The southern race nests in Britain and chooses wild moorland for its nursery, making a cuplike hollow for a nest and lining it with grass. Muddy shores are its paradise, and here it runs and probes and captures marine worms, sand-hoppers, small crabs and shrimps, etc. Sometimes great flocks of Dunlin haunt the shores, when their wonderful synchronised flying is most spectacular. Length 7½ ins.

25 WOODCOCK *Scolopax rusticola*. In Britain the Woodcock can either be a resident, a summer resident, or a bird of passage. In the mating season, at dusk and dawn, the males go through a peculiar flight display among the trees, making repeated circuits along the rides. 'Roding' is the name given to it. The nest is on the ground in woodland—a hollow lined with dead leaves. A parent, when anxious for the safety of the young, will carry them, one at a time, between the thighs, and fly to a chosen spot. The long bill is used to probe for earthworms and larvae. Length 13½ ins.

26 CURLEW *Numenius arquata arquata*. The Curlew is our largest wader. In autumn and winter it haunts the muddy shores in large numbers, and with its long bill probes for lugworms, or in the creeks seeks small crabs, shrimps and other small creatures. In summer the breeding birds leave the shore and take to the high hill pastures and moors where they make their ground nest, but some nest on low marshland and in sand dunes. Its fine impetuous flying, its trilling spring song, its wariness and fine racy appearance make the Curlew one of our most interesting birds. Length about 22 ins.

WOODCOCK

Note the peculiar position of the ear

27 GOLDEN PLOVER *Pluvialis apricaria apricaria*. In summer the Golden Plover is the nesting companion of the curlew on the high moors. There it lays its eggs in a hollow in the peat. The picture shows a male in breeding dress. In autumn, when the young are well on the wing, the 'goldens' migrate to the lowland pastures, the arable land and the mud-flats, and there spend the winter. Now they are pale-breasted birds and thus they will remain until the spring. Food consists of beetles, flies and moth, larvae, small snails, earthworms, spiders, and certain weed seeds. Length 11 ins.

223

28 TURNSTONE *Arenaria interpres interpres.* Although Turnstones may be seen all the year round on the coasts of Britain none have been proved to breed here, and we would have to visit the Arctic to see their nests. On seaweedy rocks or on shingly shore the Turnstone may be seen as it throws over pebbles and chunks of seaweed in search for food of the small creatures living underneath. I have depicted a male in summer plumage. Immature birds, females, and all winter birds are much duller in plumage. A surprising pattern of dark and light is revealed when the bird takes to wing. Length 9 ins.

29 MOORHEN *Gallinula chloropus chloropus.* On any pool of water, from the smallest marl-pit to a large mere, one may see a Moorhen. Its long toes enable it to walk over lily leaves, and also propel it when swimming. Its nest is usually near water—in a clump of rush or flag, or in tree branches. The nestlings are strange black mites with fantastic colours of red, blue and yellow on the head and bill and large feet. They can swim almost as soon as they are born. Moorhens have a varied diet from water weeds and fruits to insects, worms and larvae. Length 13 ins.

30 SPARROW HAWK *Accipiter nisus nisus.* This fierce hawk hunts by flying along the hedge-rows, and between woodland trees, hoping to take its prey, usually another bird, by sur-prise. It kills with its claws, and is swift and expert. The nest is built in a tree, and is made of twigs with sometimes a lining of leaves. Prey is brought to the nestlings ready plucked, for the hunting parent has its regular plucking place, well away from the nest, where piles of feathers may be seen during the breeding season. It is usually the male which hunts and the female which broods. Length 11–15 ins.

31 MONTAGU'S HARRIER *Circus pygargus.* Of the three harriers which visit Britain this is the most elegant. It arrives in April and leaves in October to winter in tropical and S. Africa, also S.W. Asia. While in Britain we hope that it has found some marsh or heath where it has been able to nest successfully, for egg collectors and shooters still persecute it. The male is depicted. The female is a larger, browner bird, and while she is brooding young the male hunts. On his return he flies above the nest area and calls. The female flies up and neatly takes the prey, perhaps a mouse, snake, frog, vole or small bird, from his talons. Length about 17 ins.

Kestrel nestlings

32 KESTREL *Falco tinnunculus tinnunculus.* A hovering hawk is usually a Kestrel, for only it makes a habit of hunting by hovering. It must have amazing eyes for sometimes it will descend from a high hover and pick up—a beetle! But usually it is a hunter of voles, mice and birds. Kestrels will hunt over most varieties of country, and their nest is a mere hollow on a cliff, a hole in a tree or a crevice in some ruin. No nest material is used. The male is depicted. The female is larger and browner, with no blue-grey in her plumage. Length about 13½ ins.

33 SNOWY OWL *Nyctea scandiaca.* This most impressive bird hunts in the day time and with strong, swift flight, sweeps over the coastal flats and marshes, and the moorlands, in search of mice, voles, rabbits, and even beetles, as well as birds as big as a duck. It nests on the ground in the tundras of the Arctic. This painting was made from studies of a bird which had been captured on a ship in mid-Atlantic. I drew it a few days after its arrival at a Zoo while it was still feather-perfect, and still fierce. It hissed at every move I made. In winter this owl sometimes crosses to northern parts of the British Isles. Length 21—24 ins.

34 LONG-EARED OWL *Asio otus otus.* Perched, often against a tree trunk, and in thick foliage, the Long-eared Owl spends the hours of daylight—for it is a night-hunter. It feeds on mice, voles, rats, small birds, moles and beetles. For a nest it uses old squirrel dreys, and old nests of Magpie, Crow, Sparrow Hawk, and Wood Pigeon. The so-called 'ear tufts' have nothing to do with the ears proper, but are feather tufts which the bird can raise or lower at will. They are raised only when the bird is curious, alarmed or excited. Length 13½ ins.

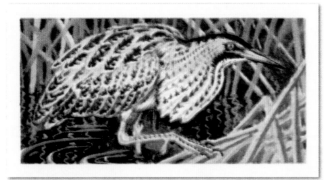

35 BITTERN *Botaurus stellaris stellaris.* A large secretive relation of the heron, the Bittern is rarely seen until it flies, for its home is in thick reed-beds. During the breeding season the male has a peculiar call, a booming sound which is not loud but which has amazing carrying power. Bitterns feed on fish, including eels, frogs, newts, voles, mice, beetles, and young water birds such as Moorhen, Coot, Water Rail etc. Norfolk and Suffolk are the strongholds of the Bittern though it occurs in a few other places in Britain. Length 30 ins.

37 PINTAIL *Anas acuta acuta.* The Pintail is best known to us as a winter visitor. In inland waters it winters in small numbers, but on the sea, and on estuaries, it may occur in larger flocks. This elegant racy duck nests in Scotland, the nest being placed on the ground among marram grass, or in heather. As in other ducks the nest hollow is lined with down from the breast of the female, and it is she who does all the incubating of the eggs. Pintail food is chiefly vegetable, but some small animal food is also eaten. Its flight is swift, and all its movements are graceful. Length 22 ins.

36 GOOSANDER *Mergus merganser merganser.* This large handsome duck is one of the 'sawbills', so named because it has saw-like edges on both mandibles, which enable it to capture and hold its slippery prey—fish. The Goosander is an expert diver and travels swiftly when submerged. In England it is usually a winter visitor and may be seen in flocks on meres and reservoirs, but in Scotland it nests. A hollow tree is a favourite nest site, but it will also use spaces among boulders. Incubation of the eggs is done by the female alone while the males gather in parties. Length 26 ins.

38 EIDER *Somateria mollissima mollissima.* A marine duck common on the coasts of Scotland and north-eastern England, and in winter off the east coast of England. The Eider nests preferably on off-shore islands and islets. The nest itself is a hollow lined with grasses, down and feathers, and it is this down that is used commercially. The female incubates the eggs and the young take to the water soon after hatching, swimming in a close-packed group at their mother's tail. The Eider is a large, heavy duck which requires to run over the water before becoming airborne. Molluscs and crustaceans form the main part of the food. Length 23 ins.

226

A Canada Goose on her nest

39 MALLARD *Anas platyrhynchos platyrhynchos.* On small woodland pools and large meres, and from coastal waters to small mountain tarns; even in London, the Mallard may be found. It is our commonest wild duck. Food comprises seeds, buds, and leaves of many aquatic and land plants, beetles, worms, tadpoles and fish-spawn. The nest is usually on the ground under cover of bushes or tussocks near the water, but sometimes in holes in trees and other unexpected places. Only the females incubate while the drakes assemble in parties. Ducklings of any species can swim soon after they are free of the egg-shell and dry. Length 23 ins.

40 BARNACLE GOOSE *Branta leucopsis.* So called because in the old days it was thought that this goose hatched from ship's barnacles, and one imaginative artist even did a drawing of this happening. It is as a winter visitor that we know this beautiful goose. In Britain its favourite haunts are the Inner and Outer Hebrides and the Solway Firth. In the Hebrides it is fond of grazing on the sweet island grass and on the herbs of the coastal stretches called 'machairs'. The flocks feed both by night and day. It appears to be a rather quarrelsome goose when feeding. It breeds in eastern Greenland, Spitzbergen, and Novaya Zemlya. Length about 25 ins.

41 CANADA GOOSE *Branta canadensis canadensis.* This species was introduced into Britain as far back as 1678. Since then it has flourished, and may be seen on many inland waters. With us it is non-migratory. The nest is constructed of reed stalks and grass etc., lined with down. Eggs are incubated by the female only, while the gander patrols the water near the nest area. Like the other geese; also swans and ducks, the adults moult all their flight feathers at one time and are incapable of flight for a period. In winter the flocks fly from one feeding area to another and often achieve very perfect 'V' formations. In North America the loud call has gained the Canada Goose the name of 'Honker'. Length 38 ins.

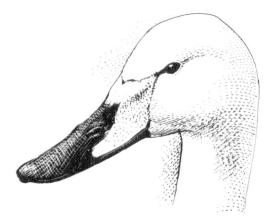

42 WHOOPER SWAN *Cygnus cygnus cygnus.* This swan is a winter visitor arriving in October and leaving in March or April. The Whooper is almost as big as the Mute Swan, from which it differs in having no knob at the base of the bill, in having yellow on the bill instead of orange and in the carriage of the neck, which is straighter than that of the Mute. It is also much more vocal and often calls loudly, especially when in flight. Like other swans it is completely vegetarian in its diet. It flies in formation, either in lines or in a wedge. Length 60 ins.

Head of a Whooper Swan

**Head of a Herring Gull
in winter plumage**

44 HERRING GULL *Larus argentatus argentatus.* This big noisy gull is very common round our shores. In summer it nests on cliffs, islands and dunes, making a large nest of any available material. The downy chicks are quite pretty, but in the first brown plumage the bird is all gull with hooked bill and predatory instincts well developed. It requires three years for this gull to acquire its bluish-grey and white plumage. In winter it wanders inland to fresh water and arable land, and it is a common sight to see the ploughman followed by a swirling white crowd. Fish, carrion, refuse, earthworms and a variety of other foods are eaten. Length 22 ins.

43 CORMORANT *Phalacrocorax carbo carbo.* The Cormorant may be found almost anywhere round our shores. It is chiefly a sea bird, but has been known to nest in inland fresh waters. Usually the nest colony is on some rocky island or cliff ledge and a smelly place it is! Nest is usually of seaweed. When first hatched the young are naked and appear even more reptilian than their parents. Food is generally fish, for the Cormorant is an expert underwater swimmer, and specially adapted for capturing them. I have depicted an adult in breeding plumage, drying his wings after diving. Length 36 ins.

45 COMMON GULL *Larus canus canus*. At first sight this gull may be confused with the Herring Gull, but the Common Gull is much smaller. In England it is far from common in spring and summer for, with a few exceptions, it goes up to Scotland to nest. In August back it comes to our lowland pastures, marshes, and sandy shores, and stays during the winter. It nests on islets in rivers and lochs, and on low coasts, sometimes on moors. The first plumage is brown and it requires three years to attain the immaculate plumage of the adult. The diet is much like that of the Herring Gull. Length 16 ins.

Egg and chick of Common Tern

**Head of an Arctic Skua
(light type)**

46 ARCTIC SKUA *Stercorarius parasiticus*. This is the commonest of our skuas, or robber gulls. They all obtain their food by chasing other sea birds in flight, following them relentlessly until their victim drops its load of fish, when the skua swoops and captures the dropping fish before it reaches the water. Chief victims are terns, and small gulls such as Kittiwakes. It breeds in Shetland, Fair Isle, Orkney and Outer Hebrides, and sparsely on the Scottish mainland. It nests on the ground. This skua is very widely distributed and spends the winter as far southward as New Zealand. Length 18 ins.

47 COMMON TERN *Sterna hirundo hirundo*. Such delicate looking birds seem hardly capable of making a journey from the west coast of Africa, yet they do this journey twice a year. They arrive here about mid-April and leave us in September or October. With us they nest and choose a variety of sites for their purpose—shingle beaches, sand dunes, headlands, salt marshes, islets, etc. Their food is almost entirely of fish which they hunt usually by hovering to sight their prey, then a quick plunge, and a mounting flight with the small fish held in the tip of the bill. Crustaceans and other water life are also eaten. This tern also lives in the New World. Length 13½ ins.

48 MANX SHEARWATER *Puffinus puffinus puffinus.* This shearwater is essentially a sea bird, though it does not travel far out to sea, and in Britain it nests in burrows, on islands off our western coasts. Because of their fear of waiting gulls the shearwaters remain off-shore until darkness falls before they dare fly to their burrows. Even so there are many casualties. One egg is laid and nesting takes place in colonies. When the nestling is a certain age it is deserted by the parents, so that in time hunger compels it to leave the burrow and make for the sea. In winter this shearwater migrates southward, probably to Spanish coastal waters. Small fish form the main part of the diet. Length 14 ins.

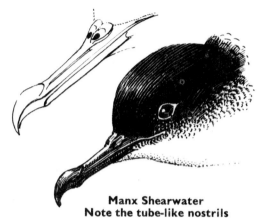

**Manx Shearwater
Note the tube-like nostrils**

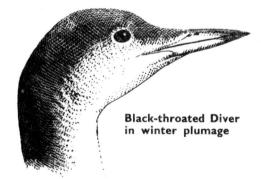

**Black-throated Diver
in winter plumage**

49 BLACK-THROATED DIVER *Colymbus arcticus arcticus.* As a nesting species in Britain this bird habitually breeds on certain deep lochs in Scotland. The nest is usually on an islet in the loch, and close to the water's edge, for divers do not walk well and progress on the ground only by using their wings also. The nest, usually, is little more than a hollow scraped in the ground. Fish and other water life are the diver's staple diet. In winter it leaves its inland waters and takes to the sea where it may be seen in many places along our coasts. Length about 25 ins.

50 GUILLEMOT *Uria aalge albionis.* Guillemots are true sea birds, not coming to shore until the nesting season. Then, in April, they begin to populate the cliff ledges. Only one egg is laid of a beautiful tapering shape, which causes it to roll in a small circle—an advantage on the sometimes narrow ledges. When the chick is ready to leave, the parents persuade it to launch itself from the nesting ledge, and with whirring tiny wings it flutters down to the waves (if no gull intervenes). Usually this launching takes place at dusk. At all times fish and other marine life are staple food. Length 16½ ins.

COMMON GUILLEMOT

The much tapered shape of the egg causes it to roll in a circle and thus prevents it from rolling off the cliff edge

The Guillemot chick frequently stands on its toes, as do the majority of birds, but the adult rarely does so, and usually rests on the whole foot as shown below

Bridled Guillemot

This is a colour phase of the Common Guillemot, scarce in the South, but becoming more frequent in the more northerly parts of the range of the Common Guillemot

Foot of a Guillemot. Note the long outer toe of the typical diving bird

THIS SERIES OF PICTURE CARDS
IS OFFERED IN THE INTERESTS
OF EDUCATION AND WILDLIFE
CONSERVATION BY

Brooke Bond

Picture cards are given with
Brooke Bond Tea
Brooke Bond Pure & French Coffees
Crown Cup Instant Coffee

Richard Ward, whose previous Brooke Bond series had included **British Butterflies** and **Butterflies of the World** was the illustrator for the 16th tea cards issue, **Transport Through the Ages** in 1966.

While the images were both interesting and colourful, they were not quite as detailed as some of the previous wildlife sets, although they covered a huge range of transport modes.

This was only the second set issued that did not focus on some aspect of nature and the first in ten years to vary from this theme. With text supplied by writer Arthur G. Bourne, the fifty cards portrayed transport as diverse as a howdah on the back of an elephant and a horse-drawn chariot to a nuclear submarine and a space rocket.

The display album includes an uncredited but concise introduction as well as a number of supplementary illustrations, with the entire inside back cover devoted to the development of waterborne transport. Even with these extra line drawings, however, the album was nowhere near as elaborate as previous publications.

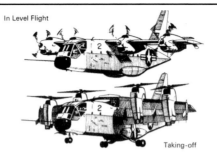

In Level Flight

Taking-off

A wall chart also accompanied this set, obtainable direct from Brooke Bond, and this was the first such chart not produced exclusively for schools. Some of the artworks for this set were used on the Canadian set of the same name and were also issued in Ireland on Musgrave Brooke Bond tea cards.

A removable order form was included to allow collectors to obtain other cards or albums and this was yet another card set that was officially reprinted in 1973, with the cards again distinct from the originals by way of the black printing on the reverse instead of blue.

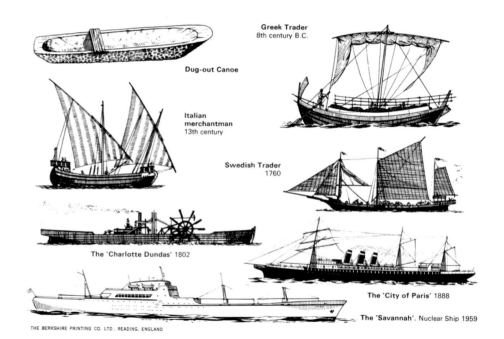

Dug-out Canoe

Greek Trader
8th century B.C.

Italian merchantman
13th century

Swedish Trader
1760

The 'Charlotte Dundas' 1802

The 'City of Paris' 1888

The 'Savannah'. Nuclear Ship 1959

THE BERKSHIRE PRINTING CO. LTD., READING. ENGLAND

BROOKE BOND
PICTURE CARDS

Transport through the ages

ILLUSTRATED BY RICHARD WARD · DESCRIBED BY ARTHUR G. BOURNE / PRICE SIXPENCE

TRANSPORT THROUGH THE AGES

Man's first power source was his own muscles. These he used on land to transport himself, carry loads, and on water to swim and to propel himself on rafts or tree trunks. Opportunities of quicker, easier transport came when he invented the wheel and learnt how to utilise the superior muscle power of animals, and on water, he discovered that sails took the labour out of paddling and rowing. Steam, electric and diesel power are commonplace today but power sources, such as atomic energy, have again opened up new vistas in transport. From muscle power to atomic power; from early man, carrying his heavy loads, to modern man, pushing his way through the depths of space, the story of transport is the story of man's conquest of his environment.

Marathon Runner 490 B.C.

The North American X-15 Research Rocket Plane

USAF

THE 50 CARDS ILLUSTRATED

ELEPHANT *Animal Muscle Power*. The domestication of the Indian elephant and its use in transport began at least 2,000 years ago. The elephant, with its great strength and docility, was an ideal choice. The use of the elephant spread west much later, where for a limited time it became a terrifying weapon of war in the armies of North African rulers. The picture shows a howdah on the elephant's back, during a ceremonial occasion. This gave rise to the familiar inn sign 'The Elephant and Castle'.

THE CAMEL *Animal Muscle Power*. The camel is called the 'Ship of the Desert', and it is essential to desert dwellers in many parts of Africa and Asia. The camel's feet are specially adapted to walking on soils of the desert and it can go without food and water for long periods. Camel caravans can still be seen in North Africa, Arabia and Asia, although motorised transport is fast superseding them.

DOG SLEDGE *Animal Muscle Power*. Eskimos inhabit the most inhospitable region of the world, the Arctic. In early times transport by land was only possible on foot, and through much of the year passage by boat was impossible. As there were no large beasts that could be harnessed, the Eskimos turned to man's oldest friend, the dog, and trained him to work in a team to pull a cart that would slide over the ice and frozen land, the sledge. This combination is still one of the most efficient ways of travelling in these regions. The Husky has proved to be one of the finest breeds of dogs for this type of work.

Early Wheel
The Sumerians
4000-1200 B.C.

CHARIOT *Animal Muscle Power*. The horse was first used as a pack animal and as a mount, but soon man learned to harness the horse to drags and wheeled vehicles, including the chariot. Unlike the ox and elephant, the horse supplied speed as well as power. In fact, in the late 18th century when James Watt wished to define the power of his steam engines in readily understandable terms, he accurately measured the amount of work a horse could do—hence the term 'horse power'. A fast, lightweight war chariot of the type used in Ancient Greece and Rome is shown in the picture.

OX WAGON *Animal Muscle Power*. In many parts of the world the slow but powerful oxen are still used. The ox, although not really stronger than the larger carthorses, has the advantage of being able to develop its power with less effort and impetus. It is therefore ideal for pulling great loads with ease, provided speed is not required. The covered wagon became famous in the 19th century when it was used with horse or oxen, by the pioneers who settled in South Africa and the American West. The picture shows the Voortrekkers of South Africa who began the 'Great Trek' in 1835.

STAGE COACH *Animal Muscle Power*. Horse drawn transport reached its zenith in the stage coach of 19th century Europe and North America. At each 'stage' of the journey fresh horses would be harnessed to the coach so as to avoid the lessening of speed that comes from tired horses. One of the most famous of the American stage coach lines, the Wells Fargo, is illustrated. Wells Fargo came into being at the time of the Great Californian Gold Rush in the 1850's. The stage coach remained a dominant factor in transport until the railroads superseded it.

HORSE TRAM *Animal Muscle Power*. Trams, that is, wheeled vehicles running on rails laid in the roadway, developed, like the railways, from the transport used in mines. The first public tramway, from Wandsworth to Croydon, was really a project for a railway, and was opened in 1803. It was horse drawn. Apart from this, the first street tramway in England was built in Birkenhead in 1860 by an American, G. F. Train. Although horse drawn trams were largely replaced by electric trams, some survived into the 20th century, including the Isle of Man horse trams which are shown on the card.

THE BICYCLE *Man Muscle Power*. The 'Hobby Horse' of 1818 was the first bicycle. On this the rider simply pushed himself along with his feet on the ground. In 1839 Kirkpatric Macmillan's bicycle came into use. It had pedals attached to the frame and connected to the back wheel with rods. The Penny Farthing is illustrated, and had, like most early cycles, its pedals fixed to the front wheel, which made going down hill a real hazard. The card also shows the Coventry Rotary 'Sociable'—a 4-wheeler. Cycling became much safer with the invention of the Safety Bicycle which had smaller wheels driven by a chain.

London Bus 1914

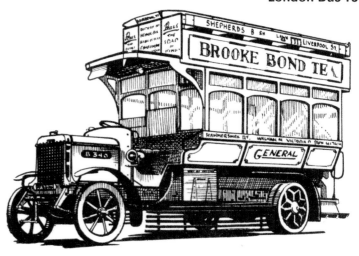

Steam Traction Engine

The Kon-tiki Raft 1947
Based on pre-Columbian
Polynesian rafts

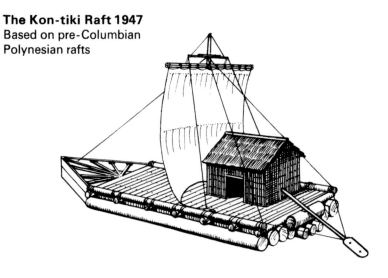

GALLEY *Man Muscle Power*. The birthplace of the galley, a ship propelled by oars, was in the Eastern Mediterranean. Ancient Greek sailors attained remarkable speeds in galleys. Thucydides recorded that 168 miles were covered in 24 hours, an average speed of 7 m.p.h. Xenophon mentions a speed of 9 m.p.h. being maintained. War galleys had a powerful ram at the bow for holing enemy ships. There was one man to each oar and the oars were arranged in banks—the trireme of the Greeks, shown in the picture, had three banks, 170 oars in all.

KAYAK *Man Muscle Power*. Many primitive craft in which the only power is that of man's own muscles remain in use to this day. The most advanced form of skin boat is the kayak used by the Eskimos of Greenland and North America. This has a frame of driftwood covered with tanned seal skins. It is also light enough for one man to carry. When the ice melts after the long winter the lone Eskimo hunter can use his fragile kayak with such skill that he is able to hunt seals and fish in some of the most dangerous waters of the world.

HORSE BARGE *Animal Muscle Power*. In Britain, the Duke of Bridgewater (1736–1803) pioneered the modern use of man-made canals. At first horses were used to pull the narrow barges. The dimensions of these boats were governed by the size of the locks of the early canals, and although only 7 ft. wide and 72 ft. long, with the very shallow draught of 3 ft. they had a capacity of 25 tons. The bargees, sometimes called 'Water Gypsies', lived with their families on the gaily painted barges, which had sleeping quarters at the stern. The advent of railways saw the decline of the canal system.

EAST INDIAMAN *Wind Power/Sail.* The discovery of the use of the sail to utilise the propulsive force of the wind is lost in antiquity. The Red Sea galleys with their auxiliary square-rigged sails were probably the forerunners of the sailing ships. The pride of the 18th century mercantile fleets were the ships of the East India Company. These sturdy ships with large cargo carrying capacities of between 400 and 1,200 tons, carried Britain's trade from the East Indies for over 100 years. The card shows the East Indiaman 'Atlas'.

TEA CLIPPER *Wind Power/Sail.* The supreme achievement of sail power was realised in the famous tea clippers, which carried tea from China to Europe. The *Cutty Sark* was one of the last tea clippers. She was built and launched at Dumbarton on the Clyde on the 23rd November 1869. She was square-rigged and had 32,000 sq. ft. of sail which could drive her at over 17 knots, an equivalent of 3,000 horse power. The *Cutty Sark* was one of the fastest ships that ever sailed the seas under the power of sail alone. The *Cutty Sark* can be seen today preserved at Greenwich, in London.

Chinese Junk

Arab Dhow

241

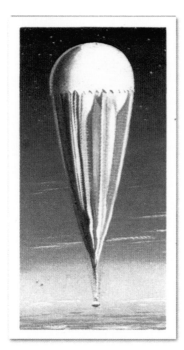

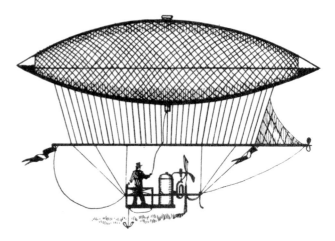

Gifford's Balloon 1852

Cayley's Glider model 1804

HOT AIR BALLOON *Wind Power*. The first balloon, made by the French Montgolfier Brothers in 1783, was filled with hot air from a fire and, using the lift provided by the lightness of the warm air, it carried a sheep, a cockerel and a duck high over Versailles and flew for 8 minutes before the air inside cooled and the balloon gently returned to earth. The Montgolfiers also made the first manned balloon which carried its passengers over Paris on the 21st November 1783. This was the first aerial voyage in history; it flew 5½ miles in 25 minutes.

GAS BALLOON *Wind Power*. A Frenchman, Professor Charles, made the first balloon to use hydrogen which was flown on the 27th August 1783. Later that year he sent up another balloon which carried 2 men for 27 miles. The English Channel was crossed not long after by hydrogen balloon in 1785. In 1935 *Explorer II*, shown on the card, carried two Americans to a height of 13·7 miles, the highest achieved by man at that time. Since then balloons have achieved even higher altitudes and in 1958 during 'Operation Man High', two U.S.A.F. pilots reached the amazing height of 100,000 ft., about 18 miles above the earth.

STEAM COACH *Steam Power*. The first steam powered vehicle was built by the French military engineer, Nicholas Cugnot, in 1769. This 3-wheeled steam machine ran for only 15 minutes and the project was abandoned. However, it was a start. Many attempts followed, including William Murdoch's steam carriage of 1786, which was successful, although only a model. In 1801 Richard Trevithick built a steam carriage which ran on the London roads. The picture shows Sir Goldsworthy Gurney's steam coach of 1830.

STEPHENSON'S ROCKET *Steam Power*. The first successful locomotive was made by Richard Trevithick for the Pen-y-darran Colliery in 1804. The first passenger railway to use steam locomotives was the Stockton and Darlington Railway of 1825 for which Robert Stephenson built *Locomotion*. The card depicts another Stephenson locomotive, *The Rocket*, built for the Liverpool and Manchester Railway, which astonished the world with its speed at the Rainhill Trials in 1829, and started the boom in railway development. *The Rocket* later attained a speed of 36 m.p.h.

STEAM WAGON *Steam Power*. The steam lorry for carrying freight was very successful. Its low running costs enabled it to survive the arrival of the petrol driven lorry until 1920 when in England, at least, steam road lorries suffered by the introduction of new taxes based on the vehicle's unladen weight which put them at an economic disadvantage compared with the lighter petrol lorries. The famous *Sentinel* steam lorry could carry sufficient water to give it a range of 40–60 miles. The card shows a Clayton steam wagon of a type produced between 1910 and 1920.

MODERN STEAM LOCOMOTIVE *Steam Power*. Steam powered locomotives developed rapidly after the success of Stephenson's *Rocket*. Pulling power increased and with power, speed. Before 1850 speeds of up to 70 m.p.h. had been achieved. The railway fever that swept England spread overseas and many countries began to develop their own railways. The world speed record for steam locomotives is 126 m.p.h. set by *Mallard* of the London and North Eastern Railway in 1938. The picture shows a very fine steam locomotive of the Canadian Pacific Railway, Class Tl.B. Selkirk, 2-10-4, No. 5921.

DIESEL LOCOMOTIVE *Internal Combustion/Diesel.* Diesel and diesel–electric locomotives are more economical than steam locomotives. Engine-driven generators produce an electric current to drive the motors which give traction to the wheels. Some of British Rail's diesel–electric locomotives can generate 3,300 horse power. The modernisation of the railways has included the improvement of carriages for the comfort of the passengers and in British Rail's new Pullman trains, shown on the card, luxury with speed has been achieved. One of these, on the run from Bristol to Paddington in 1965, took only 87 minutes for a journey of 118 miles.

THE COMET *Steam Power.* The importance of a means of propulsion which is independent of wind and tide is obvious. Although several experiments in the use of steam power had been tried in both the Old and the New World, William Symington's *Charlotte Dundas* of 1802, which worked as a tug on the Forth and Clyde Canal, was the first practical steam powered vessel, followed shortly after by Robert Fulton's *Clermont* on the River Hudson in 1807. The card shows the first commercial passenger steamer in Europe, Henry Bell's *Comet* of 1812.

GAS TURBINE LOCOMOTIVE *Internal Combustion/Gas Turbine.* In 1941 a revolutionary step was taken in locomotive engineering when the Swiss Federal Railways introduced a gas turbine locomotive. Gas turbine engines can give more horse power per foot of locomotive than any other types and they also have the advantage of low maintenance costs. The card shows a Union Pacific 61 from which was developed a mammoth locomotive, the 8,500 horse power, 420-ton locomotive of the Union Pacific Railroad in the U.S.A. which is one of the largest locomotives in the world.

MISSISSIPPI RIVER STEAMER *Steam Power.* The paddle wheel was the only successful means of propulsion for steamboats until the later 1830's, and it was the use of the paddle wheel which made possible the building of the American shallow-draught river steamers which became so famous in the Eastern States and on the Hudson and Mississippi rivers. These boats, with their huge paddle wheels, up to 25 ft. in diameter, played an important part in American history and in their own time became legend and are commemorated in the folk songs of the period. The *Robert E. Lee* is shown on the card.

THE GREAT EASTERN *Sail-assisted Steam Power*. The *Great Eastern* was designed by I. K. Brunel and launched in 1858. She made her first Atlantic crossing in 1860 at an average speed of 14 knots. With a 32,000-ton displacement she was the largest vessel afloat from 1858 to 1888 when she was broken up for scrap. She was unique in that she was propelled by both paddle wheel and screw propeller, in addition to which she carried a spread of 6,500 sq. yards of sail on her 6 masts. Although not a great commercial success she did prove that large ships of iron could be built.

MODERN OCEAN LINER *Steam Power/Turbine*. The modern liner is the queen of the seas. Her sleek outlines and sturdy build enable her to sail anywhere in the world, while her passengers enjoy the luxury of a floating hotel. 80 years ago a voyage would take months—today the same voyage may take only weeks or even days. The card depicts the 42,000 ton P & O-Orient *Oriana* which was launched in 1959. She can carry 2,180 passengers at a top speed of 32 knots.

TURBINIA *Steam Power/Turbine*. The most dramatic revolution in the history of steam propulsion was the invention of the steam turbine which enabled steam power to be produced from far smaller engines. During the Spithead Naval Review of 1897, a steam turbine launch impressed everyone with her tremendous speed of 34 knots. This launch, the *Turbinia*, was made by Charles Parsons who invented the steam turbine. In 1906 the two great steam turbine liners, *Mauretania*, which won the Atlantic Blue Riband, and the *Lusitania*, were launched.

OIL TANKER *Steam Power/Turbine*. Before the advent of the modern ship built specially to carry oil, any ship had to do and the oil was carried in individual barrels. The forerunner of the modern tanker was the *Gluckauf*, built in Newcastle in 1886 for the German-American Petroleum Co. Today the large tankers of the modern fleets rival the largest liners for size and even larger tankers, of 100,000 tons and more, are being built to carry the fuel necessary for modern industry. The card depicts the 42,000-ton British Petroleum Tanker, 'British Prestige'.

ELECTRIC TRAM *Electric Power*. The first electrically driven vehicle was built by Robert Davidson. His 7-ton electric locomotive was tried on the Edinburgh to Glasgow Railway in 1842. The first electric tramway system did not appear until 1879 when Dr. Werner Siemens's tramway opened at the Berlin Exhibition of that year. In 1888 the first practical overhead wire system was introduced by the Union Passenger Railway Company of Richmond, Virginia, U.S.A. The picture shows a double decker electric tram used in Bradford until 1950.

MONORAIL *Electric Power*. The monorail system can carry passengers at enormous speeds between short stops, in cars suspended high above the streets. Although many forms have been tried, including one driven by propellers which was tried in Glasgow in 1930, the most famous was built in 1901 in Wuppertal in Germany. Its far-sighted inventor, the engineer, Eugene Langen, built it to last, and during its life it has carried over 850 million passengers.

ELECTRIC LOCOMOTIVE *Electric Power*. Electric power is cleaner than steam power and does not require the same running attendance. It has obvious advantages for underground railways. Electricity on main lines has been in use on the Continent and in some parts of Britain for years. The modernisation of British Rail includes the electrification of the main line from London to Birmingham, Liverpool and Manchester. The picture shows British Rail's 25 KV A.C. Electric Locomotive.

Cable Cars
Swiss Alps

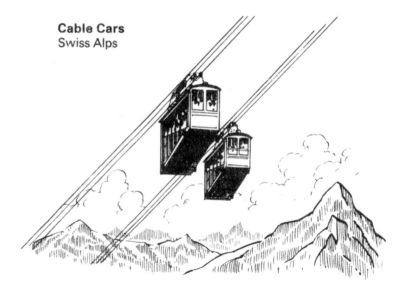

EARLY MOTOR CAR *Internal Combustion/Petrol.* The invention of the motor car was to transform modern society. The first use of the internal combustion engine was by Gottlieb Daimler in an experimental motor bicycle in 1885, which was followed by Carl Benz's 3-wheeled 'Dog Cart'. In 1896 Henry Ford built a tiny 2-cylinder car in a shed in his back yard and just over a decade later the Model T Ford, the '*Tin Lizzie*', was coming off the production line. The Model T (shown on the card) was the most popular car of all time. Over 15 million were built.

MOTOR CYCLE *Internal Combustion/Petrol.* The first practical motor cycle was the Wolfmüller motor bicycle of 1894. This machine was capable of 24 m.p.h. From then on motor cycles became one of the most popular means of individual transport, being cheap and speedy. Many developments from the motor cycle have occurred, and today there is a whole family of motorised bicycles. There are many famous makes of motor cycles and the illustration shows a Matchless 500 c.c. The fastest speed ever attained on a motor cycle was 224 m.p.h., by Bill Johnson on a Triumph Bonneville Special Streamliner at Bonneville Salt Flats, U.S.A., on 5th September 1962.

BLUEBIRD *Internal Combustion/Petrol.* The modern motor car with its smooth streamlined shape, automatic drive and comfortable seating is the product of years of scientific research and design. A great deal is learnt by the motor industry from the performances of racing cars and special speed trials like those undertaken by Donald Campbell in *Bluebird* (illustrated). On the 17th July 1964 Campbell broke the world land speed record in Bluebird with a speed of 403 m.p.h. on the salt flats at Lake Eyre, South Australia.

SNO-CAT *Internal Combustion/Diesel.* Captain Scott was the first to use motorised vehicles in the Antarctic and Sir Vivian Fuchs in his epic crossing of the Antarctic in 1955 used Sno-cats which showed good potential for the difficult Antarctic terrain. The Sno-cat is a tracked vehicle, powered by a Chrysler diesel engine which can give a speed of 15 m.p.h., and can carry up to a ton, in addition to pulling a further load of 5 tons on sledges.

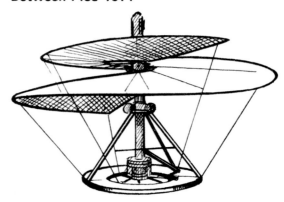

Leonardo da Vinci's
Flying Machine
Between 1488-1514

THE WRIGHT BROTHERS AEROPLANE *Internal Combustion/Petrol*. On the morning of the 17th December 1903 Orville Wright made a flight of 12 seconds over a distance of 120 feet at Kill Devil Hills near Kitty Hawk in the United States. This was the first powered, sustained and controlled flight in a heavier-than-air aircraft. Wilbur Wright in the fourth and last flight of the morning flew for 59 seconds and for a distance of 852 feet. This remained the record for four more years but the aeroplane had arrived.

AIRSHIP *Internal Combustion/Gas*. The step from the free floating balloon to a controllable airship was made in 1852 with Henri Giffard's rigid cigar-shaped balloon. By 1914 the German Count Zeppelin was building colossal airships. The *Graf Zeppelin* (illustrated) flew non-stop from Germany to Japan and in 1929 it made a round-the-world flight. Between 1931 and 1937 it was used in a regular passenger service between Germany and South America. Altogether, the *Graf Zeppelin* carried 13,789 passengers and flew 1,200,000 miles without an accident. ,

EARLY AIRLINER *Internal Combustion/Petrol*. The Imperial Airways operated services to the Continent, the Middle East and India. From 1931 to the outbreak of war in 1939 the Handley Page HP42s were used on these routes, and when introduced were the largest landplanes in regular service. The eight aircraft that made up the fleet had an aggregate of 10 million miles without a fatality. The HP42 E *Hannibal* class (illustrated) had a cruising speed of 95-100 m.p.h., and was powered by four 9-cylinder, aircooled Bristol Jupiter radial engines.

Early Airliners   The De Havilland DH16

The Boeing 247D

SUPERMARINE SCHNEIDER TROPHY PLANE *Internal Combustion/Petrol*. The Supermarine S6B seaplane won the much coveted Schneider Trophy in 1931. R. J. Mitchell designed the S6Bs from which were developed the famous Vickers Supermarine *Spitfires* that played a major role in winning the Battle of Britain in the Second World War. The S6Bs were monoplanes and their powerful Rolls Royce engines gave them speeds of over 400 m.p.h. The card depicts the S6B which made the world airspeed record of 407·5 m.p.h. in 1931.

FLYING BOAT *Internal Combustion/Petrol*. The Short S23 *Empire* flying boats of Imperial Airways (Class C is depicted) operated trans-Atlantic services before the 1939-45 War. For the first time in aircraft history they offered spacious accommodation which included room for 24 passengers, smoking room and a promenade deck, and could carry, in addition, 1½ tons of mail. The last service was run in 1947. They had a cruising speed of 165 m.p.h., and were powered by four 9-cylinder aircooled Bristol Pegasus radial engines.

TRANSPORT AIRCRAFT *Internal Combustion/Gas Turbine*. The Short *Skyvan* is a new light utility transport plane with two Turbomeca turboprop engines. It carries a crew of one and can accommodate 18 passengers or 4,000 lbs. of freight. It cruises at 180 knots at 10,000 feet, and has a range of 500 miles when carrying a 3,000 lb. load. It can also be used as a military plane for carrying paratroops.

HELICOPTER *Internal Combustion/Gas Turbine*. Among the many designs of Leonardo da Vinci was one for a helicopter, but centuries were to elapse before a practical helicopter was built. Helicopters in use today stem from the Russian-born Igor Sikorsky who designed and built the first practical single rotor helicopter. Sikorsky helicopters are world famous but years of patient experiment had to pass before the revolutionary IG-300 successfully took to the air in 1940. The picture shows a Royal Air Force Westland *Whirlwind* HCC Mk12 of The Queen's Flight, which has a gas turbine engine.

MODERN JET AIRLINER *Internal Combustion/Jet Propulsion*. Swept-back wings and tail-mounted engines help achieve greater speed and reduce noise in the passenger cabin. These features are found in the De Havilland 121 *Trident*, short-haul airliner, which made its maiden flight on the 9th January 1962. The *Trident*, has been designed to employ fully automatic landing equipment. It carries 101 passengers and has a cruising speed of 585 m.p.h. at 32,000 ft. It is powered by three Rolls Royce Spey engines.

FIRST TURBOJET AIRLINER *Internal Combustion/Jet Propulsion*. The introduction of jet propulsion enabled entirely new standards in flight to be realised; faster, smoother and longer flights became possible. The De Havilland *Comet* 4 DH 106 was the first pure jet airliner to be used on the North Atlantic route, a service which it inaugurated on the 3rd October 1958 with B.O.A.C. The picture shows the *Comet* 4. The *Comet* 4 has a range of 3,200 miles and carries 79 passengers at a cruising speed of 480 m.p.h. at 28,500 ft. It is powered by four Rolls Royce RA 29 Avon Turbojets.

VARIABLE WING AIRCRAFT *Internal Combustion/Jet Propulsion*. One way to achieve even faster speeds is to alter the shape of the aircraft's wings after it has become airborne, and the variable wing aircraft is the first step in this direction. This idea was conceived by Barnes Wallis, a British aircraft designer. The variable wing aircraft is conventionally shaped on take-off, but folds back its wings as it gains speed, until at very high speeds the wings are almost completely folded. The picture shows the American Convair F III A.

THE MESOSCAPHE *Electric Power*. The possibility of using submarine cargo and passenger carriers is coming closer to being realised. To the knowledge gained from the use of nuclear submarines has been added the ideas of the late Dr. August Piccard, who gave us the Bathyscaphe with which man can explore the deepest ocean chasm. His son, Dr. Jacques Piccard, invented the Mesoscaphe which, launched in 1964, has already carried over 25,000 fare-paying passengers beneath the waves of Lake Geneva in Switzerland.

Vertical Take-off Aircraft (Vought-Hiller-Ryan XC—1424)

In Level Flight

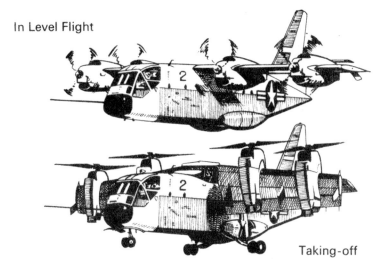

Taking-off

HYDROFOIL *Internal Combustion/Diesel*. One of the great difficulties in ship propulsion is to overcome the resistance the water exerts on the vessel's hull. A most successful way of avoiding drag, at least in small fast vessels, is to lift the hull out of the water when the ship is travelling at high speed. This has been done in the Hydrofoil, by placing lifting wings or foils under the hull near the bows, which at high speeds lift the craft's bows out of the water and enable it to plane along the surface. The picture shows the 'Vingtor' which operates between Bergen and Stavanger in Norway.

HOVERCRAFT *Internal Combustion*. The hovercraft, as its name implies, hovers over the surface, and does this by the downward draught of air that is generated by a propeller fan within the craft. The air so compressed is trapped under the vehicle by a curtain that surrounds the underside of the craft, and so lifts it off the ground or water surface. Forward motion is supplied by aero engines driving airscrews mounted on the outside. The world's first hovercraft, the SR.N1., invented by the British engineer, C. S. Cockerell, was operated in 1959. The card shows the Denny D-2 *William Denny* which can travel at 25 knots.

251

NUCLEAR SHIP *Nuclear Power*. The use of nuclear power, that is, using the energy of the atom to raise steam, is only just beginning but already great strides have been made. The first surface ship to be propelled by nuclear energy was the Russian icebreaker *Lenin*, built in 1959 with a horse power of 44,000. It is used to keep the Arctic sea lanes open during the winter. Like all icebreakers, the *Lenin* is specially designed to force its way through the pack ice; it has a reinforced steel hull and is extremely powerful. With nuclear energy, ships can stay at sea for much longer periods.

NUCLEAR SUBMARINE *Nuclear Power*. Nuclear submarines like the Royal Navy's *Dreadnought* (depicted) have heralded a new era in sea transport. Atomic energy enables these vessels to travel in the untroubled storm-free depths of the sea for months without refuelling. It was not until just before the 1914–18 war that the submarine was used in navies, but now nuclear powered military submarines have opened up the prospect of underwater cargo ships that could use the short sea route under the North Polar ice from the Atlantic seaboards to the Pacific.

SPACE ROCKET *Rocket Power*. On April 12th 1961 a Russian, Major Yuri Gagarin, was launched in the rocket spaceship *Vostok I*, and thus became the first man to go beyond the pull of earth's gravity into free orbit. The Americans, using a Mercury capsule on an Atlas booster rocket, put Colonel John H. Glenn into orbit on the 20th February 1962. This space craft is shown on the card. Since then other astronauts have orbited the earth, have walked in space free of the earth's gravity, while un-manned rockets have crashed on the moon or have travelled far beyond into space.

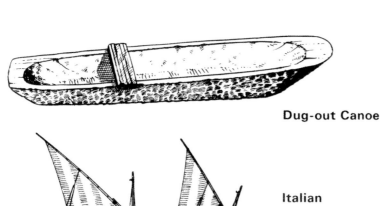

Dug-out Canoe

Greek Trader
8th century B.C.

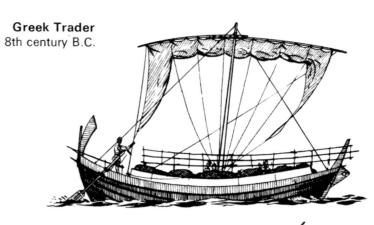

**Italian
merchantman**
13th century

Swedish Trader
1760

The 'Charlotte Dundas' 1802

The 'City of Paris' 1888

The 'Savannah'. Nuclear Ship 1959

Britain's green and pleasant land would be neither without the millions of trees that adorn our countryside, gardens, roadsides and even our streets. The 17th set of tea cards produced by Brooke Bond, *Trees in Britain* was a celebration of this hugely important part of our environment. Although only 25 different species of tree were covered in the set, there were 50 cards as, unusually, each subject had two cards devoted to it. One card provided a 'portrait' of the tree while another showed its leaves, flowers and fruit.

This set was illustrated and described by Michael Youens who was also to produce *British Costume* for Brooke Bond and a number of military themed books for other publishers. Youens' studies of the full trees showed them as they might typically be found, by a stream, on a hillside or in open parkland, while the second card of each pair was a delightfully detailed, annotated close up, referenced to the text.

The display album includes an introduction by Michael Youens and included throughout the album and on the inside of the front and back covers are a number of nicely executed black and white drawings, with a host of illustrations at the end of the album showing twigs and buds to help with the identification of deciduous trees in winter.

Note the twists and turns to the Oak's branches.

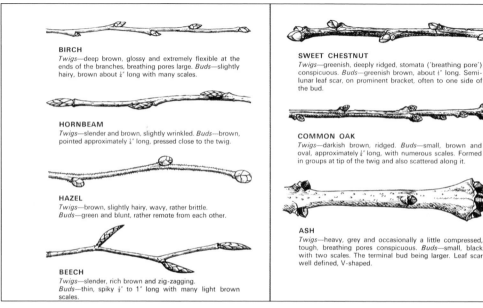

BIRCH
Twigs—deep brown, glossy and extremely flexible at the ends of the branches, breathing pores large. *Buds*—slightly hairy, brown about ¼" long with many scales.

HORNBEAM
Twigs—slender and brown, slightly wrinkled. *Buds*—brown, pointed approximately ¼" long, pressed close to the twig.

HAZEL
Twigs—brown, slightly hairy, wavy, rather brittle. *Buds*—green and blunt, rather remote from each other.

BEECH
Twigs—slender, rich brown and zig-zagging. *Buds*—thin, spiky ¼" to 1" long with many light brown scales.

SWEET CHESTNUT
Twigs—greenish, deeply ridged, stomata ('breathing pore') conspicuous. *Buds*—greenish brown, about ¼" long. Semi-lunar leaf scar, on prominent bracket, often to one side of the bud.

COMMON OAK
Twigs—darkish brown, ridged. *Buds*—small, brown and oval, approximately ¼" long, with numerous scales. Formed in groups at tip of the twig and also scattered along it.

ASH
Twigs—heavy, grey and occasionally a little compressed, tough, breathing pores conspicuous. *Buds*—small, black with two scales. The terminal bud being larger. Leaf scar well defined, V-shaped.

First issued in 1966, **Trees in Britain** was another set reprinted in 1973 and again the cards can easily be distinguished from the originals by the black text on the back. At the same time the album was also reprinted and there are a number of variations for both original and reprinted albums. The most well known album anomaly can be found next to card 15 where the second paragraph in some albums contains the word "Chestnut's" and in others the word "Chesnut's", missing out the first "t".

A collectable wall chart also accompanied this set, the chart having to be acquired directly from Brooke Bond.

Trees in Britain

BROOKE BOND PICTURE CARDS

ILLUSTRATED & DESCRIBED BY MICHAEL YOUENS PRICE SIXPENCE

Trees in Britain

Of the entire Vegetable Kingdom, two groups are of outstanding importance in human economy—the grasses and the trees. The trees provide us with timber, fuel (including coal, the fossilised remains of trees), paper, rubber, resins and many other different products. But in addition to being useful, trees are beautiful and interesting. They include the largest and oldest of living things, and species of tree still growing today reach far back into the history of life. There is fascination in getting to know them—their distinctive shapes, their bark, the form of the twigs, all of which, when known, make them as recognisable in winter as in summer when in leaf and flower. It is hoped that this series of cards will provide a stimulating introduction to dendrology, the study of trees.

Michael Youens

ILLUSTRATIONS ON ALBUM COVERS

Front Cover. *(l. to r.)* The Common Lime in Spring; the Horse Chestnut in Summer foliage; the Larch in Autumn.

Back Cover. *(Foreground l. to r.)* Spindle tree fruit; Hawthorn with with berries; Holly with berries; Rowan; group of Scots Pines. *(Middle Background l. to r.)* Two English Elms; Crab Apple; Screen of Lombardy Poplars behind farmhouse.

Note the twists and turns to the Oak's branches.

INDEX

The wood of trees, especially in temperate climates, shows distinct rings of growth which, normally being produced annually, give a guide to age. The growth rate as shown by the width of these rings has been shown to be a reliable guide to climate in past years, allowance being made for the fact that the rings naturally become narrower with increasing age.

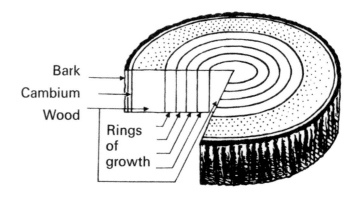

Bark
Cambium
Wood
Rings of growth

Maiden—Natural growth. *Pollard*—Lopped at the top of the trunk, sending up many side shoots. *Coppice*—Cut back at the bottom of the trunk, forming many side shoots.

MAIDEN   POLLARD   COPPICE

259

Conifers

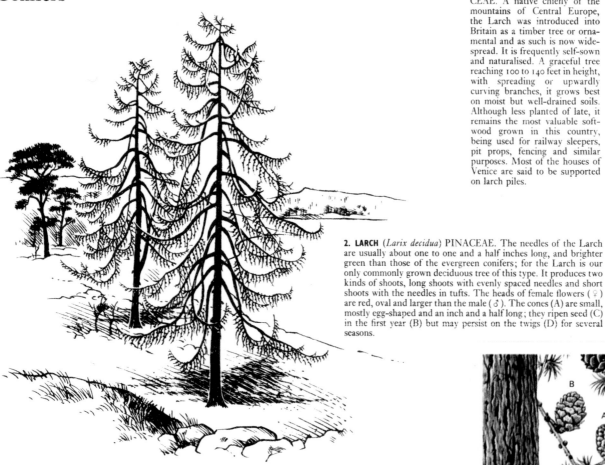

In the winter months the tall skeleton of the Larch looks almost dead, adorned only by its small, black cones.

1. LARCH (*Larix decidua*) PINACEAE. A native chiefly of the mountains of Central Europe, the Larch was introduced into Britain as a timber tree or ornamental and as such is now widespread. It is frequently self-sown and naturalised. A graceful tree reaching 100 to 140 feet in height, with spreading or upwardly curving branches, it grows best on moist but well-drained soils. Although less planted of late, it remains the most valuable softwood grown in this country, being used for railway sleepers, pit props, fencing and similar purposes. Most of the houses of Venice are said to be supported on larch piles.

2. LARCH (*Larix decidua*) PINACEAE. The needles of the Larch are usually about one to one and a half inches long, and brighter green than those of the evergreen conifers; for the Larch is our only commonly grown deciduous tree of this type. It produces two kinds of shoots, long shoots with evenly spaced needles and short shoots with the needles in tufts. The heads of female flowers ($♀$) are red, oval and larger than the male ($♂$). The cones (A) are small, mostly egg-shaped and an inch and a half long; they ripen seed (C) in the first year (B) but may persist on the twigs (D) for several seasons.

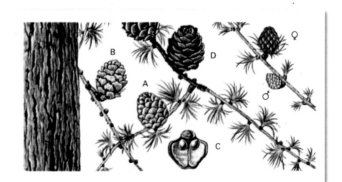

3. SCOTS PINE (*Pinus sylvestris*)
PINACEAE. Our only native pine, the Scots Pine occurs wild at the present time only in the Highlands of Scotland, but it was formerly more widespread. It is frequently planted, especially on lighter sandy soils in the S. E. of England and in East Anglia. Usually about 100 feet in height, when young the crown is pyramidal, but with age the branches become crowded at the top and the crown flattened. The Scots Pine provides a very valuable softwood timber, which was imported into this country from Scandinavia at least as early as the 9th century.

4. SCOTS PINE (*Pinus sylvestris*).
In common with all pines, the Scots Pine is an evergreen. The familiar grey-green needles are about two to three inches in length; they are distinctly twisted, and grow in pairs on short shoots from the twigs, falling complete with the short shoot after 3 or more seasons. Male flowers (♂) develop in groups at the base of a young growing shoot, and are yellowish. The cones (A), which are hard and up to 3 inches in length, are shortly stalked, and the scales (B) spread widely after the seeds are shed; the seeds (C) have large chaffy wings.

5. STONE PINE (*Pinus pinea*) PINACEAE. An attractive tree from its manner of growth, the Stone Pine is a rather squat tree from 40 to 100 feet in height. If growing in the open and not forced up by other trees it has a short trunk and a broad, spreading canopy of branches often wider than its own height. It is a native of the Mediterranean region from Portugal to Turkey and is not commonly grown in Britain, but there is a very fine specimen not far from the main gate of Kew Gardens (as illustrated). The trunk is very deeply fissured between the flattened, layered, greyish-brown segments of bark.

6. STONE PINE (*Pinus pinea*)
PINACEAE. The buds of the Stone Pine are very distinctive, the curled scales of each bud being furnished with long silvery hairs along the margins; these are interwoven so that the scales are matted together. The needles, like those of the Scots Pine, are in pairs, but are larger, being 3 to 5 inches in length; the cones (A young, B mature) are also larger. When ripe, the seeds (C) are bean-shaped and edible, and appear to have been used as food for the Roman armies of occupation in Great Britain.

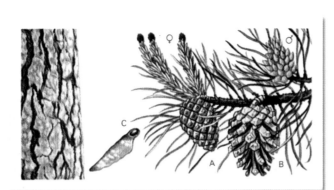

7. JUNIPER (*Juniperus communis*) CUPRESSACEAE. Occurring principally on chalk and limestone in southern England, but frequently on moors and heaths in the north and in Scotland and Ireland, the Juniper often forms a dense scrub on broken hill slopes. It very rarely becomes a tree as shown here, but is usually seen as a shrub about 6 to 10 feet in height. On the higher mountains, however, it takes up a mat form, completely flattened on the ground, and with much less prickly leaves.

8. JUNIPER (*Juniperus communis*) CUPRESSACEAE. The leaves of the Juniper are narrow and rigid with a sharply pointed tip, are up to ¾ inch in length, and grow in groups of 3, spreading round the twigs. The fruit is fleshy, a false berry formed by female (♀) scales corresponding to those forming the cone of the Scots Pine; in the Juniper, however, the scales become succulent and fuse together. The (A) 'berries' were formerly used medicinally and as an additive to gin. They are (B) black with a bluish bloom, and about the size of a currant.

10. YEW (*Taxus baccata*) TAXACEAE. The branches of the Yew are densely leafy, and the poisonous leaves, although inserted all round the twigs, are twisted below so that they spread out in two rows to form a flat surface; they are dark glossy green above with the margins recurved, and paler beneath. The male and female flowers are always on separate trees. The male flower (♂) is a small round cluster of stamens, and the female (♀) develops into a red berry-like fruit, also poisonous with a cup-like central excavation. The Yew is a favourite for topiary as it stands clipping well.

9. YEW (*Taxus baccata*) TAXACEAE. The Yew is most frequently met with in woods or thickets on limestone or chalk, usually as scattered individuals or in small groups among other trees. It normally attains about 30 to 40 feet, with a very heavy rounded crown and a massive stocky trunk often compounded of numerous risers which may be as much as 15 feet in diameter. There are many very ancient yews in Britain, but age determination is difficult as the original trunk often rots away. It was sacred to the Druids, and from the Yew (imported from the Continent since British wood was inferior) most archery bows were made.

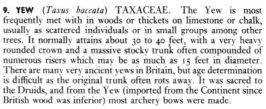

Broadleaved trees

11. COMMON LIME (*Tilia X europaea*) TILIADEAE. A familiar tree in streets, parks and avenues, the Common Lime is a tall species which may be over 100 feet high, with a wide, rounded crown. The trunk is almost smooth, but is often disfigured by large and unsightly warty projections developed upon it. It is not wild, but is generally believed to be a hybrid between our two rather uncommon native limes, *T. cordata* and *T. platyphyllos*. It produces a white, soft timber which is particularly excellent for carving and turning since it does not turn the knife blade to the direction of the grain.

12. COMMON LIME (*Tilia X europaea*) TILIACEAE. The blossom of the Lime is very distinctive, consisting of a long tongue-shaped yellowish wing or bracteole, from the central vein of which arises a stalk bearing several small yellowish-white flowers. These finally develop into almost spherical, short, hairy capsules often with 5 rather distinct ridges. The leaf of the Lime is roundish in outline with an abrupt point and is usually heart-shaped at the base; as with the Sycamore, greenfly are much attracted by the Lime, and its leaves are frequently sticky or dripping with 'honeydew'.

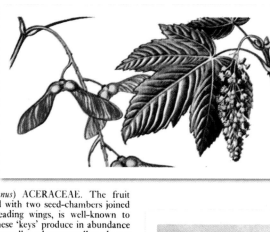

14. SYCAMORE (*Acer pseudoplatanus*) ACERACEAE. The fruit or 'key' of the sycamore, curved with two seed-chambers joined at the centre and two flat spreading wings, is well-known to children. The seedlings which these 'keys' produce in abundance are equally familiar but scarcely equally welcome to all gardeners working near sycamore trees. Before the fruits develop the flowers may be seen, hanging in cylindrical clusters at the ends of short leafy twigs; they are small and greenish-yellow in colour. The leaves are often sticky with honeydew, the upper side being much darker than the underside.

13. SYCAMORE (*Acer pseudoplatanus*) ACERACEAE. A species of maple, the Sycamore is not considered to be a native of the British Isles, but to have been introduced from Central Europe. Both on the Continent and in this country, however, it is absolutely naturalised and spreads rapidly where unchecked. It grows to about 100 feet in height and has a dense spreading crown. The bark is smooth and greyish, but tends to crack and then lift at the margins of the cracks so that large slab-like portions fall away. The wood is pale whitish yellow with a close grain and is chiefly used for veneers.

15. HORSE CHESTNUT (*Aesculus hippocastanum*) HIPPOCASTANA-
CEAE. It is one of the many mysteries of plant distribution that
a tree which is so easily grown and often self-sown throughout
Europe, temperate Asia and N. America should be restricted as a
wild species to a small area in the Balkans. The Horse Chestnut is a
stately tree with a large, round, densely leafy crown up to 100 feet in
height, and with the spread of
branches almost as great. It
was introduced into Britain
as an ornamental in the 17th
century. The wood is little
used, being soft and
perishable.

Note the upward
sweep of the Horse
Chesnut's branches,
tipped with erect
sticky buds.

18. HOLLY (*Ilex aquifolium*)
AQUIFOLIACEAE. The
flowers of the Holly occur in
short clusters in the axils of
leaves which are not of the current year's growth. They are
white and waxy in texture; male
(♂) and female (♀) flowers are
normally borne on separate trees.
The red berries which the tree
produces are too well-known to
need description. The leaves of
young holly trees and the lower
leaves of older trees are strongly
wavy-margined and very spiny;
the upper leaves of taller trees are
less spiny and often almost flat.

16. HORSE CHESTNUT (*Aesculus
hippocastanum*) HIPPOCASTA-
NACEAE. The most familiar part
of the Horse Chestnut is the spiny
seed-case, splitting open along
three 'seams' to reveal the one or
two seeds, 'conkers' (conquerors)
within. The glory of the tree as an
ornamental, however, is in the
erect cylindrical 'candles' of pink
or white flowers, each almost an
inch across and very attractive to
the bumble bees which pollinate
them. The leaves are formed of
5-7 leaflets all tapering to their
common point of insertion on the
stalks; the sticky leaf-buds are
used as winter decoration.

17. HOLLY (*Ilex aquifolium*)
AQUIFOLIACEAE. Found as a
native tree throughout most of
Britain, large Holly trees usually
occur as solitary scattered individuals; often the Holly is found
as a shrub, under the upper tree
canopy in woodland. It grows on
almost any soil, up to about 50
feet in height. The trunk is
slender, the bark dark grey and
smooth or cracking slightly in old
trees. The wood is very close-
grained and fine in texture, giving
a hard surface which takes a high
polish.

19. SPINDLE TREE (*Euonymus europaeus*) CELASTRACEAE. Occurring mainly in the south of England, but scattered through the remainder of the British Isles except northern Scotland, the Spindle is usually found as a shrub in bushy corners of woods, thickets and hedges, where it is often inconspicuous except when in fruit. Rarely it grows to tree-size, up to about 25 feet in height with a slender, grey, smooth trunk and a spreading, rounded crown. It prefers soils containing lime, and is usually found only in small numbers in any one locality. It is the only British representative of its family.

20. SPINDLE TREE (*Euonymus europaeus*) CELASTRACEAE. The most conspicuous feature of the Spindle Tree is undoubtedly the fruit, which is unlike that of any other British plant. The tree is most beautiful in autumn when laden with this unusual fruit. The bright pink, 4-lobed capsules are about half an inch long and hang in clusters on short leafy shoots. The flowers are small, greenish-white and inconspicuous, with 4 petals. The leaves taper to a sharp point, and are toothed all the way round the margin.

22. GEAN, WILD CHERRY (*Prunus avium*) ROSACEAE. In April and May the Gean, when growing in the open, is a glorious mass of white blossoms, each about an inch across, hanging in clusters which are effectively set off by the light green of the folded, developing young leaves. Cherries are formed in July and are bright or darker red in colour, with a taste varying from quite sweet to acid. The leaves when fully developed are dull green above and paler beneath, finely pointed at the tip, and have the margins regularly and neatly toothed all the way round.

21. GEAN, WILD CHERRY (*Prunus avium*) ROSACEAE. This elegant tree is frequent throughout most of Britain except for northern Scotland, growing especially on the better, well-drained soils. It prefers open woods, hedges and scrub, and attains 75 feet or more in height. The bark is reddish-brown, smooth and somewhat shining, and has a tendency to peel in papery strips. The Gean is certainly the ancestor of our cultivated cherries, either by direct descent or by hybridisation with the Sour Cherry (*P. cerasus*), which also occurs wild in Britain but is rarer. The wood is used for furniture-making.

265

23. HAWTHORN, MAY (*Crataegus monogyna*) ROSACEAE. Very common on all types of soil throughout Great Britain with the exception of northern Scotland, the Hawthorn is most familiar as the agricultural hedging for the partition of fields, retention of stock etc., for which its formidable armament of spines and ease of layering to form a dense barrier makes it very suitable. It is also the most frequent form of hill scrub. Where growing in the open, however, it will form a neat small tree up to 30 feet in height. The smooth grain of the very hard wood makes it very suitable for engraving work.

24. HAWTHORN, MAY (*Crataegus monogyna*) ROSACEAE. The Hawthorn begins to flower in May and continues into June; at this season the country air is often heavy with the sweet, cloying odour of the blossom, attractive to an extraordinarily numerous and diverse insect population. The Glastonbury Thorn, of legendary fame, is a variety (praecox) of this species which flowers and produces young leaves in winter (or, in very severe winters, in early spring) as well as flowering at the normal season. The fruit (haws) of the Hawthorn are a staple diet of birds in winter.

25. ROWAN, MOUNTAIN ASH (*Sorbus aucuparia*) ROSACEAE. The Rowan is widespread as a native tree in the British Isles, but found especially in the west and north; it is so attractive that it is also grown very widely in parks, along roadsides and in gardens. In the wild state its characteristic habitat is on heathy scrubland or on mountain rocks, where it may cling to a rock face with its roots penetrating deeply into a convenient crevice. The trunk is greyish and smooth and the crown narrow and sometimes rather scanty. The Rowan may grow to a height of 50 feet or more.

26. ROWAN, MOUNTAIN ASH (*Sorbus aucuparia*) ROSACEAE. As a decorative tree the Rowan, in common with several of its near relatives, has the great advantages of being attractive at all stages of its growth. The graceful leaves are usually divided into 6–7 pairs of narrowly oblong, regularly and sharply toothed leaflets, and dense clusters of white flowers with warm, creamy anthers are produced in May and June. In September, the bright scarlet, round fruits are conspicuous and beautiful, and the orange to scarlet autumn tinting of the leaves is also spectacular.

27. CRAB APPLE (*Malus sylvestris*) ROSACEAE. This, the ancestor of our cultivated apples, is found in woodland and hedges throughout most of the British Isles. It grows as a small tree of up to 35 feet in height with a rounded crown, and not uncommonly also as a hedge shrub. The bark is similar to that of the cultivated apple, cracking irregularly and falling off in flakes. The wood has a close grain and is hard; it needs careful seasoning, but has been employed in turning and also in the manufacture of heads for golf clubs.

28. CRAB APPLE (*Malus sylvestris*) ROSACEAE. The truly wild Crab Apple has the leaves and flower stalks and sepals hairless; a form with leaves hairy beneath and the flower stalks etc., woolly occurs, but is apparently always an offspring of cultivated trees. In most features the Crab Apple is very like the cultivated apples, but the fruit, produced in August and September, is extremely sour and unpalatable. In many country districts, however, a pleasant jelly is made from 'crabs'.

29. LONDON PLANE (*Platanus X hybrida*) PLATANACEAE. Of all the trees which have been planted in an effort to beautify our larger and smokier cities, none has been as successful as the London Plane. Its large rounded crown and straight smooth trunk, with the bark peeling off in copious flakes, is a familiar sight in most urban areas. The London Plane is believed to be of hybrid origin, produced by the crossing of the American Buttonwood (*P. occidentalis*), which does not succeed in this country, and the Oriental Plane (*P. orientalis*) of the Balkans and W. Asia, which can be grown here. It may attain 120 feet in height.

30. LONDON PLANE (*Platanus X hybrida*) PLATANACEAE. The leaves of the London Plane are not unlike some of the maples in shape (*P. occidentalis*, one of its parents, is also known as Sycamore in America), but they are thicker in texture than our Sycamore and are less coarsely and irregularly toothed, with broadly triangular lobes. Male (♂) and female (♀) flowers are separate but on the same tree. In the autumn at leaf fall the most conspicuous feature of the tree is the globular fruits (A), 2 to 6 being disposed along a pendulous stalk. The fruits disintegrate to liberate a large number of seeds (B), each provided with a 'parachute' of hairs.

Even after shedding its leaves the elm still makes an impressive sight towering above the hedgerows.

31. ENGLISH ELM (*Ulmus procera*) ULMACEAE. Probably native only in England, where it is common and characteristic except in the north, the English Elm has been planted also in Wales and Ireland, but less so in Scotland. It grows to a height of about 100 feet in hedges and along roadsides, and when isolated its tall outline, irregularly lobed especially between the heavy lower and spreading upper branches, makes it easily recognisable. Sucker shoots are abundant and the bark is hard and deeply fissured. Good elm timber is in demand for furniture, coffins, etc.

32. ENGLISH ELM (*Ulmus procera*) ULMACEAE. The leaves of the Elm are easily distinguished from those of British trees by their very unequal base, the one leaf margin being rounded and meeting the midrib at a considerably lower point than the other, which is more or less straight; they are frequently rough to the touch. The flowers (A), however, are very undistinguished, appearing in April and May before the leaves; they grow in rounded clusters, and the anthers are their most conspicuous feature. The fruit (B), produced in May and June, consists of central seed chambers (C) winged on each side.

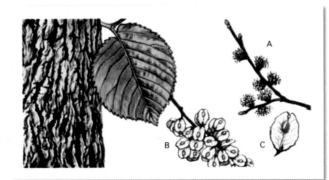

34. SILVER BIRCH (*Betula pendula*) BETULACEAE. The twigs of the birch are smooth and shining brown, bearing triangular, pointed leaves with slender stalks, so that they are easily set in motion by the wind. The leaves are irregularly toothed around the margin. Male (♂) and female (♀) catkins are produced on the same branch, the male being long and pendulous and showing yellow anthers; the female are less conspicuous, being at first shorter and erect, but when mature also pendulous (A) and producing winged seeds (B).

33. SILVER BIRCH (*Betula pendula*) BETULACEAE. The most graceful of all our native trees, the Silver Birch is also probably the best known, the smooth, silvery-white bark alone being sufficient to identify it — though in the lower part of the trunk this colour is marred by black cracks and warts; it grows to about 80 feet. The outline of the tree crown is rather narrow, the twigs pendulous. Occurring particularly on acid soils, it is seen at its best in the Highlands, where it often predominates. Much plywood is made from birch timber.

35. HORNBEAM (*Carpinus betulus*) CORYLACEAE. Less well-known than many of our native trees, the Hornbeam occurs wild principally in the Home Counties and E. Anglia, but as a planted tree it may be found throughout most of Great Britain. In cultivation the Hornbeam is a handsome tree 50 feet or more in height, with an attractively fluted trunk and a densely leafy crown. In the wild, however, it is most often seen coppiced and shrubby, like its close relative the Hazel. The timber is tough and strong and used, among other things, for piano parts and policemen's truncheons.

36. HORNBEAM (*Carpinus betulus*) CORYLACEAE. Of our other native trees the leaves of the Hornbeam most closely resemble those of the Elm, but are narrower in outline and less unequal at the base. The male (♂) and female (♀) catkins are found in different groups but on the same tree. When in fruit (A), the Hornbeam is unmistakable, as above the small seed-chamber at the base are produced two (B) 3-lobed leaf-like bracts which press closely against each other— a feature found in no other British tree.

38. HAZEL (*Corylus avellana*) CORYLACEAE. The sight of the long, pendulous male (♂) catkins of the Hazel, up to 2 inches long with bright yellow anthers, is one of the first signs of spring, produced as they are from February to April, or even earlier in mild winters. The female (♀) catkins, borne separately but on the same tree, are small and bud-like, with bright red styles and give rise at length to the well-known clusters of Hazel or Cob nuts (A & B) which are a favourite for dessert, and for making fancy chocolates etc. The leaves are oval, hairy, and narrowed to an abrupt point.

37. HAZEL (*Corylus avellana*) CORYLACEAE. One of our most familiar trees, the Hazel is almost invariably seen as a coppiced shrub forming dense thickets beneath the upper canopy of larger trees in open woods of oak and other deciduous species. It rarely attains a height of more than 15 feet, and spreads chiefly by abundant sucker shoots. Only rarely is it seen as a small tree with a smooth, thinly peeling bark. The branches of the Hazel are supple and may be used for weaving, like osiers. A Hazel twig is the usual instrument of the water diviner.

The massive twisting roots and smooth grey bark of the Beech make it an easy tree to identify.

39. BEECH (*Fagus sylvatica*) FAGACEAE. Perhaps the noblest of all our great woodland trees, the Beech is most at home on hills of chalk and limestone such as the Chilterns and the Cotswolds, where one may walk beneath giants up to 150 feet in height with massive, grey, smooth trunks. The crown is broad and densely leafy, casting a refreshing but rather sombre shade. Native only in the south, it is frequently planted elsewhere. Beech is one of our toughest native timbers, but is most suitable for domestic use, being rather perishable outdoors.

40. BEECH (*Fagus sylvatica*). FAGACEAE. Examined closely, the oval, rather shining leaves of the Beech are most attractive, with fine silky hairs around the margins and along the veins of the lower surfaces; when young they are very delicate and thin, and before leaf fall produce most beautiful autumn tints. The male (♂) and female (♀) flowers are separate on the same tree, the former being scattered in clusters along tassel-like stalks. The fruit (A), commonly known as 'beech mast', consists of one or two triangular nuts (B) in a hard prickly case which opens lengthwise along 4 'seams'.

41. SWEET OR SPANISH CHESTNUT (*Castanea sativa*)

FAGACEAE. A native of the Mediterranean region but of ancient introduction, generally believed to have been imported into Great Britain by the Romans, the Sweet Chestnut has proved very much at home in our climate and is now extensively naturalised in southern England and the Midlands, thriving best on light soils. A large tree often growing to 100 feet in height and with a wide rounded crown, it can usually be recognised by the bark alone, this being deeply fluted with the fissures ascending the trunk in a distinct spiral. The wood closely resembles that of oak.

There is no mistaking the fine twist to the sweet chestnuts' bark.

42. SWEET OR SPANISH CHESTNUT

(*Castanea sativa*) FAGACEAE. The Sweet Chestnut cannot in any way be confused with the Horse Chestnut. Instead of spectacular "candles", its flowers are attractive erect catkins, conspicuous for the bright yellow anthers of the male (♂) flowers, which are all situated at the top of each upper catkin while the female (♀) flowers are collected at the bottom; the lower catkins are male only. The leaf is not divided, but has an oblong blade regularly toothed around the margins. The fruit (A) (seed-case) is densely prickly over the whole surface, and usually contains three nuts (B)—the true chestnut commonly roasted for eating.

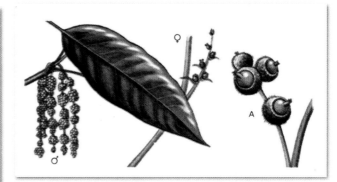

44. HOLM OR EVERGREEN OAK

(*Quercus ilex*) FAGACEAE. The dense whitish felty down of the young leaves of the Holm Oak soon vanishes from the upper surface, leaving it dark green and smooth; on the lower surface, however, it persists and darkens. The margins of the oblong leaves may be toothed or not. As in all oaks, the male (♂) and the female (♀) flowers are in different groups on the same tree, the male forming loose tassel-like catkins. The acorn (A) is similar to that of the Common Oak, but the scales of the cup are covered with short hairs.

43. HOLM OR EVERGREEN OAK

(*Quercus ilex*) FAGACEAE. Commonly planted principally in southern and central England, the Holm Oak is occasionally self-sown and naturalised. It is a native of western Europe and the Mediterranean region, and grows to a height of 70 feet. The crown is heavy and densely leafy, giving a deep shade, and is sombre in appearance from the dark leaves. The trunk is furnished with a dark greyish, scaling bark. Holm Oak timber has been used for agricultural purposes, but tends to warp in the seasoning process.

Galls, produced on the tree being attached by gall wasps, are common on oak trees. The Marble Gall illustrated is one type, the Oak Apple another.

45. COMMON OAK (*Quercus robur*)
FAGACEAE. One of our commonest and best known deciduous trees, the Common Oak thrives best on heavy and alkaline soils, the Durmast Oak (*Q. petraea*) being the more usual on lighter acid soils. The Common Oak lives to a great age (1000 years and more), many very old individuals being found in the New Forest and other relict woodlands. When growing in the open its average height is about 75 feet with a broad rounded crown, but woodland specimens may be taller and more slender. The timber is the most valuable of our native hardwoods for strength and durability.

46. COMMON OAK (*Quercus robur*)
FAGACEAE. The leaves of the Common Oak are deeply and irregularly divided with rounded lobes, and almost or quite without stalks; at the base they do not taper to the midrib but have rounded, flap-like appendages on each side. The leaves of the Durmast Oak, also common but on more acid soils, lack these appendages and have stalks up to an inch long. Conversely, the groups of acorns (A) are stalked in the Common Oak but not or only shortly so in the Durmast. Hybrids between the two species occur. The Common Oak has slender male (♂) catkins up to about $1\frac{1}{2}$ inches long.

47. STRAWBERRY TREE (*Arbutus unedo*) ERICACEAE. As a British native tree, the Strawberry Tree is found only in the mild, moist climate of S.W. Ireland, where it is common in some localities, flourishing in rocky scrub and open woodland. It is commonly found as a shrub, but may also grow to a tree up to 40 feet in height, with a broad crown and rather rough bark. It may be grown in the warmer districts of southern England, but is essentially a Mediterranean species. The wood has a hard close grain and will take a high polish; it is chiefly used for marquetry.

48. STRAWBERRY TREE (*Arbutus unedo*) ERICACEAE. As is the case with most evergreens, the narrowly oval, pointed leaves of the Strawberry Tree are dark green above and rather leathery in texture; the margins are regularly toothed. Like most of the heath family, to which the plant belongs, the flowers are urn-shaped with recurved lobes at the mouth; they are creamy-white or pinkish in colour. After almost a year they produce the conspicuous fruits which give the tree its name. These are orange-red, warty, strawberry-like and about $\frac{3}{4}$ inch across.

49. ASH (*Fraxinus excelsior*) OLE-ACEAE. A large tree of 75 to 100 feet or more, the Ash is one of our most common and widely distributed species. It has a broad, dense crown and the bark is grey and smooth, or in old trees somewhat cracked. It grows particularly well on soils containing lime, and is rarer in acid localities. The wood is of considerable value to the Economy as it has more important applications than that of any other British tree. Although difficult to season, it is particularly resistant to sudden shock, and for this reason is much used for sports equipment and tool handles.

50. ASH (*Fraxinus excelsior*) OLE-ACEAE. The flowers of the Ash are unattractive, having no petals or sepals since they are pollinated by wind and thus have no need to attract insects; they appear in April and May, and the fruit is set in October and November. This is a winged 'key' rather like half that of a Sycamore key but almost symmetrical. The clear green graceful leaves are composed of mostly 9 to 11 lance-shaped, regularly toothed leaflets. In winter and spring the most conspicuous feature of the Ash is the jet black buds, which contrast strikingly with the grey-green twigs.

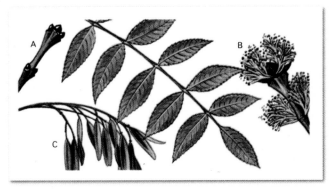

Winter identification of deciduous trees in this series

LARCH

Twigs—blackish, slender, ridged with scales and leaf scars. Spur shoots form prominent black knobs. *Buds* — small, numerous, with single bud at tip of the twig.

LIME

Twigs—greenish, slender and shiny, with tendency to zig-zag, the leaf scars small, oval. *Buds*—egg-shaped, red, with two visible scales of unequal size.

SYCAMORE

Twigs—greyish brown, ridged, leaf scars prominent, shallowly V-shaped. *Buds*—bright green, several scales turning brown at the tips. Terminal bud larger.

HORSE CHESTNUT

Twigs—stout, dark brown, wrinkled, breathing pores, horse-shoe shaped leaf scars prominent. *Buds*—large up to 1" long, sticky, with many scales.

SPINDLE TREE

Twigs—smooth and green. *Buds*—glossy, green, pointed with several scales, leaf scar very narrow.

GEAN

Twigs—brown, wrinkled, often shining, with conspicuous leaf scars. *Buds*—egg-shaped, brown and glossy, mostly gathered on spur shoots along the side of the twig, the terminal bud solitary.

HAWTHORN

Twigs—greyish brown with single thorns, leaf scars, small semilunar. *Buds*—small, rounded, with numerous scales.

ROWAN

Twigs—dark, purplish smooth or straight. Leaf scars prominent, triangular. *Buds*—fairly large, yellowish, woolly with purple-black scales, growing close to the twig.

CRAB APPLE

Twigs—brown, wrinkled, downy at the extreme tip. *Buds*—small, pointed and close to twig, scales numerous.

LONDON PLANE

Twigs—greenish brown, buds rather distant. *Buds*—large, conical, enclosed in a single bud scale. Leaf scar narrow almost surrounding bud.

ENGLISH ELM

Twigs—dark brown to blackish, wrinkled. *Buds*—small and dark.

BIRCH

Twigs—deep brown, glossy and extremely flexible at the ends of the branches, breathing pores large. *Buds*—slightly hairy, brown about $\frac{1}{4}$" long with many scales.

HORNBEAM

Twigs—slender and brown, slightly wrinkled. *Buds*—brown, pointed approximately $\frac{1}{4}$" long, pressed close to the twig.

HAZEL

Twigs—brown, slightly hairy, wavy, rather brittle. *Buds*—green and blunt, rather remote from each other.

BEECH

Twigs—slender, rich brown and zig-zagging. *Buds*—thin, spiky $\frac{1}{2}$" to 1" long with many light brown scales.

SWEET CHESTNUT

Twigs—greenish, deeply ridged, stomata ('breathing pore') conspicuous. *Buds*—greenish brown, about $\frac{1}{5}$" long. Semi-lunar leaf scar, on prominent bracket, often to one side of the bud.

COMMON OAK

Twigs—darkish brown, ridged. *Buds*—small, brown and oval, approximately $\frac{1}{4}$" long, with numerous scales. Formed in groups at tip of the twig and also scattered along it.

ASH

Twigs—heavy, grey and occasionally a little compressed, tough, breathing pores conspicuous. *Buds*—small, black with two scales. The terminal bud being larger. Leaf scar well defined, V-shaped.

THE BERKSHIRE PRINTING CO. LTD., READING, ENGLAND

Flags & Emblems of the World was the 18th set issued by Brooke bond and was first issued in 1967. This set was illustrated by G. Mussett and N. Manwaring who are described on the front cover of the display album and on the backs of the cards as "Herald Painters."

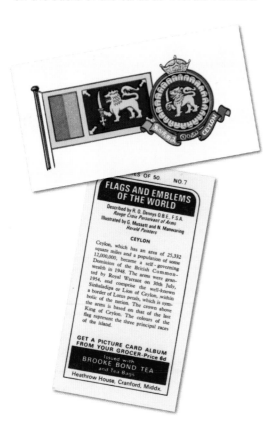

The descriptions were provided by Rodney Onslow Dennys, O.B.E., F.S.A. and Rouge Croix Pursuivant of Arms. This latter title identifies Dennys, a former Lieutenant Colonel who had a distinguished career in the Intelligence Corps during the Second World War, as an officer of the College of Arms in London and an authority on heraldic symbols. The display album includes an interesting

introduction by Rodney Dennys and a list of the countries covered on the cards. The reader is warned that, such is the rapid pace of change of these emblems "Changes have been made in the emblems of very many states in recent years and are constantly occurring; some may even have taken place in one or two of those shown here, by the time we go to press." Over 40 years later, there have certainly been changes, some small, such as the emblem of Ceylon (now Sri Lanka) and some far more radical such as the flags and emblems of South Africa and Iran. It is also interesting to see how details in the text, one of the most obvious being the populations of countries, have changed over the last four decades.

Included throughout the album are a number of black & white illustrations enhancing the details on the cards or adding extra points of interest. The inside front cover has an illustration showing the different parts which comprise "a heraldic achievement" while the back cover gives information on how Arms are granted.

Tea-picking in Assam, India

Emblems of the

HOW ARMS ARE GRANTED

In England Armorial Bearings have been granted by or under the authority of the Sovereign for the last five hundred years and more. In the case of eminent men and certain corporate bodies, Armorial Bearings are normally granted by Letters Patent of the Kings of Arms (the senior heralds), acting under the authority delegated to them by the Sovereign, and subject to the approval of the Duke of Norfolk as hereditary Earl Marshal. In the case of British Colonial Territories and of the Commonwealth Countries of which Her Majesty is Queen, Armorial Bearings are granted by Royal Warrant, signed by The Queen at the top and countersigned at the foot by the Secretary of State concerned. The Royal Warrant is

Red Cross

St. John Ambulance Brigade

Red Crescent
(Muslim equivalent of the Red Cross)

addressed to the Earl Marshal, describes the Armorial Bearings granted and assigned, and directs him to have them recorded in the Official Registers of the College of Arms, so that all concerned may have knowledge of them. Garter King of Arms advises the Commonwealth authorities on questions of heraldic practice and law and on the design of the proposed new Arms, and they also consult Garter about any changes, or the adoption of new Arms, and record their actions in the Registers of the College of Arms. In England, as in most countries, it is an offence to use or display the Royal or State Arms without authority and care should be taken not to use any of the Arms illustrated here, without first ascertaining from the authority concerned whether this is in order.

❖

THE DESIGN ON THE FRONT COVER
consists of the flags of
St. George (England), Jamaica,
St. Andrew (Scotland),
and the Sovereign Order of St. John,
with a lion of England over all

❖

❖

THE DESIGN ON THE BACK COVER
consists of an ancient compass rose,
surrounded by emblems appropriate to
different countries, and linked by
stylised foliage representing flowers
and leaves of the tea plant

❖

The display album for this 50-card set included the now familiar removable order form for buying previously issued cards and albums and was yet another set officially reprinted in 1973 with the reprinted cards identifiable by the black text on the reverse.

For collectors interested in rare or unusual elements, there was a wall chart that accompanied this set and rumours abound of a set of these cards with some of the pictures having been printed upside down.

BROOKE BOND
PICTURE CARDS

FLAGS & EMBLEMS of the WORLD

By R.O. Dennys, O.B.E., F.S.A., Rouge Croix Pursuivant of Arms
Illustrated by G. Mussett and N. Manwaring, Herald Painters

PRICE SIXPENCE

FROM EARLIEST TIMES kings and peoples have used emblems to identify themselves in battle or for government and ceremonial purposes. With the development of heraldry in Europe after the twelfth century the dynastic and hereditary emblems of the sovereigns became associated with the countries they ruled. Changes have been made in the emblems of very many states in recent years and are constantly occurring; some may even have taken place in one or two of those shown here, by the time we go to press. The first twenty-three illustrate the development of royal and state heraldry in the British Commonwealth; the next seven show the arms of other European kingdoms, followed by six European republics which have continued in modified form their ancient arms, and three which use non-heraldic devices. North and South America and South Africa carry on the European tradition, while the emblems of Israel and Egypt show similar influence. We end with three of the oldest kingdoms in the world, whose emblems have been quite uninfluenced by European heraldry.

Rodney Dennys
Rouge Croix

The Armorial Bearings of the College of Arms, London, showing the different parts which comprise a heraldic achievement

Flags & Emblems of the World
INDEX

The population figures given for each country are estimates for mid 1967. They are based upon the latest published figures adjusted in line with the average annual changes recorded by census returns, etc.

Where different authorities give varying areas for the same country the more commonly accepted has been taken.

*The Second
Great Seal of
King Richard I,
1198*

1. UNITED KINGDOM The United Kingdom of Great Britain and Northern Ireland is 94,211 square miles in area, with a population of some 54,000,000. It has remained unconquered since the Battle of Hastings, 900 years ago. King Richard I, "Lion Heart," adopted the three gold lions on red as his arms about 1198, after returning from the Third Crusade, and in later centuries different quarterings were added or abandoned for dynastic reasons. The Royal Arms assumed their present form in 1837, with England quartering Scotland and Ireland. The Union Flag began in 1707 as the combined crosses of St. George and St. Andrew, and that of St. Patrick was added in 1801.

3. AUSTRALIA The Commonwealth of Australia, inaugurated on 1st January, 1901, is 2,967,741 square miles in area with a population of some 11,550,000. The armorial bearings were granted by Royal Warrant on 19th September, 1912. We illustrate here only the shield, in order to show more clearly the very interesting quarterings, which represent the States of New South Wales, Victoria, Queensland, South Australia, Western Australia, and Tasmania. The crest is a seven-pointed star of gold, and the supporters are a Kangaroo and an Emu, both in their natural colours, usually represented with sprigs of wattle flowers and leaves.

2. CANADA The Dominion of Canada, which came into being on 1st July, 1867, is the oldest of the independent Commonwealth countries. It is 3,851,809 square miles in area with a population of some 19,500,000. The arms were granted by Royal Proclamation on 21st November, 1921, and consist of the British Royal quarterings of England, Scotland and Ireland, with the old Royal Arms of France in the fourth quarter (commemorating the countries from which Canada was mainly colonised), together with three conjoined maple leaves in base to represent the Dominion. The symbolism of the supporters and crest is similar. The National Flag came into being on 15th February, 1965.

4. NEW ZEALAND The Commonwealth Kingdom of New Zealand has an area of 103,939 square miles and a population of some 2,700,000. Captain Cook first charted the islands in 1769. British settlement followed, and a large measure of self-government was granted in 1852, with Dominion status in 1907. The armorial bearings were granted by Royal Warrant on 26th August, 1911, and contain allusions to the position of New Zealand in the South Seas and the principal products, occupations and peoples of the country. The crest was a demi-lion holding aloft the Union Flag, but in 1956 a Royal Crown was placed above the shield.

Tea-picking in Assam, India

Arms for Captain James Cook (1728-1779), South Pacific Explorer

6. PAKISTAN The Commonwealth Republic of Pakistan, with an area of 365,529 square miles and a population of some 110,000,000, was granted independence in 1947 and became a Republic within the Commonwealth in 1956. The armorial bearings were adopted on independence and the shield is comprised of charges alluding to the principal products of the country, jute, wheat, cotton and rice, while the crescent and star, by way of crest, is the symbol of Islam. The motto, which is in Urdu and Bengali, means Discipline, Unity, Fate.

5. INDIA The Commonwealth Republic of India, with an area of 1,261,597 square miles and a population of nearly 450,000,000, was granted independence on 15th August, 1947, and the constitution came into force in 1950. The lion emblem is based on the capital of the Ashoka pillar at Sarnath, erected to commemorate the place where Buddha first proclaimed his gospel of peace. The saffron yellow stripe in the flag symbolises courage and the spirit of renunciation, the white stripe purity and truth, and the green faith and fertility. In the centre of the flag is the 'Dharma Chakra' or Wheel of Law.

7. CEYLON Ceylon, which has an area of 25,332 square miles and a population of some 12,000,000, became a self-governing Dominion of the British Commonwealth in 1948. The arms were granted by Royal Warrant on 30th July, 1954, and comprise the well-known Sinhaladipa, or Lion of Ceylon, within a border of Lotus petals, which is symbolic of the nation. The crown above the arms is based on that of the last King of Ceylon. The colours of the flag represent the three principal races of the island.

8. GHANA Formerly the British Colony of the Gold Coast, Ghana was granted independence on 6th March, 1957, becoming a Republic within the Commonwealth in 1960. It has an area of 92,100 square miles and a population of some 7,700,000. The armorial bearings were granted by Royal Warrant on 4th March, 1957. The crossed stick and sword represent the administration, and the castle alludes to the national Government, while the cocoa-tree and mine-shaft allude to the main produce and activities. The red in the flag represents independence, the gold the wealth of the country, and the green the forest and farms.

9. MALAYSIA With an area of about 130,000 square miles, and a population of some 9,000,000, Malaya became an independent Kingdom within the Commonwealth in 1957. It was enlarged by the accession of Singapore, Sarawak and Sabah (formerly British North Borneo) in 1963, but Singapore seceded in 1965. The armorial bearings were adopted by the Malay Rulers and approved by The Queen on 18th March, 1952. The five golden kris in the chief of the shield represent the former Unfederated Malay States of Johore, Kedah, Perlis, Kelantan and Trengganu; while the quarterings represent the other states, before the departure of Singapore. The motto means Unity is Strength.

10. CYPRUS For long a part of the Byzantine Empire, Cyprus was conquered in 1191 by Richard I of England. He sold it to the Knights Templars who shortly afterwards sold it to the King of Jerusalem, and thereafter it became the principal Crusader Kingdom in the Eastern Mediterranean, until conquered by the Turks in 1571. It came under British administration in 1878 and was annexed in 1914, as a Crown Colony, becoming a Republic within the Commonwealth in 1960. It has an area of 3,572 square miles and a population of some 600,000. Since independence, an emblem of a dove bearing an olive branch has been used.

*The Queen's Personal Flag
for use in Sierra Leone*

11. NIGERIA The Federal Republic of Nigeria has an area of 356,669 square miles and a population of some 60,000,000. It was granted independence on 1st October, 1960, and became a Republic within the Commonwealth in 1963. The armorial bearings were granted by Royal Warrant on 28th April, 1960. The shield represents the two major rivers, Niger and Benue, with their confluence in the middle of the country. The eagle crest is symbolic of strength and determination, while the "coctus specta-bilis" flowers are commonly found in Nigeria. Each of the Regions, Northern, Eastern, Mid-Western, and Western, also has its own armorial bearings.

13. TANZANIA The United Republic of Tanzania (formerly Tanganyika and Zanzibar) was granted independence on 9th December, 1961 and became a Republic within the Commonwealth a year later. Its total area is about 362,688 square miles, with a population of around 10,300,000. The armorial bearings were granted by Royal Warrant on 6th December, 1961. This was the first occasion on which an African warrior's shield was used to display the charges, which allude to the country and its sea and lakes, while the torch of freedom and knowledge is within linked rings representing the unity of the principal races.

12. SIERRA LEONE Becoming a Commonwealth Kingdom on 27th April, 1961, Sierra Leone has an area of some 27,925 square miles and a population of about 2,350,000. The armorial bearings were granted by Royal Warrant on 1st December, 1960. The lion on the shield and the chief "dancetty of three points" are plays upon the name of the country; the wavy blue and white in base represents the sea, which has played such a large part in its history, while the torches denote education. The palm trees allude to the palm oil, which is one of the principal products of the country.

Sir Henry Morgan (c.1635-1688), the buccaneer who became Lieutenant-Governor of Jamaica

15. TRINIDAD AND TOBAGO With a combined area of about 1,980 square miles and population of some 1,000,000, the Territory was granted independence as a Commonwealth Kingdom on 31st August, 1962. The very attractive arms were granted by Royal Warrant on 9th August, 1962. Humming birds abound in the islands, while the three ships represent part of the fleet of Christopher Columbus, who discovered the islands in 1496. The ship's wheel upon the Royal Helm alludes to their maritime interests, while the Scarlet Ibis represents Trinidad and the Cocrico Tobago.

14. JAMAICA With an area of 4,411 square miles and a population of about 1,800,000, Jamaica has been British since 1670, and was granted independence on 6th August, 1962. It was a famous base for the buccaneers. The first Seal made under a Warrant dated 3rd February, 1661/2, shows the arms surmounted by a Royal Helm. A new Royal Warrant was issued on 8th April, 1957, specifying the armorial bearings. The motto was altered in 1962 to its present form. The pineapples on the red cross of St. George allude to the principal fruit of the island, and the crest to its largest reptile. The supporters represent the aboriginal inhabitants, the peace-loving Arawak Indians.

16. UGANDA With an area of 93,981 square miles and a population of some 8,000,000, Uganda was granted independence on 9th October, 1962, and became a Republic within the Commonwealth a year later. The arms were granted by Royal Warrant on 3rd September, 1962, upon an African warrior's shield, with two spears of estate crossed behind it. The drum symbolises the kingdoms and the traditional culture of Uganda, and the sun refers to the fact that it lies astride the Equator; the blue and white allude to the great lakes, sources of the Nile. The kob and the crested crane are indigenous.

A ship of the time of Columbus

Arms of Philippe Villiers de l'Isle Adam, Grand Master when the Knights of St. John were granted Malta in 1530

17. KENYA With an area of 224,960 square miles and a population of some 9,500,000, Kenya was granted independence on 12th December, 1963, and became a Republic within the Commonwealth a year later. The arms, granted by Royal Warrant on 15th October, 1963, are borne on an African warrior's shield. The colours refer to the people, the struggle for independence and the agriculture of the country; the cockerel holding an axe is regarded, according to local tribal customs, as heralding a new and prosperous life. The motto, in Swahili, means Work Together.

19. MALTA, G.C. The islands of Malta, Gozo and Comino, 122 square miles in area with a population of nearly 330,000, form the Commonwealth Kingdom of Malta. The white and red shield is of great antiquity, while the George Cross in the top corner was awarded in 1943 to commemorate the heroism of the people in withstanding ceaseless German air attacks. The crest represents the castle of the Knights of Malta, who withstood the famous Turkish siege of 1565, and their cross hangs below the shield. The dolphins supporting the shield, which rests on the Island of Malta, reflect its maritime interests.

18. MALAWI Formerly the Nyasaland Protectorate, Malawi has an area of 45,747 square miles and a population of around 4,300,000. It was granted independence on 6th July, 1964, becoming a Republic within the Commonwealth on 6th July, 1966. The arms were granted by Royal Warrant on 30th June, 1964, and reflect the principal features of the country. The lion and the leopard are indigenous to Malawi, as is the fish-eagle in the crest. The compartment on which the supporters stand represents the Mlanje Mountain.

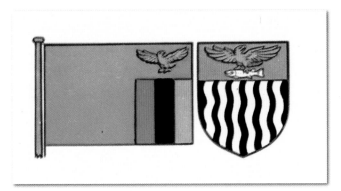

20. ZAMBIA Formerly Northern Rhodesia, the Commonwealth Republic of Zambia, which has an area of 290,586 square miles and a population of about 4,000,000, was granted independence on 24th October, 1964. The original arms, illustrated here, were granted by Royal Warrant on 16th August, 1939. Since these were printed, the Government of Zambia has altered the arms by removing the chief with the eagle and making the latter into a crest, with a hoe and pick below it, and adding as supporters an African workman and a woman in traditional dress. These have not yet been registered at the College of Arms.

A Carthaginian ship

Arms of Sir Stamford Raffles (1781-1826), founder of Singapore

22. SINGAPORE The town and colony of Singapore was founded in 1819 by Sir Stamford Raffles, and soon became one of the most important trading cities of South-East Asia. The island is 224 square miles in area, with a population of about 2,000,000. It was granted independence on 16th September, 1963, when it joined the Federation of Malaysia, but seceded from it on 9th August, 1965, although remaining in the Commonwealth. The arms were granted by Royal Warrant on 26th November, 1959. The symbolism of the arms alludes to brotherhood and virtue, with aspirations of a young country towards its ideals. The motto means Onwards Singapore.

21. THE GAMBIA The west coast of Africa was explored by Hanno, the Carthaginian, about 520 B.C., and the Portuguese were there in 1447; in 1588 the first British Africa Company was granted a charter to trade in The Gambia. Some 4,003 square miles in area, with a population of about 325,000, The Gambia was granted independence within the Commonwealth on 18th February, 1965. The armorial bearings were granted by Royal Warrant on 18th November, 1964, and comprise a Locar axe and a Mandinka hoe crossed in saltire. The crest is an oil palm nut tree, which is indigenous to the country.

*Arms of
the former
British Guiana*

24. BELGIUM The Kingdom of Belgium, with an area of 11,775 square miles and a population of some 9,500,000, has had a turbulent history. It was at Bruges that Philip the Good, Duke of Burgundy, founded the famous Order of the Golden Fleece in 1430. The Low Countries later passed by succession to the Hapsburg Emperors. Conquered by the French in 1794, they finally achieved independence in 1814. In 1830, the southern portion broke away to form modern Belgium, when the arms illustrated here were adopted. They are encircled by the chain of the Order of Leopold.

23. GUYANA Formerly British Guiana, with an area of some 83,000 square miles, a population of about 650,000, and extensive mineral wealth, Guyana became an independent Kingdom within the Commonwealth on 26th May, 1966. The armorial bearings were granted by Royal Warrant on 21st January, 1966, and consist of a Victoria Regia lily-leaf and two flowers, one open and the other opening, and in base a Canje Pheasant. The crest is a Cacique's crown between two diamonds, while the supporters are emblematic of the country.

*Badge of the
Order of the
Golden Fleece,
founded at
Bruges by
Philip the Good,
Duke of
Burgundy,
1429/30*

25. THE NETHERLANDS The Kingdom of the Netherlands, with an area of about 13,500 square miles, and a population of some 12,300,000, has played an important part in the history of Europe. Under the leadership of the Princes of Orange it was in the forefront of the struggle for freedom in the sixteenth century against the Hapsburgs. The States-General of the Netherlands used a Lion on their seal in 1578. The gold lion on its blue shield strewn with billets, of the Princes of Orange, became the basis of the arms of the Kingdom of the Netherlands formed in 1814, when it was given its well-known sword and sheaf of arrows.

A Viking ship

26. DENMARK The Kingdom of Denmark, which has an area of 16,608 square miles and a population of some 4,600,000, is one of the ancient kingdoms of Europe, and was once joined to England under King Cnut. The arms are very old, and are found in the twelfth century, in a form not unlike that in use today. The small coat of arms, here illustrated, is used by Danish Government authorities and is the national emblem. The Royal Arms contain this coat in the first quarter, with other quarterings and inescutcheons relating to the duchies and provinces forming the kingdom.

28. NORWAY The Kingdom of Norway, which has an area of 125,181 square miles and a population of some 3,700,000, is one of the oldest kingdoms in Europe. The lion was adopted about the end of the twelfth or early in the thirteenth century, and the present form of the shield came into use about 1285. The battle-axe was the principal weapon of the Vikings, who sailed from the rocky shores of Scandinavia to colonise eastern England and Normandy, and whose raids are so vividly described in the Anglo-Saxon Chronicle.

27. SWEDEN The Kingdom of Sweden, with an area of 173,436 square miles and a population of some 7,650,000, is of considerable antiquity. The shield with the three crowns first appears in 1364 on the seal of Albrecht of Mecklenburg, when he became King of Sweden. For reasons of space we show only the shield of the present Royal Arms, which have as supporters two crowned lions of gold, the whole upon a "pavilion" of red lined with ermine, and which are known as the Great Coat of Arms. The second and third quarters contain the arms of the ancient Folkung dynasty, and in the centre are the arms of the present Bernadotte dynasty.

29. GREECE With an area of about 51,182 square miles and a population of some 8,700,000, the Kingdom of Greece (Hellas) achieved its independence from the Ottoman Empire in 1821. The State Arms, shown here, are supported by two figures of Hercules. The Royal Arms, adopted in 1863, reflect the Danish origins of the present dynasty, but have not been shown here as they are too complicated for reduction to such a small size. They are, however, the same as the present Royal Arms of Denmark, and displayed in an escutcheon placed upon the Greek National Arms.

An ancient Greek warrior

30. MONACO The Principality of Monaco, on the shores of the Mediterranean, with an area of only some 360 acres and a resident population of about 22,500, is one of the smallest independent states in the world. The Grimaldi family has been associated with Monaco since the early Middle Ages, although the country changed hands on several occasions until 1297, when it was recaptured by a ruse, Francesco Grimaldi and his men-at-arms entering the castle disguised as monks. The supporters of the princely arms are in allusion to this. The descent has passed on occasion through heiresses, each family assuming the ancient name.

Arms of the City of Berne, capital of Switzerland

31. SWITZERLAND The Confederation of Switzerland, with an area of 15,950 square miles and a population of some 6,100,000, is one of the oldest republics with a continuous history. Practical independence of the Holy Roman Empire was achieved in 1499 and formal independence in 1648. As a result of the Geneva Convention of 1864, the distinctive arms of Switzerland suggested the Red Cross, by reversing the colours. Heraldry flourishes in the Republic and the arms of the cities of Switzerland provide many interesting examples, those of Berne, the capital, being shown in the album.

33. AUSTRIA The Austrian Federal Republic, first formed in 1918 on the break-up of the old Austro-Hungarian Empire, and re-established as a Sovereign State in 1955, after occupation by the victorious Powers, has an area of 32,376 square miles and a population of some 7,275,000. The Hapsburgs ruled Austria from the thirteenth century, and it later became the nucleus of the Austro-Hungarian Empire until 1918. The present State Arms, based on the ancient Hapsburg Royal Arms, were first adopted after the First World War, the broken chains on the eagle's legs being added after the Second World War.

32. PORTUGAL The Republic of Portugal has an area of 34,500 square miles and a population ,of some 9,000,000. Originally a fief of the Kingdom of Leon, the early Counts achieved independence after a series of wars with their overlords and against the Moors, between 1095 and 1279. Prince Henry the Navigator (1394-1460) initiated a series of brilliant discoveries along the West African coast and down to the Cape. The present State Arms continue the old Royal Arms, set upon an armillary sphere, an ancient nautical instrument, in memory of these Portuguese maritime discoveries.

34. POLAND The Polish People's Republic, established in 1952, has an area of 121,000 square miles and a population of some 32,000,000. The eagle has been the heraldic emblem of the Polish Kings since the early Middle Ages, and a very fine example of it appears on the Great Seal of Casimir the Great (1333-1370). The present State Arms, based on a sixteenth century design, were adopted in 1927 by the pre-war Republic and retained by the post-war Communist Government, thus continuing a traditional link with Poland's turbulent past, in which on more than one occasion it was a bastion of western civilization.

Arms of Maximilian I, Holy Roman Emperor (1459-1519)

Arms of the Kings of France, before the Revolution

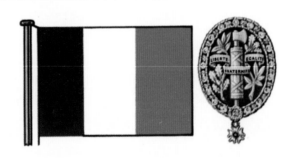

36. GERMANY The Federal Republic of Germany, with an area of some 95,958 square miles and a population of about 61,000,000, was formed in 1949 from the fusion of the three occupied Western Zones. The rise of the Hohenzollerns to Electors of Brandenburg, then Kings of Prussia and in 1871 Emperors of Germany, is a matter of history. The very ancient, and consequently simple, arms of this family were borne on an inescutcheon upon the breast of an eagle and, instead of supporters, the whole was shown upon the breast of an imperial eagle with outspread wings. The black eagle of the Federal Republic recalls its past royal emblems.

35. IRELAND The Republic of Ireland, with an area of 26,600 square miles and a population of some 2,750,000, achieved complete independence from Great Britain in 1937. Since 1172 the Kings of England had been recognised as Lords of Ireland, and the Anglo-Norman settlement brought with it many feudal institutions. In consequence, heraldic practice in Ireland has followed closely that of England. Originally the three antique gold crowns on a blue shield (now the arms of the Province of Munster) were regarded as the arms of Ireland, until Henry VIII and Elizabeth I adopted the well-known gold harp on blue, which has been retained by the present Republican Government.

37. FRANCE The French Republic has an area of 212,895 square miles and a population of some 48,700,000. The fleur-de-lys has been a royal emblem since the Dark Ages, but the golden fleur-de-lys strewn on a blue shield were only much later adopted as the Royal Arms. In 1376 the lilies were reduced to three, and remained the Royal Arms until the Revolution of 1789. Napoleon I adopted a gold eagle with outspread wings standing upon a thunderbolt, on a blue shield. Although the emblem of the Republic is officially only the flag, the device illustrated here is frequently used officially by the Fifth Republic.

Arms of the Hohenzollern Emperors of Germany

38. U.S.S.R. The Union of Soviet Socialist Republics, with its fifteen constituent federal republics, has a total area of 8,650,000 square miles and a population of some 235,000,000. The facts of geography and the chances of history tended to orientate the Russians towards Byzantium, and it is not surprising, therefore, that Ivan the Great adopted as his arms the two-headed eagle of the empire, whose heirs the Grand Dukes of Muscovy had long felt themselves. The Revolution of 1917 swept away all vestiges of the Romanoffs, and the new government adopted the non-heraldic emblem here illustrated.

Arms of the Vatican City State

39. ITALY The Italian Republic, with an area of some 131,000 square miles and a population of about 51,000,000, came into being in 1946, on the abdication of the King. The Royal Arms of the House of Savoy ceased, in consequence, to be used and the emblem shown here was adopted by decree on 5th May, 1948. This is a complete break with the past for a country with such a long and flourishing heraldic tradition. The Vatican City State, seat of the Pope, occupies a small enclave in Rome enjoying independent sovereignty, and the head-quarters of the Sovereign Order of the Knights of Malta are also there.

Arms of George Washington, First President of the U.S.A.

40. U.S.A. The United States of America, with an area, excluding overseas possessions, of 3,548,974 square miles and a population of some 200,000,000, achieved independence of Great Britain in 1783. The first President was George Washington, the descendant of an ancient English family whose arms, illustrated in the album, are believed to have suggested the design of the American arms and flag. The Congress of 20th June, 1782 adopted the design for the armorial bearings to be used on the first Great Seal of the republic, which have remained substantially unchanged from that day to the present. The thirteen stars above the eagle and the arrows in its claws record the founder States.

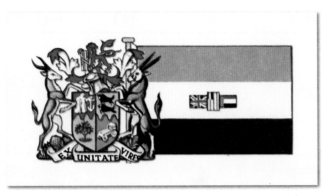

41. SOUTH AFRICA The Republic of South Africa has an area of 472,359 square miles and a population of some 18,500,000. The Union of South Africa was established in 1910, combining the earlier Boer republic and the old colonies of the Cape and Natal. The armorial bearings were granted by Royal Warrant on 17th September, 1910, and the four quarters of the arms include symbols alluding to the four provinces. The Cape is represented by the Virgin or Lady of Good Hope, and Natal by the two wildebeeste, while the orange tree alludes to the Orange Free State and the ox-waggon to the Transvaal.

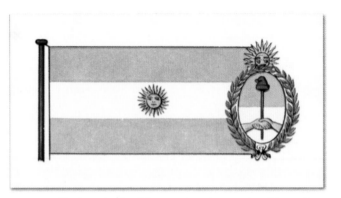

42. ARGENTINE The Argentine Republic, occupying a large portion of the southernmost part of the South American continent, has an area of 1,079,965 square miles and a population of about 22,500,000. First discovered in 1515 and gradually colonised by Spain during the succeeding century, the Argentine finally achieved independence from the mother country in 1816. The armorial emblem had been adopted in 1813 during the war of independence, and its symbolism was clearly inspired by that of the French Revolution, with the cap of liberty and clasped hands, symbolic of brotherhood and unity.

43. BRAZIL The Republic of the United States of Brazil, with an area of 3,289,440 square miles and a population of some 84,000,000, was originally colonised by the Portuguese in the early sixteenth century. In 1822 it became an independent Empire, under Dom Pedro, son of the King of Portugal, but his successor was dethroned and a republic declared in 1889. The emblem adopted shortly afterwards is an interesting example of the non-heraldic kind of devices frequently favoured by revolutionary governments. The stars in the centre represent the Southern Cross while the chaplet is composed of the leaves of coffee and tobacco plants.

44. MEXICO The United States of Mexico, once the cradle of an ancient civilization which was overthrown by the Spaniards under Cortes shortly after 1519, has an area of 760,000 square miles and a population of some 40,000,000. Following a successful revolt from Spain in 1821, a republican government was established. In 1862 the French installed Maximilian as Emperor, but he was executed five years later, and the republic was restored. The revolution of 1910 changed the social structure. The present emblem, first adopted in 1823 and re-approved in 1934, is based on old Indian symbolism.

*Detail of the
Imperial Crown
of Iran*

45. ISRAEL The Republic of Israel, with an area of some 7,992 square miles and a population of about 2,600,000, occupies a little over two-thirds of the total area of Palestine. The British mandate was relinquished in 1948 when Israel became an independent state. The seven-branched candelabrum, known as the Menorah, was proclaimed the official emblem of Israel on 10th February, 1949. It is one of the oldest Jewish religious symbols, and blue is of almost equal antiquity with it as a national colour, while the Star of David in the middle of the flag has been associated with the Jews since the Middle Ages, if not before.

47. IRAN The Empire of Iran (more generally known in England as Persia), has an area of 628,000 square miles and a population of some 23,000,000. One of the most ancient kingdoms in the world, with a recorded history going back several centuries B.C., Persia has played an important part in the affairs of Asia and eastern Europe. This very attractive emblem is surmounted by the Pahlavi Crown, one of the most striking of all royal crowns. The National Flag consists only of the three horizontal bands of colour, but in the Ensign and Military Flag the Royal Emblem is placed in the middle.

46. EGYPT The United Arab Republic was established on 1st February, 1958, following a union between Egypt and Syria, the former country having become a Republic in 1953 after a coup d'etat the previous year. Syria seceded from the union in 1961. The total area of Egypt is about 386,110 square miles, with a population of some 26,000,000. The arms, which show some European influence in their design, were adopted by Presidential decree on 25th October, 1958. The principal emblem of the Republic is the "Salaheddin Eagle" and the name of the U.A.R. is written in Kufi script beneath it.

48. ETHIOPIA The Empire of Ethiopia, with an area of approximately 395,000 square miles and a population of some 22,000,000, is one of the most ancient Christian kingdoms in the world. The Emperor claims descent from King Solomon and the Queen of Sheba. The Royal Emblem alludes to this with the Throne of Solomon depicted in the centre with a royal orb upon it, and two angels on either side as supporters. In front of the throne stands the Lion of Judah supporting a cross, a motif which is repeated on the National Flag. Below the emblem, in Amharic, is the legend "The conquering lion of the tribe of Judah."

A Japanese samurai

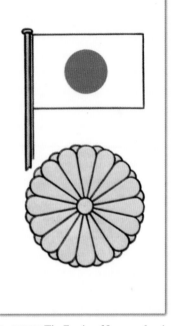

Flag of the North Atlantic Treaty Organisation

THE BERKSHIRE PRINTING CO. LTD., READING, ENGLAND

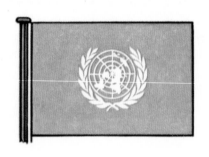

50. UNITED NATIONS The United Nations Organisation was brought into being on 24th October, 1945, and its permanent headquarters are at New York. The principal organs of the U.N.O. are the General Assembly, the Security Council, the Trusteeship Council, the International Court of Justice, and the Secretariat. Its simple flag is emblematic of the world interests embraced by the organisation. Other international bodies of a more regional kind are the Consultative Assembly of the Council of Europe, the North Atlantic Treaty Organisation, the Central Treaty Organisation, and the South East Asia Treaty Organisation, all of which have their own distinctive flags.

49. JAPAN The Empire of Japan, or Land of the Rising Sun, has an area of 142,505 square miles and a population of about 100,000,000. Japan's continuous history as a kingdom goes back some two thousand years, and its rulers claimed divine descent. The chrysanthemum of sixteen petals was the emblem of the Imperial House, but in recent years has come to be regarded as a national emblem as well. In Japan there is a well-developed system of family emblems, or "mon," which, like the heraldic emblems of Europe, were hereditary and used as a means of personal recognition in war and for identifying property in peace.

HOW ARMS ARE GRANTED

In England Armorial Bearings have been granted by or under the authority of the Sovereign for the last five hundred years and more. In the case of eminent men and certain corporate bodies, Armorial Bearings are normally granted by Letters Patent of the Kings of Arms (the senior heralds), acting under the authority delegated to them by the Sovereign, and subject to the approval of the Duke of Norfolk as hereditary Earl Marshal. In the case of British Colonial Territories and of the Commonwealth Countries of which Her Majesty is Queen, Armorial Bearings are granted by Royal Warrant, signed by The Queen at the top and countersigned at the foot by the Secretary of State concerned. The Royal Warrant is

Emblems of the

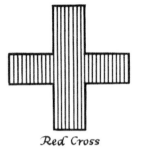

Red Cross

St. John
Ambulance
Brigade

Red Crescent

(Muslim equivalent of the Red Cross)

addressed to the Earl Marshal, describes the Armorial Bearings granted and assigned, and directs him to have them recorded in the Official Registers of the College of Arms, so that all concerned may have knowledge of them. Garter King of Arms advises the Commonwealth authorities on questions of heraldic practice and law and on the design of the proposed new Arms, and they also consult Garter about any changes, or the adoption of new Arms, and record their actions in the Registers of the College of Arms. In England, as in most countries, it is an offence to use or display the Royal or State Arms without authority and care should be taken not to use any of the Arms illustrated here, without first ascertaining from the authority concerned whether this is in order.

❖

THE DESIGN ON THE FRONT COVER
consists of the flags of
St. George (England), Jamaica,
St. Andrew (Scotland),
and the Sovereign Order of St. John,
with a lion of England over all

❖

❖

THE DESIGN ON THE BACK COVER
consists of an ancient compass rose,
surrounded by emblems appropriate to
different countries, and linked by
stylised foliage representing flowers
and leaves of the tea plant

❖

Technical illustrator Kenneth Rush provided the images that were used in Brooke Bond's 20th card set, *History of the Motor Car*, while motoring author Peter Hull supplied the text, Brooke Bond again bringing together two experts in their fields to produce a stunning collection. They were not, however, the only experts involved with this set.

The display album includes a foreword by Walter Owen Bentley, the famous "W.O." who founded the Bentley car company and designed the Le Mans winning Bentley and Lagonda cars in the 1930s. When *History of the Motor Car* was issued, "W.O." was 80 years old and it would have been difficult to find a more distinguished or respected personality to write the album's foreword. He outlined the difficulties of car design and acknowledged that he was "glad to see the designers of the different cars in the series are often named, though car designing is essentially a team effort…"

The vehicles featured on the cards are arranged in historical order starting from Cugnot's 3-wheel steam tractor in 1770 and the 12 mph petrol-driven Benz of 1885 all the way up to the four-wheel-drive Jensen sports car and Wankel-engined NSU Ro-80 of 1968. Adding to the appeal of each card, the manufacturer's logo is also included beside each car. This set is considered by many to be one of Brooke Bond's finest and heralded a new age for card collectors.

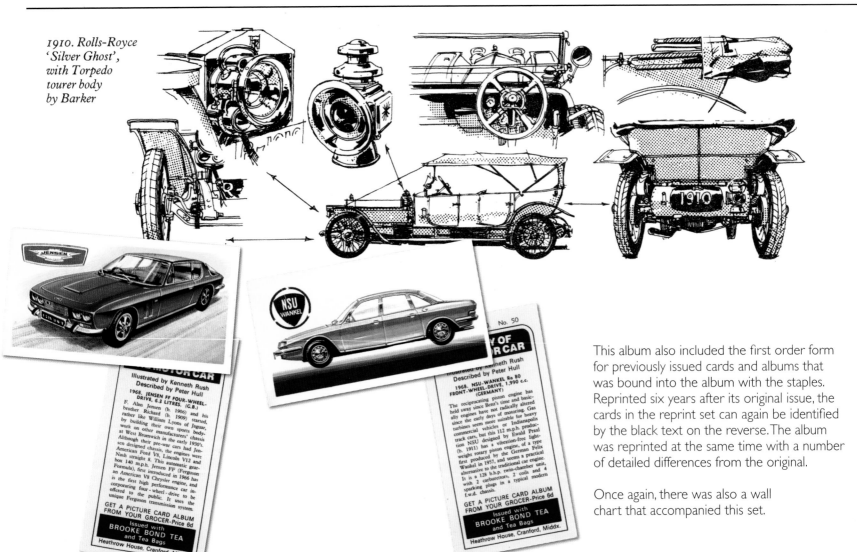

1910. Rolls-Royce 'Silver Ghost', with Torpedo tourer body by Barker

MOTOR CAR
Illustrated by Kenneth Rush
Described by Peter Hull
1968. JENSEN FOUR-WHEEL-DRIVE, 6.3 LITRES. (G.B.)
F. Alan Jensen (b. 1906) and his brother Richard (b. 1909) started, rather like William Lyons of Jaguar, by building their own sports body-work on other manufacturers' chassis at West Bromwich in the early 1930's. Although their pre-war cars had Jensen designed chassis, the engines were American Ford V8, Lincoln V12 and Nash straight 8. This automatic gear-box 140 m.p.h. Jensen FF (Ferguson Formula), first introduced in 1966 has an American V8 Chrysler engine, and is the first high performance car in-corporating four - wheel - drive to be offered to the public. It uses the unique Ferguson transmission system.

GET A PICTURE CARD ALBUM FROM YOUR GROCER-Price 6d
Issued with
BROOKE BOND TEA
and Tea Bags
Heathrow House, Cranford, Middx.

No. 50
...Y OF ...OR CAR
Illustrated by Kenneth Rush
Described by Peter Hull
1968. NSU-WANKEL Ro 80 FRONT-WHEEL-DRIVE, 1,990 c.c. (GERMANY)
The reciprocating piston engine has held sway since Benz's time and basic-ally engines have not radically altered since the early days of motoring. Gas turbines seem more suitable for heavy commercial vehicles or Indianapolis track cars, but this 112 m.p.h. produc-tion NSU designed by Ewald Praxl (b. 1911) has a vibration-free light-weight rotary piston engine, of a type first produced by the German Felix Wankel in 1957, and seems a practical alternative to the traditional car engine. It is a 128 b.h.p. twin-chamber unit, with 2 carburettors, 2 coils and 4 sparking plugs in a typical modern f.w.d. chassis.

GET A PICTURE CARD ALBUM FROM YOUR GROCER-Price 6d
Issued with
BROOKE BOND TEA
and Tea Bags
Heathrow House, Cranford, Middx.

This album also included the first order form for previously issued cards and albums that was bound into the album with the staples. Reprinted six years after its original issue, the cards in the reprint set can again be identified by the black text on the reverse. The album was reprinted at the same time with a number of detailed differences from the original.

Once again, there was also a wall chart that accompanied this set.

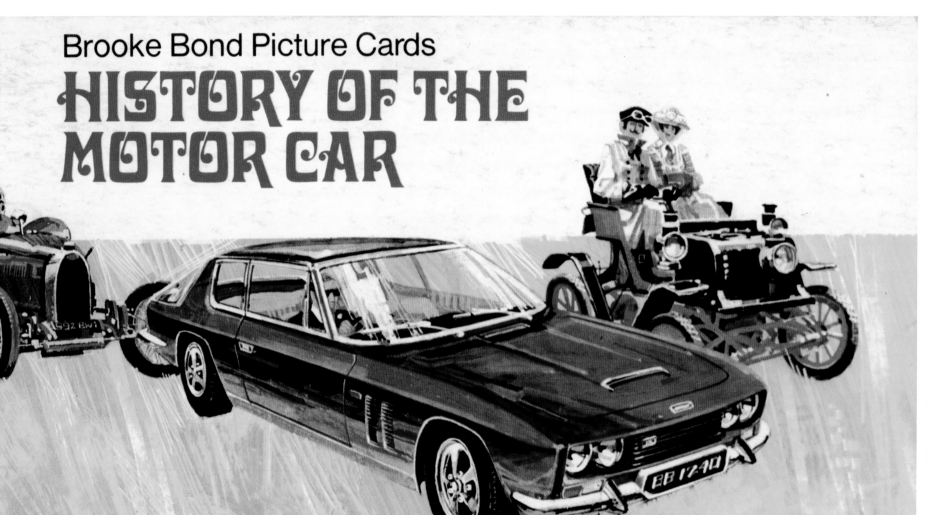

Brooke Bond Picture Cards

HISTORY OF THE MOTOR CAR

Illustrated by Kenneth Rush. Described by Peter Hull.

PRICE SIXPENCE

In recent years I have often entertained young people of school age to tea at my home, and have been surprised at their interest in the cars I designed nearly 50 years ago, as well as in the cars of today. These 'History of the Motor Car' cards cover the first 80 years of car production, with a glance at the steam road carriages which came before. Not all the famous makes could be included, of course, but generally the examples shown were either typical of their period, or else were leaders in some advanced feature of design.

It is unfortunate that originality in design costs money and does not necessarily lead to commercial success, though without it there would be no progress; and in this connection it is an interesting fact that it is far more difficult to think up a good simple design than a complicated one to achieve the same end.

I am glad to see the designers of the different cars in the series are often named, though car designing is essentially a team effort with one man, who knows exactly what the team is aiming at, taking overall responsibility. Frequently he shows what he wants by means of rough sketches, leaving the detail work to his team. I used to make a habit of driving 600 miles a day in the prototype of any new car I was responsible for, and at the end of the day when I was getting tired, any faults revealed seemed to be almost shouting at me for rectification.

As you read the text in this album and study the fascinating drawings, I hope you will be entertained as well as instructed—I know I was!

1914. D.F.P.

1939. Le Mans V12 Lagonda.

1930/31. 8 litre Bentley.

THE 50 CARDS ILLUSTRATED IN THIS ALBUM (cover illustrations are identified opposite card no. 50)

1 1770 Cugnot's 3-wheel Steam Tractor. (France)
2 1885 Benz 3-wheeler, 1.7 litres. (Germany)
3 1895 Panhard et Levassor 4 h.p., 1.3 litres. (France)
4 1898 Renault 1¾ h.p., 240 c.c. (France)
5 1899 'La Jamais Contente' Electric Car. (France)
6 1901 Mercedes 35 h.p., 6 litres. (Germany)
7 1902 Napier 35 h.p. Gordon Bennett Racing Car, 6.4 litres. (G.B.)
8 1903 Lanchester 12 h.p., 4 litres. (G.B.)
9 1903 Oldsmobile 5 h.p., Curved Dash, 1.5 litres. (U.S.A.)
10 1907 Rolls-Royce 40/50 h.p., Silver Ghost, 7/7.4 litres. (G.B.)
11 1908 Ford Model T, 2.9 litres. (U.S.A.)
12 1911 Fiat S.74 Grand Prix, 14.1 litres. (Italy)
13 1912 Peugeot Grand Prix, 7.6 litres. (France)

14 1913 Bébé Peugeot, 850 c.c. (France)
15 1914 Mercer Type 35 Raceabout, 5 litres. (U.S.A.)
16 1912 Duesenberg Grand Prix, 3 litres. (U.S.A.)
17 1921 Talbot-Darracq Voiturette, 1½ litres. (France)
18 1922 G.N. Cyclecar 1.1 litres. (G.B.)
19 1922 Baby Austin, 7 h.p., 696/747 c.c. (G.B.)
20 1922 Trojan, 1½ litres. (G.B.)
21 1922 Vauxhall 30/98 E Type, 4½ litres. (G.B.)
22 1923 Sunbeam Grand Prix, 2 litres. (G.B.)
23 1924 Bentley 3 litres. (G.B.)
24 1924 Morris Cowley 'Bullnose', 1½ litres. (G.B.)
25 1925 Leyland-Thomas Special, 7.2 litres. (G.B.)
26 1925 Lancia Lambda, 2.1 litres. (Italy)
27 1927 Bugatti Grand Prix Type 35B, Supercharged 2.3 litres. (France)
28 1927 Riley Nine Monaco Saloon, 1.1 litres. (G.B.)

29 1927 Delage Grand Prix, Supercharged 1½ litres (France)
30 1928 Miller Front-Wheel-Drive, Supercharged 1½ litres. (U.S.A.)
31 1928 Alvis Front-Wheel-Drive, Supercharged 1½ litres. (G.B.)
32 1931 Hispano-Suiza Type 68 V12, 9½ litres. (Spain)
33 1933 Napier-Railton Track Car, 24 litres. (G.B.)
34 1934 Morris 8, 918 c.c. (G.B.)
35 1934 E.R.A., Supercharged 1½ litres. (G.B.)
36 1934 Lagonda 4½ litre Saloon. (G.B.)
37 1934 Auto-Union Grand Prix Car, Supercharged 4.3 litres. (Germany)
38 1935 Campbell Special 'Bluebird' Supercharged 36.5 litres. (G.B.)
39 1935 Volkswagen V3 Prototype, 996 c.c. (Germany)

40 1936 B.M.W. 328, 2 litres. (Germany)
41 1938 Alfa Romeo Type 158A Racing Car, Supercharged 1½ litres. (Italy)
42 1948 Jaguar XK120, 3.4 litres. (G.B.)
43 1955 Citroën DS 19 Front-Wheel-Drive, 1.9 litres. (France)
44 1958 Vanwall Grand Prix, 2.5 litres. (G.B.)
45 1958 Cooper-Climax Grand Prix, 1.96 litres. (G.B.)
46 1959 Morris Mini Minor, Front-Wheel-Drive, 848 c.c. (G.B.)
47 1959 Rover-B.R.M. Le Mans Gas Turbine Car. (G.B.)
48 1967 Ferrari P4, 4 litres. (Italy)
49 1958 Jensen FF Four-Wheel-Drive, 6.3 litres. (G.B.)
50 1958 NSU-Wankel Ro 80 Front-Wheel-Drive, 1,990 c.c. (Germany)

1. 1770. CUGNOT'S 3-WHEEL STEAM TRACTOR. (FRANCE)

The first road vehicles were powered by steam, and this one built in Paris by Nicholas Joseph Cugnot (1723-1804) would only run for 15 minutes at about 6 m.p.h. The drive was through the front wheel, and the weight of all the mechanism made it difficult to steer, so it was very unsafe. Big coal-fired steam coaches ran surprisingly well in Britain around 1830, but steam engines were generally too heavy and too complicated to operate successfully in private cars, though four firms, Serpollet in France and White, Stanley, and Doble in the U.S.A. built practical liquid-fired cars – the latter two as late as the 1920's.

1837. Amédée Bollées L'Obéissante (steam carriage, France)

2. 1885. BENZ 3-WHEELER, 1.7 LITRES. (GERMANY)

Siegfried Marcus (1831-1898), an eccentric Austrian inventor, built three petrol driven cars between 1873-5, that ran at under 5 m.p.h. but he never developed them or influenced later designs. The true fathers of the automobile were the Germans, Gottlieb Daimler (1834-1900) and Karl Benz (1844-1929). Both built experimental cars in 1885, but Benz was the first to manufacture them for sale to the general public in 1888. The early 3 and 4-wheeled Benz cars had a single cylinder horizontal engine in the rear of a tubular frame built on bicycle principles, a 2 speed transmission by belts and chains, and a maximum speed of 12 m.p.h.

3. 1895. PANHARD ET LEVASSOR 4 H.P., 1.3 LITRES. (FRANCE)

In 1887 the wood-working machinery firm of Panhard et Levassor started making Gottlieb Daimler's engines under licence in France. In 1891 they built a car incorporating the now famous 'système Panhard', with the V-twin cylinder Daimler engine at the front of a wooden chassis, a friction clutch, a sliding pinion 3 speed gearbox and chain drive to the rear wheels, thus setting a basic design pattern for most cars that followed. In 1895 Emile Levassor drove a very similar car single-handed for 48¾ hours to win the 732 mile Paris-Bordeaux-Paris race at an average of 15 m.p.h. The car had solid rubber tyres and tiller steering.

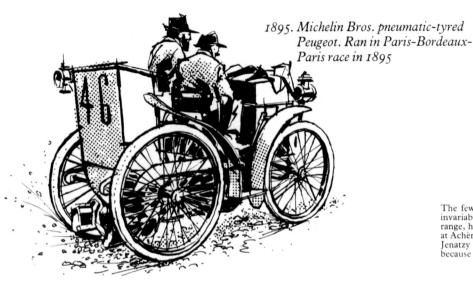

1895. Michelin Bros. pneumatic-tyred Peugeot. Ran in Paris-Bordeaux-Paris race in 1895

5. 1899. 'LA JAMAIS CONTENTE' ELECTRIC CAR. (FRANCE)

The few electric cars that have been built have invariably been for town use due to their short range, heavy batteries, and low speed. However, at Achères in France in 1899, the Belgian Camille Jenatzy (1868-1913), known as the 'Red Devil' because of his red beard, became the first driver officially to exceed 60 m.p.h. when he reached 65·7 m.p.h. and set up an early Land Speed Record on this electric car of his own design. Note the pneumatic tyres, first used on a competition car in the 1895 Paris-Bordeaux-Paris race by the Michelin brothers on their Peugeot.

4. 1898. RENAULT 1¾ H.P., 240 c.c. (FRANCE)

The great town-to-town races in France flourished in the 'nineties, and the initiative in motor manufacture passed from Germany to France, with Panhard the premier make. In 1898 a Frenchman, Louis Renault (1877-1944), mounted a single cylinder engine from his De Dion tricycle at the front of a tiny tubular chassis, and gave his first car a shaft drive transmission (no chains), and a gearbox with direct drive in top gear, setting another design trend. A big 13·4 litre 4 cylinder Renault won the first French Grand Prix at Le Mans in 1906, and today Renault is France's largest car manufacturer.

6. 1901. MERCEDES 35 H.P., 6 LITRES. (GERMANY)

The first Mercedes, built by the German Daimler firm at Cannstatt, was designed by Wilhelm Maybach (1846-1929) with the help of Gottlieb Daimler's son Paul, and was named after the daughter of a rich Austrian called Emile Jellinek, who financed it. Often called the first modern car, it had a pressed-steel frame, a smooth 4 cylinder engine, a honeycomb radiator, gate gearchange, mechanical inlet valves and a jet carburettor. Later models were called Mercedes-Benz after Daimler's amalgamation with the Benz firm in 1924, but there is no connection with the English Daimler Company of Coventry.

NAPIER

1907. Stanley Steamer (cockpit showing large lamp on steering column facing boiler gauge glass)

7. 1902. NAPIER 35 H.P. GORDON BENNETT RACING CAR, 6.4 LITRES. (G.B.)

In the early years of the century the Napier was the premier British make, and produced the first successful 6 cylinder car engine in 1903. Their designer was Montague Napier (1870-1931), grandson of the founder of David Napier & Sons of Lambeth, London, originally makers of coin-weighing machinery. The Australian driver, S. F. Edge, won the 1902 Gordon Bennett International race from Paris to Innsbruck in this 4 cylinder Napier, after his French rivals in faster cars had fallen by the wayside. This was the first international racing victory by a British car.

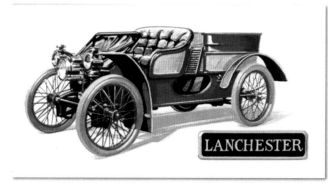

LANCHESTER

OLDSMOBILE

8. 1903. LANCHESTER 12 H.P., 4 LITRES. (G.B.)

Dr Frederick W. Lanchester (1868-1946) designed and built the first practical British 4-wheeled petrol vehicle in 1895. His production cars were scientifically designed and owed little to their competitors, who had hardly any influence on a genius like Lanchester. This 1903 car had a balanced 'vibrationless' 2 cylinder horizontal engine set amidships in the chassis with two counter-rotating crankshafts, electric ignition, 3 speed epicyclic gearbox with pre-selector control, tiller steering and a worm drive back axle. A rigid chassis and soft suspension gave excellent and comfortable roadholding.

9. 1903. OLDSMOBILE 5 H.P. CURVED DASH, 1.5 LITRES. (U.S.A.)

Although the first American car was built by the Duryea brothers in 1893, Ransom Eli Olds was the first to produce cars for a mass market. This 'Merry Oldsmobile' of the song was a typical American 'gas-buggy' with a centrally mounted single cylinder horizontal engine, a 2 speed epicyclic gearbox, and chain drive to the rear axle. It was not really rugged enough for very long journeys, and maximum speed was 20 m.p.h. After 1904 wheel steering replaced the tiller, and a dummy bonnet was fitted instead of the curved dash to make the car look more European.

1907. Sizaire Naudin — 'voiturette' (France). Very early independent front suspension with transverse leaf spring

11. 1908. FORD MODEL T, 2.9 LITRES. (U.S.A.)

Henry Ford (1863-1947) was an American of Irish-English immigrant stock, and built his first car, with 4 bicycle wheels and a 2 cylinder engine, in Detroit in 1896. He made a name for himself for a time designing and driving racing cars, and in 1903 started the Ford Motor Co. In 1908 he brought out his famous Model T, which stayed in production until 1927 by which time 15 million had been sold. This remarkable car had a 4 cylinder side-valve engine, a flywheel magneto for ignition (and, later, lighting) and 2 speed epicyclic transmission. It was cheap, strong, reliable and easy to maintain.

10. 1907. ROLLS-ROYCE 40/50 H.P. SILVER GHOST, 7/7.4 LITRES. (G.B.)

In 1904 a racing car officially exceeded 100 m.p.h. for the first time (Rigolly on a 13½ litre opposed-piston Gobron-Brillié). After 1904 cars were no longer primitive veterans incorporating belt drive, tiller steering and hot tube ignition. This Rolls-Royce epitomises the best cars of the Edwardian era. Henry Royce (1863-1933), later Sir Henry, was apprenticed to the Great Northern Railway Co., and formed Rolls-Royce in 1906 with the Hon. C. S. Rolls, racing driver and pioneer airman. The 6 cylinder Silver Ghost was in production 19 years, and it set a new standard in mechanical refinement and quiet running – hence its name!

12. 1911. FIAT S.74 GRAND PRIX, 14.1 LITRES. (ITALY)

Town-to-town racing ceased after accidents in the 1903 Paris-Madrid race caused the event to be stopped at Bordeaux, and the Gordon Bennett contests were then held on closed circuits until 1905. Although Grand Prix races from 1906 were held under formulae limiting fuel consumption, weight, or cylinder bore, generally the engines got larger and cars more unmanageable. This huge 4 cylinder single overhead camshaft Fiat, designed by Avocato Carlo Cavalli, was one of the last of the chain-driven monsters, and won the 1911 American Grand Prize at Savannah at 74.45 m.p.h. driven by the wealthy 23 year old American amateur David Bruce-Brown.

13. 1912. PEUGEOT GRAND PRIX, 7.6 LITRES. (FRANCE)

The pioneer Peugeot firm had been successful in 'voiturette' (small car) races with their Lion-Peugeots, named after their trademark the Lion of Belfort. Their 1912 G.P. car marked a watershed in racing engine design with the first twin overhead camshaft high efficiency engine, and brought the monster racing car era to an end with a win over the S.74 Fiats in the 1912 two-day French G.P. The cars were designed by the Swiss draughtsman Ernest Henry (1885-1950) together with the French driver/engineers Georges Boillot (winner of the 1912 French G.P.), and Jules Goux, with the Spaniard Paul Zuccarelli.

14. 1913. BEBE PEUGEOT, 850 c.c. (FRANCE)

The little Bébé Peugeot was notable for two things, firstly it was the original 'miniature' car and thus the forerunner of the Baby Austins and Morris Minors of the 1920's, and secondly it was designed by the famous artist/engineer Ettore Bugatti. The 1912 version had a 2 speed transmission, increased to 3 speeds in 1913. Open cars were capable of 35 m.p.h., but this little saloon was limited to 27 m.p.h. and roadholding was not up to recognised Bugatti standards. In the 1920's the bigger Peugeots had sleeve-valve engines. Peugeot and Renault are the only French manufacturers still surviving from this period.

1910. Rolls-Royce 'Silver Ghost', with Torpedo tourer body by Barker

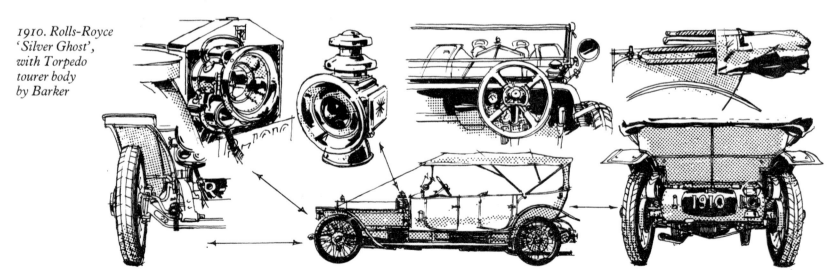

15. 1914. MERCER TYPE 35 RACEABOUT, 5 LITRES. (U.S.A.)

Some of the finest American cars ever built were the 1910-16 sports cars, typified by the Stutz 'Bearcat', Lozier, Locomobile, and the Type 35 Mercer. The Mercer Co. of New Jersey, was started in 1909 by the Roebling family, whose firm built the Brooklyn Bridge. The Type 35 was designed by Finlay Robertson Porter (1872-1964), and in its 4 cylinder engine the side-valves were in T formation. The Type 35 was successfully raced, amongst its drivers being Washington Roebling II, son of the firm's founder, who was drowned in the 'Titanic' disaster in 1912.

16. 1921. DUESENBERG GRAND PRIX, 3 LITRES. (U.S.A.)

The brothers Fred and August Duesenberg were born in Germany, but went to the U.S.A. as children in 1885 when their parents emigrated. They built racing cars before the first World War, and this post-war straight 8 cylinder Duesenberg was the only American car to win a European G.P. between the wars, when it won the 1921 French G.P. at Le Mans, driven by Jimmy Murphy. The engine was inspired by Bugatti aero-engines developed by the Duesenbergs during the war, and the car featured hydraulic 4-wheel brakes using glycerine and water. After making expensive touring cars, Fred died in 1932, aged 53, and August in 1955.

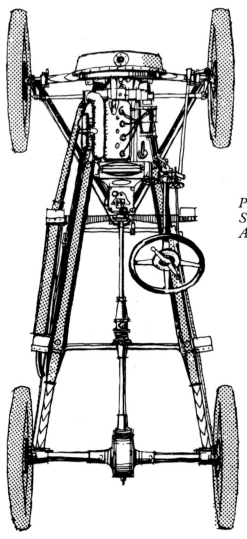

Pre 1933.
Simplicity of the
Austin 7 chassis

17. 1921. TALBOT-DARRACQ VOITURETTE, 1½ LITRES. (FRANCE)

The French Darracq firm absorbed the British Talbot and Sunbeam companies in 1919/20 to form the Sunbeam-Talbot-Darracq combine. The 4 cylinder Talbot-Darracq shown here had an engine which was virtually half the straight 8 fitted to rather unsuccessful 3 litre G.P. cars built by the S.T.D. combine for Indianapolis and the French G.P. in 1921. These Talbot-Darracqs were unbeatable in voiturette races up to 1925 and dominated the Brooklands 200 mile races of the period, Henry De Hane Segrave and Kenelm Lee Guinness being prominent drivers.

19. 1922. BABY AUSTIN, 7 H.P., 696/747 c.c. (G.B.)

Herbert Austin (1866-1941), later Lord Austin, began as a designer for Wolseleys in 1896. He drove a Wolseley in the 1903 Paris-Madrid race, and started his own firm in 1906. It is said he designed the Austin 7 in 1921 on his billiard table, though his chief designer from 1919-1941 was A. J. Hancock (1882-1959), who had been with him at Wolseleys. The memorable Austin 7 ousted the cyclecars, and brought motoring to thousands who otherwise could never have afforded it. In December, 1922, it cost £165, had a side-valve 4 cylinder engine, 3 speed gearbox, electric lighting, and rather feeble 4-wheel brakes.

18. 1922. G.N. CYCLECAR 1.1 LITRES. (G.B.)

Cyclecars, consisting of air-cooled one or two cylinder engines in simple belt or chain driven chassis were popular immediately before and after the 1914-18 war, and bridged the gap between the motor-cycle and sidecar and the small car. One of the best was the G.N., built by a firm founded in 1910 by two young men in their early twenties, 'Archie' Frazer-Nash (1889-1965) and H. R. Godfrey (b. 1887). The cars featured V-twin engines with belt drive and 2 speeds and wire and bobbin steering on early models, and 3 speeds and chain drive on later ones. Sports and racing models were very successful in competitions.

20. 1922. TROJAN, 1½ LITRES. (G.B.)

There has never been a car like the Trojan. Designed by Leslie Hounsfield (1877-1957) before the Great War as a really simple and economical car, it was manufactured by the Leyland lorry firm and sold well in the 1920's when it cost little more than the Austin 7. The engine was a horizontal 4 cylinder, but 2 plug, 'duplex' 2-stroke situated under the front seat, and started by pulling an internal lever. The punt-like chassis was pressed-steel, the gearbox 2 speed epicyclic and the bonnet housed only the petrol tank and carburettor. Solid tyres were optional and the Trojan, though slow, would climb any hill.

21. 1922. VAUXHALL 30/98 E TYPE, 4½ LITRES. (G.B.)

Laurence H. Pomeroy (1883-1941), the designer of the 30/98 Vauxhall, was apprenticed to the North Western Locomotive Works at Bow when aged 16. The side-valve 4 cylinder E Type 30/98, catalogued from 1919-1922, was basically Edwardian in design and developed from the pre-war Prince Henry Vauxhall. Highly successful at sprints and hill-climbs and at Brooklands, before the days of the big international sports car races, the E Type cost £1300, and was the fastest British sporting car of its day, capable of 80-100 m.p.h.

23. 1924. BENTLEY 3 LITRES. (G.B.)

Walter Owen Bentley (b. 1888) was apprenticed to the Great Northern Locomotive Works in Doncaster at 16, and successfully tuned and raced motor cycles and French D.F.P. cars before the Great War. During the war he designed the BR1 and BR2 rotary aero-engines, and immediately after the war the 3 litre Bentley. This had a 4 cylinder single overhead camshaft engine, and a 3 litre won the Le Mans 24 Hour Race in 1924 and 1927, whilst bigger Bentleys (4½ and 6½ litres) won there from 1928-30 inclusive. Rolls-Royce took over the old Bentley firm in 1931, and in 1935 W. O. Bentley went to Lagonda.

22. 1923. SUNBEAM GRAND PRIX, 2 LITRES. (G.B.)

Driven by Henry (later Sir Henry) Segrave, this 6 cylinder car won the 1923 French Grand Prix at Tours, the only British car to win this important race in a period of over 50 years. Modelled on the unbeatable 1922 2 litre G.P. Fiat, it was actually designed by the Italian Vincent Bertarione, who had been on the Fiat design team, and built by Sunbeam at Wolverhampton under their chief engineer, Frenchman Louis Coatalen. The rival Fiats pioneered superchargers at Tours, which gave trouble and caused their retirement. A supercharged 2 litre Sunbeam won the 1924 Spanish G.P. the following year.

24. 1924. MORRIS COWLEY 'BULLNOSE', 1½ LITRES. (G.B.)

William Richard Morris (1877-1963), afterwards Lord Nuffield, began as a cycle repairer in Oxford, and built his first Morris Oxford in 1913. It was an 'assembly job' with the main components bought from outside firms, the engine being made by White & Poppe. The Cowley was born on the liner 'Mauretania' in August, 1914, when Morris and Hans Landstad commenced its design whilst on their way to buy engines from Continental of Detroit, at £18 each. After the war Morris had this 4 cylinder side-valve engine made in the French Hotchkiss Company's factory at Coventry.

25. 1925. LEYLAND-THOMAS SPECIAL, 7.2 LITRES. (G.B.)

The first banked motor racing track in the world was opened during 1907 at Brooklands, Weybridge, Surrey. A star driver who raced there in the 1920's was also a great designer, the Welsh born John Godfrey Parry Thomas (1885-1927). This racing car was developed from the luxury Leyland 8 touring car, which Parry Thomas designed with his young assistant Reid Railton, and it lapped Brooklands at 129.36 m.p.h. in 1925. The engine was a straight 8 cylinder with an overhead camshaft, and the chassis featured anti-roll torsion bars. Parry Thomas was killed during a record attempt in 1927.

27. 1927. BUGATTI GRAND PRIX TYPE 35B, SUPERCHARGED 2.3 LITRES. (FRANCE)

Ettore Bugatti (1881-1947) was born in Milan, and has been described as the last of the artist/engineers. He had no formal scientific training, only a natural mechanical ability. His factory at Molsheim, in Alsace-Lorraine, had a country estate atmosphere, and his love of thoroughbred horses is shown in the Bugatti horseshoe-shaped radiator. Bugatti manufactured racing cars for private sale, so more Bugattis took part in races – and won them – than any other make. The most successful was this 120 m.p.h. 35B, with a supercharged straight 8 single overhead camshaft engine and alloy wheels.

26. 1925. LANCIA LAMBDA 2.1 LITRES. (ITALY)

The burly, cheerful, Vincenzo Lancia (1881-1937) was an ace racing driver for Fiat until 1906. His forceful driving often meant he took the lap record and then retired, leaving final victory to his less exuberant team-mate Felice Nazzaro. When he started his own car firm in Turin in 1907, he adopted the lance ('lancia') as his trademark, and one of his most famous models was the Lambda, designed in 1921 and first produced in 1923. Its advanced specification included sliding pillar independent front suspension, integral body and chassis, and a single overhead camshaft V4 engine with an alloy block.

28. 1927. RILEY NINE MONACO SALOON, 1.1 LITRES. (G.B.)

The Riley firm of Coventry originally made weaving machinery, but Percy Riley (1883-1941), who built his first car shortly after leaving King Henry VIII Grammar School, was responsible for the design of the 4 cylinder Riley 9 in 1926 with his brother Stanley (1884-1952). The outstanding light car of its day, the Riley 9 was remarkable for Percy Riley's cylinder head with hemispherical combustion chambers, and overhead valves operated via pushrods by two high set camshafts. The fabric body, being light and rattle free, was popular in the late 1920's. A racing version of the Nine, called the Brooklands, was developed by Parry Thomas and Reid Railton.

29. 1927. DELAGE GRAND PRIX, SUPERCHARGED 1½ LITRES. (FRANCE)

Louis Delage (1874-1947), the son of a station-master in Cognac, lost the use of one eye at birth, but became an engineer at Peugeot and started his own firm in 1906. It was successful until 1935, but Delage was to die in poverty. He made a pilgrimage from Paris to Lisieux on foot and to Lourdes by bicycle when nearly 70. This success-ful 128 m.p.h. straight 8 Grand Prix Delage, de-signed by Albert Lory, had a complicated 'watch-like' engine with 21 timing and auxiliary gears driving camshafts, magneto, oil pumps, etc. In 1936 a rebuilt 10 year old example was still winning important races.

31. 1928. ALVIS FRONT-WHEEL-DRIVE, SUPERCHARGED 1½ LITRES. (G.B.)

At the same time as Miller in the U.S.A. was designing an f.w.d. track car, two Britons evolved an f.w.d. sprint car for Alvis of Coventry. These were G.T. Smith-Clarke (1884-1960), who com-menced his career with the Great Western Rail-way, and a Scot, W. M. Dunn (b. 1885), who was apprenticed as a marine engineer. The sprint car was more successful than the f.w.d. Grand Prix cars built in 1926/27, and the design culminated in this advanced single overhead camshaft, 4 cylinder sports car with all four wheels independ-ently sprung. Despite some racing successes, Alvis only developed the independent suspension aspect of their sports f.w.d. project, which they abandoned in 1930.

30. 1928. MILLER FRONT-WHEEL-DRIVE, SUPERCHARGED 1½ LITRES. (U.S.A.)

Harry Armenius Miller (1875-1943) was born in Wisconsin of a German father and a Canadian mother. His engine building talent was apparent in 1915 when he and his assistant, Fred Offen-hauser, rebuilt a 1913 Henry Peugeot engine which performed better than the original. Later he built conventional chassis to house his straight 8 racing engines, but he is most famous for his track race winning front-wheel-drive design which first appeared in 1925. In 1939 Miller built a four-wheel-drive rear engined racing car, and 4 cylinder Offenhauser engines, based on Miller's concept, were still winning at Indian-apolis in the early 'sixties.

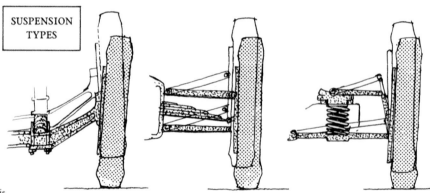

SUSPENSION TYPES

Normal front axle   *Parallel radius arms (independent) with transverse spring*   *Unequal radius arms with helical springs*

32. 1931. HISPANO-SUIZA TYPE 68 V12, 9½ LITRES. (SPAIN)

Marc Birkigt (1878-1953) was a Swiss, born in Geneva, and went to Barcelona to work on electric locomotives. In 1904 he started his car factory with Spanish finance, hence the name Hispano-Suiza. His 'Alfonso' sporting model of 1912 achieved fame, and during the 1914-18 war he designed the V8 aero-engines fitted to the SE5 fighter aircraft, as used by Guynemer's Stork Squadron. Birkigt adopted the stork as his mascot on his post-war cars, commencing with an overhead camshaft 6 cylinder. This magnificent 100 m.p.h. V12 was built in the Paris factory from 1931-38. The engine was also used to power fast railcars.

34. 1934. MORRIS 8, 918 c.c. (G.B.)

The Morris 8, designed by Boyle and Westbury, is typical of the smaller British family cars of the 1930's. In 1927 Morris Motors took over Wolseley and the single overhead camshaft on the original Morris Minor engine of 1928 was a Wolseley feature. This engine and chassis also formed the basis of the famous M.G. M-type Midget. In 1931 the side-valve Morris Minor replaced the overhead camshaft model, but this Morris 8 was longer and wider than the previous 4-door Minor saloon, and its side-valve engine survived in the early post-war Morris Minor, immediate predecessor of the Morris 1000 of today.

33. 1933. NAPIER-RAILTON TRACK CAR, 24 LITRES. (G.B.)

After the first World War some of the fastest cars raced at Brooklands were made by putting ex-wartime aeroplane engines into large pre-war chain-drive chassis, Count Louis Zborowski's 'Chitty-Chitty-Bang-Bangs' being typical examples. Much more sophisticated was this car built for the famous driver John Cobb, using a 450 h.p. Napier Lion 12 cylinder aero-engine in a special shaft-drive chassis designed by Reid Railton. When Brooklands closed in 1939 it held the ultimate lap record at 143·44 m.p.h., and amongst its long-distance records was one of 24 hours at 150·6 m.p.h. at Bonneville Salt Flats, Utah, in 1936.

35. 1934. E.R.A., SUPERCHARGED 1½ LITRES. (G.B.)

E.R.A. stood for English Racing Automobiles. Although Austin and M.G. built some fine 750 c.c. and 1100 c.c. racing cars in the 1930's, the E.R.A.s scored the major British victories at home and abroad in the 1½ litre voiturette class in which their main rivals were the Italian Maseratis. The designer of the E.R.A. was Peter Berthon (b. 1906), who used a racing adaptation of the 6 cylinder Riley engine with a pre-selector gearbox in a chassis which received development by Reid Railton. Racing drivers Raymond Mays and Humphrey Cook were behind the E.R.A. project and Mays and Berthon went on to build the B.R.M. after the war.

36. 1934. LAGONDA 4½ LITRE SALOON. (G.B.)

A light sports version of this handsome saloon won the 1935 Le Mans 24 Hour Race. This Cranmer designed M45 model used a conventional chassis fitted with a proprietary 6 cylinder pushrod overhead valve engine designed by R. S. Crump (b. 1894) and built by the Henry Meadows Co. of Wolverhampton. When W. O. Bentley joined Lagonda in 1935 he developed the M45 into the more refined LG45. After the war a new 6 cylinder Lagonda engine designed by Bentley was fitted to the David Brown Aston-Martin, a famous British sporting make, which won the 1959 Le Mans race.

1937. W125 Mercedes
(the most powerful Grand Prix car ever built, over 600 b.h.p.)

37. 1934. AUTO-UNION GRAND PRIX CAR, SUPERCHARGED 4.3 LITRES. (GERMANY)

Some of the greatest German and Austrian cars from the early years of the century until the 1950's - Austro-Daimler, Mercedes-Benz, Auto-Union, Volkswagen and Porsche - were designed by one man, the Austrian Dr Ferdinand Porsche (1875-1952). This Auto-Union was designed for the 1934-37 Grand Prix formula, limiting weight to 750 kgs. (about 14 cwt.). It had a V16 cylinder engine and was chief rival to the successful Mercedes G.P. cars of the era. Its unique rear-engined layout made the Auto-Union tricky to handle, and only three drivers really mastered it.

38. 1935. CAMPBELL SPECIAL 'BLUEBIRD', SUPERCHARGED 36.5 LITRES. (G.B.)

The first man to exceed 200 m.p.h. in a car was Segrave in 1927 at Daytona Beach, Florida, driving a 45 litre 3¾ ton chain-driven Sunbeam Special, fitted with two old 1914/18 war 'Matabele' aero-engines, one in front and the other behind the driver. First over 300 m.p.h. was Sir Malcolm Campbell in 1935 on the Bonneville Salt Flats, Utah, in this 5 ton 'Bluebird' designed by Reid Railton and fitted with a new Schneider Trophy-winning Rolls-Royce 'R' racing aircraft engine. It was customary to paint British and American crossed flags on British cars record-breaking in U.S.A.

39. 1935. VOLKSWAGEN V3 PROTOTYPE, 996 c.c. (GERMANY)

This prototype of Dr Porsche's Volkswagen (Peoples' Car) does not look very different from the famous 'beetle' still selling in huge numbers (one million were built in 1966 alone) over 30 years later. On the production cars the rear mounted air-cooled engine with 4 horizontally opposed cylinders was increased to 1.2 litres capacity, with 1·3, 1·5 and 1·6 versions being introduced more recently. The advanced suspension was independent all round using torsion bars as the springing medium, a system also adopted on the Auto-Union G.P. car.

41. 1938. ALFA ROMEO TYPE 158A RACING CAR, SUPERCHARGED 1½ LITRES. (ITALY)

The first designer for this great Milan firm from 1910-26 was Giuseppe Merosi (1872-1956), originally trained as a building surveyor. More famous was his successor, Vittorio Jano (1891-1965), who designed various Alfa Romeos that proved world beaters in both Grand Prix and sports car racing up to 1937. This straight 8 158A was the work of Gioacchino Colombo (b. 1903). Originally built for voiturette racing, it achieved its greatest fame when developed into a Grand Prix car for the first post-war formula, and was unbeatable for most of the time it was racing between 1946 and 1951. In its final 200 m.p.h. Type 159 form, it developed 400 b.h.p. and used fuel at the rate of 1½ m.p.g.

40. 1936. B.M.W. 328, 2 LITRES. (GERMANY)

This 100 m.p.h. German car, made in Munich by the Bayerische Motoren Werke, could be called the prototype of the modern sports car, with its smooth body contours and light construction. The B.M.W. was one of the first sports cars with enveloping bodywork, and had a tubular chassis, rack and pinion steering and independent front suspension. Known in England as the Frazer Nash B.M.W., its 6 cylinder engine used an ingenious system of transverse push-rods to give many advantages of the more costly twin overhead camshaft design. This engine was used in the early post-war Bristol cars.

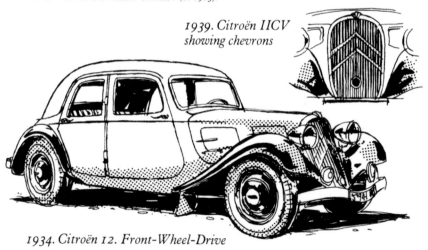

1939. Citroën 11CV showing chevrons

1934. Citroën 12. Front-Wheel-Drive

42. 1948. JAGUAR XK120, 3.4 LITRES. (G.B.)

The Jaguar Company was founded by Sir William Lyons (b.1901) who originally manufactured sidecars, and then special 'Swallow' bodywork on various manufacturers' chassis. His first pre-war SS (Standard Swallow) cars introduced in 1931 had Standard chassis and engines, but the XK120 was entirely manufactured by Jaguar Cars Ltd. with Claude Baily (b. 1902), William Heynes (b. 1903) and Walter Hassan (b. 1905) forming the design team. From it sprang the famous 'C' and 'D' type Jaguars, Le Mans winners in 1951, 1953 and 1955-57. The 120 m.p.h. plus XK120 had a 6 cylinder twin overhead camshaft engine.

44. 1958. VANWALL GRAND PRIX, 2.5 LITRES. (G.B.)

Despite brave efforts by old E.R.A.s in the 1940's and by H.W.M. and Connaught in the early 1950's, Britain did not have a competitive G.P. car between the Sunbeams of 1923/4 and the Vanwalls of 1957/8. G. A. Vandervell (1900-1967), the bearing and accessory manufacturer, sponsored a 4½ litre Ferrari known as the 'Thin-wall Special' in the early 1950's on which his team of Vanwalls was to some extent based. Norton motor-cycle racing experience was incorporated in the fuel injection 4 cylinder engine, whilst the chassis was developed by Colin Chapman (b. 1928) of Lotus fame, and Frank Costin.

43. 1955. CITROEN DS 19 FRONT-WHEEL-DRIVE, 1.9 LITRES. (FRANCE)

When Citroën produced their f.w.d. Twelve in 1934 it was considered revolutionary, but the DS 19 in 1955 was thought to be even more so. The 4 cylinder push-rod engine was a more powerful version of the previous Light 15 engine, but the chassis was entirely new. The most interesting feature of the car was the hydraulic power supplied by an engine-driven pump, to assist the steering and brakes, operate the clutch and gear change, level the hydro-pneumatic suspension, and adjust its height automatically. It was also the first production car to have disc brakes on the front wheels only.

45. 1958. COOPER-CLIMAX GRAND PRIX, 1.96 LITRES. (G.B.)

John Cooper (b. 1923) with his father Charles had built very successful little 500 c.c racing cars immediately after the war, with rear mounted motor-cycle engines. After building front engined Formula 2 (voiturette) Bristol-engined cars, they entered the Grand Prix field with this basically Formula 2 Coventry-Climax mid-engined car under the sponsorship of Rob Walker, and with its low weight and small frontal area it beat the larger 2½ litre front engined cars early in 1958 in the Argentine and Monaco G.P.s. Within 3 years the Cooper layout with the engine behind the driver was universal in G.P. racing.

46. 1959. MORRIS MINI MINOR, FRONT-WHEEL-DRIVE, 848 c.c. (G.B.)

1951 saw a merger between Morris and Austin and these two makes, plus M.G., Wolseley and Riley, all came under the new British Motor Corporation. The B.M.C. Mini, designed by Alec Issigonis (b. 1906), was the first really revolutionary mass-produced British car. The 4 cylinder engine was not fundamentally new, and the rack and pinion steering was like that on the Issigonis designed Morris Minor, so the remarkable features of the Mini were its unique f.w.d. design with a transverse engine enclosing the 'gearbox' in its crankcase to give more passenger space, tiny 10 inch wheels and all independent variable rate rubber suspension.

47. 1965. ROVER-B.R.M. LE MANS GAS TURBINE CAR. (G.B.)

This rear-wheel-drive car was a product of Rover's car gas turbine research and B.R.M's chassis design experience in G.P. racing, the first gas turbine car ever to be raced, and it finished the 1965 Le Mans race in 10th place at 98·75 m.p.h., and averaged 13·52 miles to the gallon. Rover's Noel Penny was responsible for the engine design and David Bache for the styling, whilst the B.R.M. chassis was designed under A. C. Rudd of the Owen Organisation.

Citroën single-spoke steering wheel

Citroën constant ground clearance device

1953. This XK Jaguar holds the fastest recorded speed by that type (172 m.p.h.)

48. 1967. FERRARI P4, 4 LITRES. (ITALY)

With its V12 engine situated behind the driver, this Ferrari is a typical modern sports/racing car. Although Ferraris won at Le Mans from 1960-65, they had to give best to the larger 200 m.p.h. G.T. 40 7 litre Fords in 1966 and 1967. Enzo Ferrari (b. 1898) managed Alfa Romeo's racing affairs from 1929-1937, but he achieved greater fame since the 1939-45 war with his own racing and sports cars made at the works near his birthplace at Modena. The shield depicting the Ravenna horse was originally presented to Ferrari after he had won the 1923 Circuit of Savio race on an Alfa Romeo.

49. 1968. JENSEN FF FOUR-WHEEL-DRIVE, 6.3 LITRES. (G.B.)

F. Alan Jensen (b. 1906) and his brother Richard (b. 1909) started, rather like William Lyons of Jaguar, by building their own sports bodywork on other manufacturers' chassis at West Bromwich in the early 1930's. Although their pre-war cars had Jensen designed chassis, the engines were American Ford V8, Lincoln V12 and Nash straight 8. This automatic gearbox 140 m.p.h. Jensen FF (Ferguson Formula), first introduced in 1966 has an American V8 Chrysler engine, and is the first high performance car incorporating four-wheel-drive to be offered to the public. It uses the unique Ferguson transmission system.

50. 1968. NSU-WANKEL Ro 80 FRONT-WHEEL-DRIVE, 1,990 c.c. (GERMANY)

The reciprocating piston engine has held sway since Benz's time and basically engines have not radically altered since the early days of motoring. Gas turbines seem more suitable for heavy commercial vehicles or Indianapolis track cars, but this 112 m.p.h. production NSU designed by Ewald Praxl (b. 1911) has a vibration-free lightweight rotary piston engine, of a type first produced by the German Felix Wankel in 1957, and seems a practical alternative to the traditional car engine. It is a 128 b.h.p. twin-chamber unit, with 2 carburettors, 2 coils and 4 sparking plugs in a typical modern f.w.d. chassis.

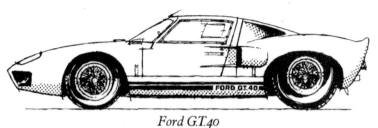

Ford G.T.40

COVER ILLUSTRATIONS (left to right)

1967. Formula 1 B.R.M. Grand Prix 2½ litres V.12
1967. Rolls-Royce Convertible (see also card no. 10)
1908/10. Panhard et Levassor (see also card no. 3)
1967. Mini Mark II (see also card no. 46)
1927. Isotta-Fraschini Type 8
1927. Type 37 Bugatti (see also card no. 27)
Jensen FF. Winner of 1967 CAR magazine 'Car of the Year' award (see also card no. 49)
1901. Columbia

1904. Gobron Brillié.
1st over 100 m.p.h.
at 103.56 m.p.h.

1965. Spirit of America.
Present holder of World Land
Speed Record. (Driver: Craig
Breedlove) at 600.60 m.p.h.

1927. Sunbeam.
1st over 200 m.p.h.
at 203.79 m.p.h,

Further reading

An interesting booklet explaining the working principles of the motor car in simple language is Know Your Car (Iliffe Books Ltd), which costs 3/6. The following paperbacks and cheap editions would make a good basis for a motoring library of your own: Veteran and Edwardian Motor Cars by D. Scott-Moncrieff and The Racing Car by Clutton, Posthumus and Jenkinson (both Batsford Paperbacks at 5/- each). Also recommended are The Racing Car Pocketbook by Jenkinson and The Veteran Motor Car Pocketbook by Bird and Hutton-Stott (Batsford cheap editions at 3/6 each). Nearly all public libraries today have an excellent selection of more expensive motoring books on their shelves which you can borrow.

Motor museums

The following museums have cars on display:
LONDON—The Science Museum, South Kensington, SW7
BIRMINGHAM—The Science Museum, Newhall St, Birmingham 3
COVENTRY—Herbert Art Gallery and Museum, Jordan Well
GLASGOW—Art Gallery and Museum, Kelvin Grove, C3
HULL—The Transport Museum
BRIGHTON—The Motor Museum, Madeira Drive
HAMPSHIRE—Montagu Motor Museum, Beaulieu
HERTFORDSHIRE—Shuttleworth Collection, Old Warden Aerodrome, Biggleswade
SOMERSET—Cheddar Veteran and Vintage Car Museum, Cheddar

How to see old cars in action

There are more old racing and sports cars in England than in any other country in the world, and these are regularly raced at meetings organised by the Vintage Sports Car Club. If you would like details of these meetings so that you can watch the races, write enclosing a stamped addressed envelope to The Secretary, The V.S.C.C., Bone Lane, Newbury, Berks. This Club specialises particularly in Vintage cars, i.e. those built between 1919 and 1930.

The Veteran Car Club specialises in Veteran Cars, i.e. those built before 1905, and also in Edwardian cars built between 1905 and 1918! For details of events held by the Veteran Car Club, write enclosing a stamped addressed envelope to The Secretary, The V.C.C., 14 Fitzhardinge St, London W1.

THE BERKSHIRE PRINTING CO. LTD., READING. ENGLAND

This series of Picture Cards is offered in the interest of education by **BROOKE BOND**

Picture Cards are given free with Brooke Bond Tea and Tea Bags